CHARISMA

CHARISMA
Charles Lindholm

Basil Blackwell

Copyright © Charles Lindholm 1990

First published 1990

Basil Blackwell, Inc.
3 Cambridge Center
Cambridge, Massachusetts 02142, USA

Basil Blackwell Ltd
108 Cowley Road, Oxford, OX4 1JF, UK

ISBN 1 55786 021 1

British Library Cataloguing in Publication Data
A CIP catalogue record for this book is available from the British Library.

Library of Congress Cataloging in Publication Data

Lindholm, Charles, 1946–
    Charisma / Charles Lindholm,
      p. cm.
    Includes bibliographical references.
    ISBN 1–55786–021–1
    1. Leadership. 2. Charisma (Personality trait) 1. Title.
HM141.L553 1990
303.3′4–dc20
                                  90–32760
                                      CIP

Typeset in 10 on 11½ pt Sabon
by Photo·graphics, Honiton, Devon
Printed in Great Britain by T.J. Press, Padstow

Contents

Part IV Conclusion

Acknowledgements

My study of charismatic phenomena has benefited from the advice and help of many people in many disciplines. Because of the cross-disciplinary nature of this book, I've painted in broad strokes what my specialist colleagues would have drawn in a far more nuanced manner. I hope they will forgive me for the simplifications that result, and accept my thanks for their help. Those who have been most influential include: my friend and advisor during my graduate work at Columbia, Abraham Rosman, who always encouraged my interests; Richard Christie, for whom I first wrote about charisma; Richard Castillo, who advised me on altered states of consciousness; Patrice Birenberg and Lewis Wurgaft, who helped me think about some of the material on psychology. Peter Dougherty, my original editor at Basil Blackwell, encouraged me to write this manuscript, and provided me with good advice throughout. My research assistants at Harvard, Laurie Hart-McGrath and Krzysztof Kowalski, were of immeasurable help, especially in my research on cults, Blythe Horman was a superb fact-checker and bibliographer, while in the earlier stages of the book John Borneman and Nikhil Singh did considerable work on collecting Nazi material. I am grateful to them all not only for their efforts, but for their ideas; and to the Clark and Milton funds for their support of my research. I am very grateful as well to John A. Hall, who generously read an earlier draft and gave me a valuable and exhaustive critique, which was extremely useful in cutting and reworking the material. I would also like to give special thanks to my colleagues and the students of my two departments at Harvard, Anthropology and Social Studies, where I have met with the sort of encouragement and intellectual stimulation that makes academic life worthwhile. Finally, I want to thank my wife, Cherry Lindholm, who argued with me, encouraged me, pressed me to write more clearly and logically, helped to find a way to shape and trim my ungainly original manuscript, and worked with me to edit the final page proofs. Without her this book would never have been finished.

This book is dedicated to my father,
Wilbur T. Lindholm,
with love and respect

Part I

Introduction

1

Introduction

In 1969 the brutal murders committed in Southern California by the followers of Charles Manson riveted the attention of the American public. The apparently senseless killings of ten people were explained by the media as the result of the strange hypnotic power exercised by Manson, who had convinced the disciples that he was Christ incarnate. Manson, on the other hand, argued that he was nothing more than a mirror, reflecting society's own dark fantasies.

Nearly ten years later, the residents of Jonestown, a commune isolated in the jungles of Guyana, killed a visiting member of the United States House of Representatives and some of his entourage. Then, at the request of their leader, Jim Jones, nearly all of the hundreds of men, women and children of the Temple drank cyanide-laced kool-aid and died in the greatest mass suicide of modern history. At first it was assumed that the suicides were forced, but evidence indicated instead that these people willingly killed themselves and their children in order to accompany their beloved leader, whom they worshipped as a god on earth.

Behind these frightening outbursts lurks the spectre of Adolf Hitler, who inspired his supporters to similar violent acts, and who also proclaimed himself a living god. But where Manson touched only a few dozen followers, and Jones less than a thousand, Hitler inflamed an entire nation with his paranoid vision, precipitating the greatest war and the most horrible atrocities of the century.

In these terrible events, the concepts of cult, charisma, and diabolical evil seem inextricably intertwined. Our fear of such Hitler-like movements has been reawakened by the rise of religious fanaticism as a mode of government on the international scene, while domestic incidents of mob violence and hatred, as well as surges of apparently irrational cultic fervor, undermine our faith in the power of reason. Even within the mainstream of Western society, passionate evangelical figures exhorting their congregations from television screens stir apprehensions about the rationality of the public, and about the possibility of resurgent cultism. Such movements make it hard to believe that human beings – at least human beings in groups gripped by enthusiasm – are reasonable creatures.

In fact, it is evident that leaders such as Hitler, Jones and Manson exert an influence on their followers that goes far beyond ordinary logic or self-interest. Immersed in a crowd that seems to have a dynamic of its own, the followers are completely devoted to their leader and are prepared to do anything he commands – even kill others, or themselves. Meanwhile, the individuals who inspire this incredible loyalty appear to the public in general as extraordinary half-mad figures, driven by violent rages and fears that would seem to make them repellent rather than attractive, while their messages look, from the perspective of the outsider, to be absurd melanges of half-digested ideas, personal fantasies, and paranoid delusions.

How is it possible to understand these extraordinary occurrences? This question has been one that has fascinated me for a very long time, partly because of the importance of charismatic relations in recent history, partly because of the intellectual challenge such movements offer to social theory. But the problem of understanding charisma and the mentality of the group also has personal relevance because I know something of it from my own experiences, experiences which I share, at least to a degree, with many of my generation.

My first awareness of the raw impersonal power of a group was during student riots in the late sixties. I was momentarily lost in the excitement of a violent crowd, and found myself facing armed policemen, who became in turn an equally angry mob. The riot that ensued was frightening, but also exhilarating, as the participants lost their inhibitions against violence along with their "instinct" for self-preservation in the confrontation.

During this same era I also witnessed the transformation of apparently ordinary, reasonable people into acolytes who wore ludicrous uniforms, practiced odd rituals and proclaimed their exotic leaders to be avatars of God on earth. These devotees told me with their faces shining that they had discovered meaning and great happiness in their attachment to these living deities. Their conversion made me realize that people were not only vulnerable to momentary immersion in a riot, but also to radical involvement in new and completely different life courses. Reality was far more malleable than I had imagined, and my own perceptions of what was reasonable and rational had to be rethought.

A third factor derived from my travels through South Asia after I graduated from college. My idea was that in a different society, surviving without the baggage of my own identity, I could live more intensely and escape the alienation I felt from American culture. But I discovered even more poignantly the degree to which my worldview was limited, and how little I understood the well-springs of people's actions.

This revelation led me to study anthropology in order to learn how to put my experiences of other worlds and cultural standards into social and historical perspectives. And, to a degree, this effort was successful. However, when I did my fieldwork in northern Pakistan, I found that the tribal people I worked among, although almost fanatically egalitarian, historically had periodic charismatic revivals, where nearly the whole population would rise and follow an ecstatic religious practitioner. This made me wonder about the paradoxical connection between egalitarianism and charismatic involvement, and more generally about the role of passion in arousing collective action within a specific cultural context.

As a result of these personal experiences I became interested in the study of charisma as the source for emotionally grounded action. The collective energies and selfless communal fervor I had felt in the riots of the sixties seemed to me to be best understood in terms of the dynamics of a charismatic group, and charismatic leadership certainly had impelled a few of my friends to become immersed in cults. I also believed that it is not through rational argument, but primarily through forms of charismatic commitment, that people achieve the levels of self-sacrifice necessary for revolution and social transformation.

But what meaning did any of this have? Was the word "charisma" just a way to categorize and thereby pretend to capture an emotional experience that is really completely inexplicable? A number of commentators have argued that this is indeed the case – that charisma is actually a meaningless term, completely useless for analysis. Unfortunately, they put nothing in its place, and we are left with the naked events, and bereft even of a word to describe them. The question then is whether we can discover the outline of a theoretical framework within the discourse about charisma that can help us make sense of what appears senseless. We can begin this task by asking just what is entailed in the popular definition of charisma.

Virtually unknown a generation ago, the word "charisma" is now a part of the vocabulary of the general public, and obviously fills a felt need to conceptualize and categorize exactly the sorts of cultic commitment and extraordinary crowd phenomena I mentioned above. However, its meaning has been extended to cover not only the astonishing commitment of cultists and fanatics, not only the fervour of the mob, but also the adulation offered to glamorous movie stars, exciting sports heroes, and Kennedyesque politicians – adulation which goes far beyond mere admiration of someone with special expertise.[1]

Nor does the popular use of the term stop there. The social theorist Bertrand de Jouvenel echoes mass opinion when he explains that informal relationships in any group are a product of one individual's "naked capacity of mustering assent," a capacity that has nothing to do with position, or power, or advantage, but emanates solely from an inherent personal magnetism (1958: 163). When such a person enters

a room, heads turn, and those who are without this magical attribute
try to be close to the one who has it; they want to be liked by her, to
have her attention, to touch her. The hearts of the onlookers race when
the attractive other comes near. This capacity is thus a quality admired
and envied; and imagined, perhaps accurately, to lead to success in love
and work. In the West, we define and "explain" this magnetic
attractiveness of others by referring to it as "charisma."

Even in the most intimate personal relationships the concept of
charisma is used, since the powerful attraction of the beloved in the
first flush of romantic love is also portrayed in Western popular culture
as "charismatic." The beloved, in romantic imagery, is understood as
having the same sort of intrinsic magnetic quality, outside the range of
ordinary thought and logic, and is believed by the lover to be special,
extraordinary, remarkable in every way. Because of these imputed
qualities, the lover wants to obey the beloved, just as the follower wants
to obey the leader. The parallel between love and charisma is deep, and
I will return to it in the conclusion.

But for the moment, I simply want to argue that in Western culture
the idea of charismatic attraction is a way of talking about certain
emotionally charged aspects of social interaction, both at the level of
mass movements, and in small-scale, everyday social life. At each level,
from the personal to the public, there remains the concept of a
compulsive, inexplicable emotional tie linking a group of followers
together in adulation of their leader, or tying the lover to the beloved,
which is commonly symbolized in the imagery of charisma.

In my analysis, I accept the subjective validity of these moments – I
do not wish to "explain" charismatic attraction as an illusion, or deny
it by claiming it to be a reflection of something more fundamental.
Instead, my effort will be to understand what involvement in a
charismatic movement means emotionally and psychologically, for
leaders and followers.

There are limits, however. Even though I am an anthropologist, in
this book I stay primarily within a Western context, though I do use
material from very simple non-Western societies as a base-line for
comparison. Cross-cultural research into more complex social formations
would undoubtedly be useful for developing a more complete theory of
charisma, but I felt that what was needed first was a model built from
the material that is the most familiar to us, and is most readily available.

Secondly, the study is unfortunately quite male-centered. This is a
consequence of the ethnographic accounts, which are almost always
about male leaders, and because of a male bias in the theoretical and
popular models of charisma. The study of charismatic women is a task
I have not been able to undertake, though I hope my work will provide
a base for later research.

Let me begin then by assuming that popular discourse about the subjective experience of charisma reflects a reality that must be taken seriously. Obviously crucial to this popular imagery of charisma is the presence of a compelling charismatic individual whose innate qualities attract others. This magnetic quality that is the essence of charisma is one that a few people are thought to "have" as a part of their basic character: charisma is not learned – it exists, just as height or eye color exist.

But unlike physical characteristics, charisma appears only in interaction with others who lack it. In other words, even though charisma is thought of as something intrinsic to the individual, a person cannot reveal this quality in isolation. It is only evident in interaction with those who are affected by it. Charisma is, above all, *a relationship*, a mutual mingling of the inner selves of leader and follower. Therefore, it follows that if the charismatic is able to compel, the follower has a matching capacity for being compelled, and we need to consider what makes up the personality configuration of the follower, as well as that of the leader, if we are to understand charisma.

There is yet another aspect aside from the mutual interaction of leader and follower. Since the crowd gathered around the leader (or the lover attracted to the beloved) has particular characteristics of excitability, selflessness and emotional intensity which are beyond those of the ordinary consciousnesses of the individuals involved, and because the attracted feel their personal identities lost in their worship of the charismatic other, charisma in Western society is felt to be a "strong force," as physicists say; it binds people together in ways that transcend and transmogrify the selves of the followers – and, quite possibly, the self of the leader as well.

Understanding charisma thus implies not only a study of the character of the charismatic and the attributes that make any particular individual susceptible to the charismatic appeal, but an analysis as well of the dynamic of the charismatic group itself in which the leader and follower interact. This dynamic, we can note from the outset, is felt to be one that is extremely powerful and strikingly ambivalent, greatly desired and greatly feared, and is morally conceived both as the peak of altruistic love and as the abyss of violent fanaticism.

Finally, we can also say that charisma has an implicit structural form as a process that takes place over time and under certain conditions, as participants become more or less committed, fall in and out of love. And, since it is evident as well that charismatic commitment not only varies for a particular follower and leader, but is more prevalent in some historical periods than others, and appears more among some social groups than others, we also need to contextualize any study of it, showing the connection between circumstances and the prospects of a charismatic relation.

Obviously, the notion of charisma, though amorphous, does have a content that offers the parameters for further analysis. And it is from this basic concept that I start the task of making sense of the subjective experience of charisma by exploring theoretical paradigms, some of which attempt to understand the appeal of the leader; others focus on the dynamic of the group; and others again try to develop a synthetic and contextual model of charismatic excitement. And, as we shall see, like the popular conceptualizations, all of these theories have a moral content, finding in charisma either salvation, or damnation.

My purpose in this survey is not only to write an essay on the history of ideas, but also something more pragmatic; that is, the extraction of a model of the emotions that can both provide us with a rudimentary paradigm for hierarchizing basic human needs, and allow us to conceptualize the complex historical, social and psychological aspects of the extraordinary experience of selflessness and transcendence that we mean when we say "charisma."

Having formulated a way of thinking about the charismatic experience, the next section uses cases to test how well this model works. As my ethnographic illustrations I have chosen some of the most excessive instances of charisma in the modern era and contrasted them with each other, and with the simplest forms of charismatic revelation in small-scale societies. The movements which coalesced around Charles Manson, Jim Jones and Adolf Hitler will be placed against the examples of charisma offered by shamanism and the group trance of the !Kung Bushmen. By analyzing this varied material and by using first-person accounts, I will try to discover the inner dynamic that binds the leaders and the group, and the way this interaction is constructed by the social context.

In the concluding chapter, I consider ways in which the impulse to self-loss and charismatic participation is diffused and domesticated in modern society through alternatives such as identification with the nation, hero worship, religion, and especially through intimate personal relationships. I also discuss the possibility that, if alternative forms for achieving a momentary escape from the prison of the self are delegitimized, charismatic relations are likely to have a greater influence and a more central place in the future. If this is so, then it is especially necessary to understand what this experience entails.

Let me begin then at the beginning, and introduce the reader to the ideas that can help us to construct a model for charisma.

Part II

Theory

2

"Human Beings As They Really Are": Social Theories of the Passions

Making a convincing model of charismatic attraction rests on producing an equally convincing model of the roots of human action. Trying to develop such a model has not only been a preoccupation of Western thought but also has inspired and exasperated thinkers and dreamers in every human society. The effort to resolve this existential question lies at the core of all religion and myth, where human life is imagined as a struggle to reach a higher end, escaping the boundaries of humanity as it is to become humanity as it might be.

In modern Western society, however, the erosion of tradition and the collapse of accepted religious belief leaves us without a *telos*, a sanctified notion of humanity's potential. Bereft of a sacred project, we have only a demystified image of a frail and fallible humanity no longer capable of becoming god-like. Niccolo Machiavelli was perhaps the first to articulate this new, disenchanted, pragmatic perspective when he promised his Princely patron that he would describe human beings not as they ought to be, not as they wish they were, but "as they really are." His ambition too was practical. Only by understanding and manipulating the unadorned and unappetizing reality of the human condition, he said, can the Prince hope to rule, and society gain stability. The unflattering portrait he drew of human cowardice and greed may be contested. Nonetheless, the effort Machiavelli made to replace the sacred teleological ideal with a more realistic image of humanity "as it is" has continued to be the general thrust of Western social thought.

However, this "naturalistic" concept of humanity is threatened by the phenomenon of the charismatic relationship, wherein the followers make exactly the claim that modern social thought denies, namely that the leader is a deity, and that membership in the charismatic group surrounding the leader offers a vitalizing *telos* in itself. But as modern, rational observers we cannot permit the participant's attribution of a supernatural aura to the leader to be an explanation for the charismatic state, even though we must give credence to the subjective reality of the leader's holiness for the follower. If we are not to succumb to canonization (or demonization) of the object of our study we must instead begin with the Machiavellian premise of a demystified and disenchanted human character.

The Triumph of Passion over Reason: David Hume

But what does this naturalistic model of humanity consist of? At least from the time of the Greeks, Western thought has portrayed human beings as double creatures torn by a war between passion and reason. There are then two choices for making a "realistic" image of humanity. The first approach is to place the human capacity for reason in the forefront. From Plato, and on through the Christian tradition and into the Enlightenment, this has been the general strategy. The passions have been regarded as inchoate internal drives, felt rather than known, which impel men and women to act, often against their better judgement.[1] Reason then has been invoked as a superior faculty with the power to rein in the passions and turn them to higher ends. Within this vision, reason is given sacred qualities; humanity, although dragged down by brute desire, could be redeemed by the intellectual quest for unity with divine rationality.

But the reign of reason proved susceptible to the assaults that bombarded it as the traditional view of the world lost its accepted validity and coherence, allowing the emergence of disquieting skepticism about the taken-for-granted foundations of daily experience. René Descartes had already written in the early seventeenth century that:

> Inasmuch as reason persuades me already that I must avoid believing things which are not entirely certain and indubitable, no less carefully than those things which seem manifestly false, the slightest ground for doubt that I find in any, will suffice for me to reject all of them .... The destruction of foundations necessarily brings down with it the rest of the edifice. (1972: 95)

At the same time, Blaise Pascal asserted that the best reason can do is to realize that all human beliefs are founded on nature, custom and habit. Reason, Descartes and Pascal argued, is primarily a calculative faculty, only capable of speaking of means, never of ends, and is easily swayed by circumstances. In dethroning reason, they hoped to stimulate a renewed faith in a higher, transcendent religious truth, but instead they laid the groundwork for a new perspective that recognizes only personal sensations and emotions.

This second strategy for understanding human beings is associated especially with David Hume,[2] who set out not only to destroy the traditional reign of reason, but also to replace it with the primacy of feelings. "I shall endeavour," he wrote in 1737. "to prove *first*, that reason alone can never be a motive to any action of the will; and *secondly*, that it can never oppose passion in the direction of the will" (1978: 413). And a few pages later, even more radically, he claims that "reason is, and ought to be, the slave of the passions, and can never pretend to any other office than to serve and obey them" (1978: 415).

Hume justified his position by taking a strongly empiricist view of human nature. The consciousnesses of men and women, he said, are nothing more than "a bundle or collection of different perceptions, which succeed one another with an inconceivable rapidity, and are in a perpetual flux and movement" (Hume 1978: 252). The apparent continuity and coherence of the world that is at the heart of rational thought is an illusion, a result of innumerable separate reflective impressions arising in response to the sensations caused in the individual by external sources or by the inner workings of the body. Therefore, one cannot convincingly argue for any reliable regularity or taken-for-granted systemic coherence whatsoever.

Hume showed reason to be in the power of passion, and that each passion is equally valid as a reflection of multiple sensations; furthermore, because of differing experiences and histories each person will have different passions. Humean philosophy thus effectively disintegrated all belief systems that claimed to rest upon received wisdom or transcendent inspiration. In this way Hume contributed to validating the demystification of tradition and religion, while providing as well a philosophical basis for the pragmatic data collection and debunking spirit characteristic of the scientific method.

But Hume's own ambition was to discredit moral extremism and emotionally compelling rhetoric and to plead for tolerance and moderation. In this he was reacting not only against the prejudices and rigid morality of his own bigoted Scottish Calvinist upbringing, but also against the larger climate of the preceding century, when European society had been rent asunder by kings passionately bent on gaining their own personal glory through the force of arms, and by civil wars between religious fanatics possessed by fervent belief in their own versions of holy truth.

Hume was temperamentally repulsed by such excesses. He described himself as "a man of mild Dispositions, of Command of Temper, of an open, social and cheerful Humour, capable of Attachment, but little susceptible of Enmity, and of great Moderation in all Passions" (quoted in Letwin 1965: 17). He was repelled by the fiery ardor that burned in the hearts of the Huguenot Prophets and by the zeal of the crowds of Levellers of the previous generation. And we can be certain that he was horrified by the convulsions of the Jansenists (who were active in Paris while he was in France in 1734) and the equally extraordinary paroxysms of the Methodists in England (which began in 1739).

Hume was completely unable to sympathize with the motivations behind these effusive displays of enthusiasm, and attributed them to

hypocrisy. "Men dare not avow, even to their own hearts, the doubts
which they entertain on such subjects. They make a merit of implicit
faith; and disguise to themselves their real infidelity, by the strongest
asseverations and the most positive bigotry" (Hume 1964: vol. 2, 348).
From his point of view, all intense emotional states are simply invitations
to danger:

> The most sprightly wit borders on madness, the highest effusions of
> joy produce the deepest melancholy, the most ravishing pleasures are
> attended with the most cruel lassitude and disgust, the most flattering
> hopes make way for the severest disappointments. And, in general,
> no course of life has such safety (for happiness is not to be dreamed
> of) as the temperate and moderate, which maintains as far as possible,
> a mediocrity, a kind of insensibility in everything. (Hume quoted in
> Letwin 1965: 77).

But even though strong passions are perilous, Hume thought they
could be controlled relatively easily and with little social disruption. He
assumed that most people's desires would naturally be relatively
harmless, like his own. As Ernest Gellner asks, "With such passions,
who would not gladly be their slave" (quoted in J.A. Hall 1987: 72).
Any disruptive, violent feelings could be balanced by cultivating
inherently calming passions, such as avarice, which had the virtue of
being doggedly methodical and conducive to social order (Hirschman
1977).

In consequence, despite the apparent radicalism of his philosophy,
Hume was in fact a relatively conservative Hanoverian gentleman who
preached tolerance, who opposed all forms of zeal in favor of the
pleasures of good company, and who believed the public would naturally
realize the necessity of following social rules and maintaining decorum
for the purpose of enjoying their mild personal desires with the minimum
of interference. For him, understanding "men as they are" meant
diversity, adaptation to circumstances, balancing of desires, a willingness
to accept compromises.

Passion and Teleology: The Utilitarians

Hume's contemporaries and successors have struggled ever since
with the logical implications of his empiricism, while simultaneously
attempting to make some moral order out of the motley realm of pure
sensation he had presented them as a substitute for a coherent world
ruled by divine rationality. On the one hand, in Germany Immanuel
Kant reacted by attempting to resuscitate the power of reason through
his claim for the existence of categorical imperatives which every human
being will necessarily understand and act upon. This essential imperative

is expressed in the famous maxim that one should treat oneself and others as an end, not as a means. What this signifies is that one should influence others by offering rational reasons for acting, thus giving credit to the rationality and freedom of the other, and one should refrain from influencing others in non-rational ways, thereby denying the other's rationality and agency.

But Kant's effort was bound to fail, both logically and practically. Logically it floundered because it is perfectly possible for a person to say "let everyone else be treated as a means, let me be treated as an end." And practically it is evident, as we shall see in the course of this volume, that people are often more than willing to be convinced by non-rational arguments, while rational discourse often fails dismally to achieve any consensus.[3]

In England, on the other hand, Hume's premises gained greater acceptance. In particular, Jeremy Bentham, starting from Hume's argument in favor of the primacy of sensation, claimed to have discovered in the passions a new teleology to replace the discarded sacred framework. Where Hume saw multiple desires, Bentham's contribution was to reduce them to two: the desire to avoid pain, and the desire to gain pleasure. The next step then was to calculate what acts and policies would give the most pleasure and the least pain, and Bentham bent his astonishing energies to discovering a psychology that could measure the duration, intensity and amount of these primary sensations in order to build a social system in which everyone's pleasure would be scientifically maximized according to the principles of his new science of Utilitarianism.

As the Utilitarian theory developed, the Humean premise of incommensurate and varied personal feelings was more and more attenuated and disguised; thinkers dismayed by the confusion implicit in Hume's picture of human nature attempted to build instead a more orderly model of society by increasingly constricting their vision of natural desires and passions. The culmination of this tendency came when Adam Smith argued that the pursuit of wealth meets all the deepest needs of human beings.[4]

This constriction had highly significant consequences, since it meant that the character of humans, derived from the essential passion of greed, was portrayed by Utilitarians as dogged, methodical, predictable and self-aggrandizing; a far cry from, for instance, the selfless and fiery, but evanescent, involvement of passionate love.

As a result of this narrowed psychology, social interaction was now imagined to be constructed through a series of rational calculations for the sake of maximizing personal desires (utility functions) in a world of other competing maximizers. The advantage of this severe reduction of the passions to avarice was that theorists could now envision human life as economic exchange, susceptible to the same kinds of rule-like mathematical formulae as the rest of the market.

In this image of humanity each individual is regent, a small island empire with special needs, wants, and desires. But it is assumed that each imperial individual will be able to calculate trade-offs in the value of any object, including the value of personal relationships, and it is assumed as well that there will be consistency in relationships and exchanges. This concept of humans as self-interested rational calculators coincides too with a belief in functionalism; that is, that every part has its place within the larger whole, as the orderly "unseen hand" of the marketplace maintains social equilibrium and a moral world despite the struggle of each against all.

But the rub is that this apparently simple philosophy rests, as we have seen, on a shifting base. Utility seems concrete enough, but the common-sense premise of utility actually disguises the fact that pleasures derived from the disparate emotional desires of individuals are polymorphous, complex, and often contradictory. Within the atomizing mode of thought provided by empiricism there is no way to rank pleasures or place them within any hierarchy, nor can the pursuit of one pleasure instead of another be logically validated or justified. Furthermore, the taken-for-granted world, even as it is desacralized and placed within the frame of the marketplace, proves to be less functional, less consistent and less reducible to rational calculation of means to ends than the more vulgar Utilitarians imagined.[5]

Aside from its deep logical difficulties, in practice Utilitarianism suffered considerable setbacks when Bentham found his ameliorative social schemes repudiated by the aristocracy who ought to have, by his logic, realized their utility. Meanwhile, the French Revolution shattered the Utilitarian image of the primacy of acquisitiveness and calculation in human nature. Under the inflaming influence of Revolutionary rhetoric, people's sensations and passions no longer seemed quite as mild and pliable as they had been portrayed by the young Hume, nor did these passions seem reducible to rational calculation, as Smith had argued.

In this atmosphere, it is no wonder that the Utilitarian moral theorist Henry Sidgwick found to his dismay that beliefs cannot in fact be rationally argued upon Utilitarian grounds, but must rest solely on personal "intuition." His plaintive cry was that "where he had looked for Cosmos, he had in fact found only Chaos" (quoted in MacIntyre 1981: 63). But in fact chaos is the only possible consequence of the welter of fundamentally incommensurate and equally compelling personal desires that lie at the core of the Humean paradigm.

But despite philosophical and practical difficulties, the imagery of "possessive individualism" remained deeply embedded within the thought of Western society because it correlates with and serves to validate the economic structure. It is the paradigm for human character held, for professional reasons, by economists, and it remains a generally accepted folk model for human action, "explaining" and unmasking all behavior as an attempt to "get something" for the self.

The Philosophy of the Superior Man: Mill and Nietzsche

There is, however, an alternative model of human character that we can discover in muted form in the philosophy of John Stuart Mill, and far more clearly in the heated writings of Friedrich Nietzsche. Mill, who dominated English social thought throughout much of the nineteenth century, made a last-ditch attempt to bring philosophical order out of the chaos of Utilitarianism. He was a complex thinker who realized early on that a strict calculation of pleasure was inadequate for the complexity of human life. But despite his misgivings, Mill retained the Benthamite ambition of building a good society from a scientific understanding of human needs. The complexity of the inputs and sensations in any individual case meant such a science could never be complete, but the model for it, in Mill's mind, remained completely individualistic, concrete and pragmatic. However, Mill's science of human nature was never written, and his portrait of the good society remained, like that of the other Utilitarians, "without firm ontological rooting" (J.A. Hall 1987: 30).

But there was another side to Mill which moved toward a quite non-Utilitarian resolution to the problem of developing a moral world out of an understanding of human nature. This side is revealed in his concept of genius. The genius, he thought, stands outside the realm of ordinary people as a kind of magic beacon, a unique and inexplicable phenomenon. More ardent than the rest of us, but with a powerful will that can turn desire into "the most passionate love of virtue and the sternest self-control" (Mill 1975: 57), the superior man is described as active, strict, isolated from ordinary humanity, idiosyncratic, energetic, and selflessly struggling to transform the world in accordance with an inner ideal of perfection. The genius described by Mill looks, in fact, a great deal like Mill himself. Such people, he says, are like the "Niagara River," and cannot be constrained by the "Dutch Canals" of ordinary rules and norms (1975: 61).[6] Instead, they have the "freedom to point the way" for the rest of humanity (Mill 1975: 63).

The superior individual, according to Mill, has another important characteristic. He or she is naturally more receptive to higher pleasures than ordinary men and women. These "higher" pleasures, he believed, following the wisdom of his era and class, are poetic, artistic, and inspiring; those who feel such pleasures are above commoners motivated by mere animal sensation. Mill thus tried to solve the problem of evolving a morality and social order by arguing for an intrinsic hierarchy of pleasures and claiming that the genius would "naturally" promote these higher pleasures and lead other, lesser mortals to experience them as well, thus raising the level of society by increasing the quality and social usefulness of enjoyment.

By introducing this moral hierarchy of pleasure along with the notion of the genius, Mill broke away from Hume's tolerant view of the equality of passions, away from the egalitarianism of the Utilitarians, and away from the Smithian reduction of all passions to the "interest" of avarice. He argued instead in favor of a new teleology – a teleology based on the apotheosis of those who ardently manifest higher feelings.

Mill's glorification of genius is obviously a precursor to the modern notion of charisma, and is redolent of the romantic rebellion against mechanism and empiricism led in England by Samuel Coleridge and Mill's erstwhile friend and mentor, Thomas Carlyle. Even more striking, however, is Mill's similarity to Friedrich Nietzsche, who also apotheosized the genius – the *Übermensch* – albeit in far more fervid tones.

But where Mill linked the genius together with moral uplift through the dubious concept of the genius's naturally poetic soul, Nietzsche repudiated such an image. Unlike Mill and other Utilitarians, Nietzsche confronted and fully accepted the modern absence of any sacred *telos* or normative order. Without such an order, there can be, he said, no talk of "higher" passions, no logical way to construct a morality out of the natural constitution of human beings.

In his absolute skepticism about all systems Nietzsche resembles Hume more than he resembles any other British philosopher. But Nietzsche is far from being an amiable Hanoverian gentleman; his mental state, unlike Hume's, was radical and highly colored, shaped by the revolutionary ardor of his times, by the romantic images of the German tradition, and especially by his own febrile, passionate and contradictory character. Consequently, Nietzsche's vision of human nature, which he discovered not through study, but by introspection, is far less balanced and mild – and more in tune with our modern experience – than that proposed by the even-tempered Hume or the Calvinistic Mill.

For Nietzsche, himself a life-long invalid, humanity is "the sick animal," and human history is nothing but the story of the smoldering resentment of slaves warring against the fiery and ruthless will of the master. The difference between the two categories of humanity is simply that the master accepts and embraces his predispositions, and pursues pleasure with all his might, while the slave tries to justify his own weakness and take revenge on the strong by the invention of morality. Nietzsche thus accepts wholeheartedly the Humean formula of the primacy of impulse, but he rejects the efforts to build a morality out of these impulses as nothing more than a pious fraud perpetrated by those infected with slave mentality.

The genius, portrayed by Mill as a poet and connoisseur, is then for Nietzsche essentially a warrior; his virtue is, quite simply, his sheer overwhelming vitality. "Great men, like great epochs, are explosive material in whom tremendous energy has been accumulated" (Nietzsche 1977: 97). This explosiveness is the expression of what Nietzsche calls the "will to power." The content of the "will to power" is defined as "above all an *affect* and specifically the affect of the command" (Nietzsche 1966: 25). Those who express this elemental, transvaluing, explosive power of command naturally dominate the weak. They are the heroes who make their own laws outside of convention, based on the authentic impulses of their personal desires. This innate capacity to command is pictured as the ultimate value in a world lacking any other values:

> What is good? – All that heightens the feeling of power, the will to power, power itself in man.
> What is bad? – All that proceeds from weakness.
> What is happiness? – The feeling that power *increases* – that a resistance is overcome. (Nietzsche 1977: 115).

With this radical disavowal of liberal morality and affirmation of the right of the strong to rule, Nietzsche repudiates as well the Benthamite accountant's view that pain and pleasure vary inversely, and derides the Humean belief in the mildness of the passions. For him it is evident that increased pleasure also implies increased pain, and he takes as his paradigm the orgy, which he imagines as "an overflowing feeling of life and energy within which even pain acts as a stimulus" (Nietzsche 1977: 110). Nietzsche says that it is exactly in the erupting flood of *intense* sensations aroused in the orgy that the *Übermensch*'s will to power is released and revealed. His feelings are stronger than others'; it is precisely his emotional vitality that makes him the *Übermensch*.

Blond Beasts and Rational Calculators

Nietzsche's worship of the voracious, intense, and commanding "tropical monsters" and "blond beasts," surely the most notorious aspect of his philosophy of authenticity and emotional expression, seems far from the rational-calculator paradigm of human life assumed by Utilitarianism, and even further from the tolerant good-fellowship and pragmatic politics of David Hume. But there is a hidden connection between these philosophies; a connection that derives from their shared premises of the primacy of human desire in an age in which reason has been dethroned and custom has lost its legitimacy.

As we have seen, the Utilitarians, despite the rationalistic orientation of their theory, build their entire model of human good upon the shifting grounds of Hume's analysis of atomistic individual passions. The underlying reference to inchoate personal feelings logically implies what MacIntyre has defined as "emotivism," namely "the doctrine that all evaluative judgements and more specifically all moral judgements are *nothing but* expressions of preference, expressions of attitude or feeling, insofar as they are moral or evaluative in character" (1981: 11).

Eighteenth- and nineteenth-century English philosophy used this idea about the emotional base of action and attempted to transform it into a rational paradigm of human nature, founded on assumptions about the calculability of pleasure, the blandness and malleability of the sentiments, and the centrality of avarice, recast as "interest," and envisioned as a calm and methodical passion conducive to social harmony. This paradigm offered apparent order, but at the cost of painfully shrinking the range and complexity of human desire while simultaneously favoring a mechanistic market model of interpersonal relationships. Human beings became cost-accounting machines, calculating means, but without any way to judge what ends are worth striving for.

Nietzsche took another tack, accepting completely the consequences of the logic of emotivism, apotheosizing the only element he felt sure of: the urgent emotional intensity of the *Übermensch*. This intensity provides the *telos* lacking in the "rational man" model, and Nietzsche's struggle was to become himself such a potent figure. Yet in arguing that the force of the individual's passions is truly all that really matters, Nietzsche can be seen to be carrying the Humean premises of the primacy of preference and emotion that underlie Utilitarian thought to their logical conclusion (a conclusion also reached, although in a muted and hedged fashion, by Mill).

The claim made by Nietzsche is simply that if desire is all that exists, then let desire be gargantuan, and may the more powerfully passionate devour the world to fill their insatiable appetites. And it follows as well that other people then become quite overtly the instruments for pleasure that they are covertly assumed to be in Utilitarian thought. "A great man . . . asks for no 'compassionate' heart, but servants, instruments; in his dealings with men his one aim is *to make* something out of them" (Nietzsche 1964: 366–7).

Thus Nietzsche's acclamation of the great leader as a revelation of primal irrational vitality, and the model of man as a rational calculator, both originate as responses to Hume's corrosive insistence on relativistic personal preference as a substitute for any sacred human mission. As

MacIntyre writes, the "great man" "represents individualism's final attempt to escape from its own consequences" (1981: 241). The supreme irony is that Hume, who had a rounded and sophisticated view of human nature, and who hated demagogues, prepared the ground both for the two-dimensional "rational man" and for the volatile Superman.

We have then two models of humanity. One is built upon the way people exchange and interact with one another in order to gain their desires, and results in a concept of human beings as rational calculators who know how to weigh means, but have no way to measure ends; the other emphasizes the strength of desire and the primal emotion of the will to command as absolute values in themselves and leads to an apotheosis of the vitally charged "great man."

But despite their different directions, these models are deeply linked in their fundamental premises: demystification of the sacred and the primacy of personal emotional preferences. And it seems as well that, if those premises are accepted, only the intensity of a Nietzschean "great man" offers any hope of breaking the logical grip of a worldview in which passion has been reduced to "interest," and love to a "utility function."

3

The Sociology of the Irrational: Max Weber and Emile Durkheim

In the last chapter, we saw how the theory of a human nature resting on passions evolved in the eighteenth and nineteenth centuries, and moved in two contradictory and opposed directions: one a restricted Utilitarian paradigm in which "interest" and calculation of exchange from the point of view of the rational actor are the primary concern; the other a Nietzschean model of emotional intensity and the will to power of the superior man. According to the logic of these models humanity was envisioned either as a corporate body of reasonable maximizers or alternatively as resentful slaves ruled by larger-than-life "tropical monsters."

The Utilitarians, and to an even greater extent their economistic successors, felt no need to take cognizance of extraordinary passions or persons that did not fit their increasingly mechanistic models, since their image of people as rational calculators was in harmony with the dominant capitalist mode of production. They and their descendants increasingly occupied themselves with technical problems of charting preferences and exchanges in a world that apparently made good common sense – despite its absence of any transcendent human goal and its impoverished image of human nature. Only Mill, as we have seen, had any discussion of the importance of passion and genius, and this aspect of his thought was never integrated into his central theory of human nature, which remained resolutely Benthamite.

Nietzsche's theory, however, stood opposed to the rationalizing movement of capitalism, and he was obliged to say why the great geniuses and warriors he admired so much were no longer dominating the world. This problem led him to argue that the passionate Nietzschean man is a primitive form of humanity, who has been tamed and rationalized by the movement of civilization. Nietzsche therefore saw civilization as a diminution of human capacity, and called for a revolutionary and transcendent revaluation of all values. In his last days, as he verged on insanity, he came to believe that he himself was the Messiah sent to redeem humanity from its modern pettiness.

The challenge offered by Nietzsche to the ordinary common-sense world led sociologists to attempt to accommodate his corrosive insights into their worldviews. In this chapter, I want to talk about two such efforts. One, argued brilliantly by Max Weber, tries to retain and explicate the superman, but simultaneously diffuses the superman's power by placing him in contradistinction to a process of increasing rationalization of the world; the other, associated with Emile Durkheim, radically translates the Nietzschean, vitalizing, urge to power away from the *Übermensch*, and locates it instead within the community itself. Taken together, these two perspectives provide a new base for a more complete understanding of the actual character of the charismatic moment.

Max Weber and the Charisma of Paroxysm

Max Weber, whom we will consider first, accepts with little alteration Nietzsche's basic assertion of the willful genius who is regarded as the font of human feeling and of creativity. And Weber accepts as well the opposition between the genius and the constraints of civilization. But unlike Nietzsche, in the general thrust of his work Weber puts himself on the side of civilized constraint, despite his belief that this constraint is destructive of all that is glorious, animated, and emotionally compelling in the world. Where Nietzsche is energetically heroic in his ambitions and tragic in his failure, Weber is marked by the pathos and nostalgia of one who feels himself cut away from the vital source of life. As he tells his lover, "Fate had drawn a veil between him and the reality of things" and he laments that he is "like a tree stump, which is able to put out *buds*, again and again – without playing the part of being a whole tree" (quoted in Green 1974: 164, 114).

The sense of self-estrangement and inner deadness that is at the core of Weber's life is compensated for and well masked in his work by his disciplined intellectual powers which permitted him to rigorously control his despairing emotional states. In his study, he gained a creative capacity to escape from himself, presenting all cases and cultures "objectively," laden with the detail and insights into the rationality of human motivations that are the result of his extraordinary scholarship. More than any other writer, Weber's task was to conquer the world for rationality, removing all mystery from existence.

In consequence, Weber's sociology was above all the study of social action that is consciously planned, consistent, goal-oriented and purposive, and his great achievement lay in expanding the Utilitarian model beyond its original framework. His method was to demonstrate that much of what seems irrational in history and in other societies can be grasped by understanding the situation from the viewpoint of the actor, who is enmeshed in a particular cultural configuration, with its special values and beliefs.[1] The nobleman may exhaust his patrimony

in ostentatious entertainment, while the entrepreneur saves his money
in order to invest it. The result in the first instance is greater status-
honor, and in the second instance a larger bank account, but the
underlying motives are the same; each regent individual is seeking to
maximize a valued good according to his or her personal preferences
as structured by culture. Weber thus showed that instrumental economic
rationality is not the only form of rational thought, but that other
possible types of rationality exist.[2] In this way he greatly increased the
ability of the Utilitarian model to explain action that seemed outside
the range of reason.

Yet even as his project expanded rationality to encompass ever-wider
realms of human action, Weber also notoriously admitted into his
system two other modes of power and behavior orientation which are
quite outside the dominant realm of planned, meaningful action by
individuals seeking a desired end. The first instance of non-rational
behavior, tradition, is portrayed by Weber as an endless cycle of
repetition; actors in the pure type of traditional society supposedly have
no awareness of the meaning of their actions, but function as unthinking
robots, compulsively repeating what has been done before, simply
because it has been done before. The non-rationality of tradition is not
the non-rationality of passion, but that of inertia and lethargy. It is
conservative, predictable, and oriented toward mechanical reproduction
of itself.[3]

It is, however, the second type of non-rational action orientation
which is of interest to us. This is action organized by charisma. In fact,
Max Weber was the first to introduce the term "charisma" into
sociology, the first to attempt to analyze the inner content of the
charismatic's character, the first to argue that charisma implies a
relationship between the great man and the followers, and the first to
place the charismatic within a social context.

But charisma is not easily defined in Weber's work.[4] In particular,
he writes about two distinct forms of charisma, which in fact are quite
opposed to one another. One form is institutional charisma, which can
be inherited, or passed along with accession to an office, or invested in
an institution. This is the charisma that gives an aura of sacred power
to any individual who has the right to wear the bishop's robe, or sit
on the king's throne, regardless of actual personal characteristics. In
this case, charisma is a force for the legitimization of powerful
institutions and individuals. These particular institutions and persons
claim, and are believed by the public, to have a connection with the
sacred, and to therefore have charisma.[5]

Weber spends most of his time discussing this form of charisma, but
that does not mean that he thinks it is the primary form, only that it
is relatively rational and therefore more amenable to his type of
sociological analysis. Actually, he insists that the alliance of charisma

with the maintenance of what exists is a purely secondary phenomenon. Instead, the genuine and prior type of charisma is a negating, emotionally intense, undercutting force which "is opposed to all institutional routines, those of tradition and those subject to rational management" (M. Weber 1946: 52).

In its primal form charisma does not have any fixed lines of authority; those involved make no allowance for orderly provisioning, they despise economic trading and profit, and they aim at the overthrow of all structure, the disintegration of all the chains of custom. Charisma of this type is revolutionary and creative, occurring in times of social crisis, opening the way to a new future. In charismatic movements people no longer obey custom or law; instead the followers submit to the imperious demands of a heroic figure, whose orders are legitimated not by logic, nor by the hero's place in any ascribed hierarchy, but solely by the personal "power to command" of the charismatic individual:

"Charisma" shall be understood to refer to an *extraordinary* quality of a person, regardless of whether this quality is actual, alleged, or presumed. "Charismatic authority," hence, shall refer to a rule over men, whether predominantly external or predominantly internal, to which the governed submit because of their belief in the extraordinary quality of the specific *person*. (M. Weber 1946: 295).

Jesus's words, "It is written . . . But I say unto you," are the core of the charismatic relation for Weber. Whatever the leader says, whatever he asks, is right, even if it is self-contradictory. It is right *because the leader has said it*. The basis of the leader's legitimacy is in the immediate "recognition" of his miraculous quality, and the disciple is lost in complete personal devotion to the possessor of this quality, "a devotion born of distress and enthusiasm" (M. Weber 1946: 249). Self-sacrifice is the cardinal virtue of the charismatic follower, and selfishness the greatest vice.

In his outline of charisma as a very peculiar type of personal authority exercised by a leader who is thought to have supernatural qualities, Weber breaks with Nietzsche, who, like Mill, often pictured the genius as an outsider, perhaps as someone rejected by the crowd because of his superior character which sets him apart. But as a sociologist, Weber is concerned only with man in community, as a social creature. The charismatic, for him, can exist only in relationship to his adoring followers. Weber thus is obliged, as Nietzsche was not, to think why the charismatic's character should attract disciples, and this is where he makes his most important contributions.

Weber's thoughts about the source of the charismatic's magnetism are revealed in those he designates as prototypical charismatic leaders: shamans, epileptics, berserk warriors, pirates, demagogues, prophets.

According to Weber these figures are charismatic in that they are marked by a unique and innate capacity to display highly colored emotions, of whatever kind. Charismatic figures are imagined by Weber, as they were imagined by Nietzsche, to be more vivid than ordinary mortals; they appear to exist in an altered and intensified state of consciousness that is outside of mundane patterning, and that is more potent than ordinary emotional life.

Weber seems to believe that it is precisely the enhanced expressiveness of the charismatic, revealed in the rolling eyes of the epileptic, the frenzied fury of the warrior, the ranting of the demagogue, the preternatural calm of the exemplary prophet, that appeals to the follower.[6] The intense emotional state of the charismatic is transmitted spontaneously to onlookers, infecting them with enthusiasm and a feeling of vitality. As Liah Greenfeld puts it, "genuine charisma thus means the ability to internally generate and externally express extreme excitement, an ability which makes one the object of intense attention and unreflective imitation by others" (1985: 122).

To achieve this end, the charismatic practitioner may be aided by techniques of ecstasy: frenzied dancing and singing, mortification and self-mutilation, oratory. Following Nietzsche, all these are seen as lessened forms of the paradigmatic technique for stimulation of the charismatic moment: the erotic orgy (M. Weber 1978: 401). In the physical paroxysm the devout, intoxicated and ecstatic, can escape from their ordinary miseries by dissolving their separateness in the "objectless acosmism of love" (M. Weber 1946: 330).[7]

The participatory communion offered by the charismatic leader is understood by Weber as having an absolute value for human beings:

> They have been considered specifically consecrated and divine because of their psychic extraordinariness and because of the intrinsic value of the respective states conditioned by them. . . . for the devout the sacred value, first and above all, has been a psychological state in the *here and now*. Primarily this state consists in the emotional attitude *per se*. (1946: 278)

As a visceral truth, this charismatic moment is at the emotional heart of the religious experience, and "enforces the inner subjection to the unprecedented and absolutely unique and therefore Divine" (1978: 1,117).

But despite his interest in such extraordinary states, Weber's theory of them was rudimentary and covert. His stated social psychology of human actors elaborating infinitely variable credos and life styles, spinning cultural webs of meaning, is one in which the individual remains always locked within his or her skin, consciously calculating advantage. It is precisely this struggle of the active agent for meaning that accounts for society insofar as society can be understood at all. The charismatic, and the crowd around him, are both as remote from this rationalistic model of sociological understanding as is the convulsion of the epileptic.

Not only is the hunger for the ecstatic release of the erotic or charismatic beyond discussion, but any such hunger is also doomed to inevitable starvation in the modern world. For Weber, such intense desires are inevitably at war with the world of bureaucratic action and the instrumental rationality of economic maximizers. It is a battle in which bureaucracy is by far the stronger of the adversaries, since bureaucratically rationalized institutions favor greater production and a more efficient economy, and will mercilessly crush all spontaneous attraction, all the immediacy of vivid emotional ties, in favor of the cool and calculated, instrumentally rational relationships necessary for a technically sophisticated social order:

> Thus, discipline inexorably takes over ever larger areas as the satisfaction of political and economic needs is increasingly rationalized. This universal phenomenon more and more restricts the importance of charisma and of individually differentiated conduct. (M. Weber 1978: 1,156)

> The routinized economic cosmos, and thus the rationally highest form of the provision of material goods which is indispensable for all worldly culture, has been a structure to which the absence of love is attached from the very root. (M. Weber 1946: 355)

Weber's picture of the human adventure is then one in which not only charisma and tradition are bound to fade, but also all other forms of rational action, submerged by the most restricted Utilitarian model of humanity as economic calculator. This is hardly a future he welcomes – only one that is inevitable. "Not summer's bloom lies ahead of us," he prophesies, "but rather a polar night of icy darkness and hardness" (1946: 128). The only hope for escape lay in the hands of the very figures who are excluded, a priori, from sociological analysis; that is, in the advent of "entirely new prophets" (1958: 182). Thus Weber, the most sophisticated and disenchanted of rational thinkers, fell prey in the last analysis, and very much despite himself, to a desperate worship of the charismatic hero.

Emile Durkheim and the Charisma of the Collective

At the same time that Weber was formulating his demystified picture of a mechanical future and yearning for a heroic redeemer, the great French sociologist Emile Durkheim was developing quite a different paradigm for the human condition – one that leads to an opposing yet complementary concept of charisma. Durkheim, an idealistic man who was heavily influenced by the transformative secular religion of the French Revolution and by the ameliorative social science tradition of Comte, begins his work not with nostalgia for the vitality that has been lost, but instead with a strong faith in the eternal power and goodness of the potent and equalizing affective bonding that ties social groups together, as well as a deep distrust of the Weberian focus on the socially contextualized, but always individualistically motivated, actor. Durkheim's concern is with the dynamics of the group itself as an entity *sui generis*, and for him the job of the sociologist is to construct theories about the general rules of group life, which very definitely "are not those of individual psychology" (Durkheim 1959: 312).

Durkheim's insights and investigations into the characteristics of generic group life are many. He developed statistical measures demonstrating that alienation and anomie afflict a community in which social embeddedness is lacking; he demonstrated the transformative effect of an increasing division of labor on every aspect of social life; he prefigured much modern linguistic and structural analysis in his insistence that symbols are patterned and based on formal social structure.[8] But my interest here is in his crucial, though not greatly elaborated, discourse on the nature and origin of the collective itself.

In Durkheim's view, the collective is the type case of the sacred. He imagines it as existing above and beyond those who make it up: timeless, encompassing, vital, emotionally compelling, it evokes from its members a deeply felt commitment and provides them with a sense of surpassing value. In fact, for Durkheim, individuals actually become human beings only insofar as they escape from their individual selves, which he envisioned as inevitably solipsistic and antisocial, and submit to absorption in the moral entity of the suprapersonal group. "Insofar as he belongs to society, the individual transcends himself, both when he thinks and when he acts" (Durkheim 1965: 29).[9] Men and women therefore had two fundamental kinds of consciousness: "Far from being simple, our inner life has something that is like a double center of gravity. On the one hand is our individuality – and, more particularly, our body in which it is based; on the other is everything in us that expresses something other than ourselves. . . . [These] mutually contradict and deny each other" (1973: 152).

The opposition between the individual and group self carries with it the extraordinary implication that the individual agent is not an irreducible social fact. "We do not admit that there is a precise point at which the individual comes to an end and the social realm commences . . . we pass without interval from one order of facts to the other" (1966: 313). This means that instead of a person-centered sociology that accepts the primacy of the self and assumes the individual actor consciously manipulates a web of social meaning or acts on his impulses and personal desires, Durkheim proposes a social psychology of a continuous ebb and flow between selfish singularity and immersion in a community.

Durkheim is therefore at odds with all the other theorists we have written about so far in his portrait of the human condition. Weber, Nietzsche, the Utilitarians, and Hume all take as given the emotivist principle of the primacy of individual passions and preferences, however these are interpreted and evaluated. But Durkheim proposes a radical alternative. The passions and desires of individuals, he says, are often subordinate to those of the group, and the drives that motivate the group are quite different in type and character from those that motivate the individuals who make it up. They are of a higher order, and transcend petty interests and personal appetites.

Durkheim thus originates the principle of conflict between the moral world of the group and the desires of the person that will later be elaborated by Freud in the concept of the superego. He offers as well the possibility of social action which is unconscious – a new idea. But more importantly he proposes an escape from the logical dilemma of emotivism by his premise that there are indeed universally compelling laws governing human choices and actions within a group. Scientifically understanding and validating these suprapersonal laws is the first task of sociology, as Durkheim envisioned it. The second task, in the tradition of Comte and the Enlightenment, is to promote the conditions that will lead to a properly organized and healthy community where men and women can escape from their disparate and animalistic personal selves – and where thought escapes from the fruitless task of deriving a moral world from disparate human desires.

Because of his first premise of the priority of the suprapersonal community, it follows that Durkheim is not interested in understanding Mill's genius, nor the Nietzschean superman, nor in charisma as Weber understood it; that is, as an emotional effusion arising in a specific individual which then inspires the group that surrounds him. Durkheim, in fact, does not use the term charisma at all, and consistently downplays the importance of all forms of leadership and personal attachment in his discourse. For him the creative principle is shared participation in highly charged and depersonalizing rituals of the sacred; rituals which serve to integrate all the communicants into a unit. Where Weber postulates an instigating magician who is the precursor of the priest, Durkheim begins with the ritual group, which is the archetype of the church.

Ostensibly Durkheim took his understanding of this primal ritual communion from ethnographies of cultures he felt were the most "primitive" and therefore showed the ancestral form of worship: the Australian aborigines as described by Spencer and Gillen, Robertson-

Smith's brilliant work on the ancient Semites, and French research on the contemporary Kayble tribes of colonial Algeria. But in the back of Durkheim's mind was the French Revolution, which he referred to several times as the prototypical example of a depersonalizing and invigorating ritual in the modern era. The Revolution demonstrates, he tells us, that the emotional essence of religion is not related to gods or creeds, but rises out of spontaneous mass celebrations and the collective passions these generate.

In this he follows the image of Revolutionary enthusiasm propounded most notably by the great romantic historian Jules Michelet, who writes in a highly Durkheimian manner (but five years before Durkheim's birth) of Revolutionary fervor overwhelming individuals and transporting them beyond themselves into transcendent realms of community. "There are no longer any mountains, rivers, or barriers between men. Their language is still dissimilar, but their words agree so well that they all seem to spring from the same place – from the same bosom. Everything has gravitated towards one point, and that point now speaks forth; it is the unanimous prayer from the heart of France. Such is the power of love. To attain unity, nothing was able to prove an impediment, no sacrifice was considered too dear" (Michelet 1967: 444).[10]

Durkheim's work is animated as much as Michelet's by an implicit faith in the equalizing and energizing experience of community, but unlike his predecessor he tries to say something about the source and shape of the moment of communion. His theory, following his ethnographic material, was that such emotional effusions of selflessness are engendered automatically whenever people are put into "closer and more active relations with one another" (Durkheim 1965: 241). He argued that when a certain density of people gather, the actual physical intimacy and propinquity of the crowd inevitably obliges people to feel a sense of sharing rather than solitude, cooperation rather than competition, power rather than weakness, likeness rather than difference. The similarity of the crowd members is accentuated by their physical closeness; they begin to feel their individual identities disintegrating under the influence of the crowd massed around them. Under these circumstances Durkheim thought that collective ecstasy is bound to occur regardless of any cultural differences, since "the fundamental process is always the same; only circumstances colour it differently" (Durkheim 1965: 460).

Durkheim also believed the physical energies of the primal crowd are naturally inspired by spontaneous movements and outcries of participants who are emotionally stimulated by the gathering. These impulsive outbursts contagiously spread as they are immediately imitated, magnified, and synchronized within the group as a whole. According to his theory, the participatory unity created by these echoing and heightened responses mechanically stimulates strong states of emotion, creating "a force that stirs up around us a whole whirlwind of organic and psychological phenomena" (Durkheim 1984: 53). Durkheim called this automatic physical experience of exaltation, intoxication and self-loss "collective effervescence" and named it "the very type of sacred thing" (Durkheim 1965: 140), the prototype for all religious ritual, and the core for all forms of human community.[11]

Even though Durkheim stresses the automatic, unthinking character of this process, individuals also have a pragmatic reason for submitting themselves to this experience and even for actively seeking it, since participants feel a surge of renewed vitality when they are disintegrated into the larger body of the ecstatic group. They are strengthened and expanded, according to Durkheim, because as "each one is borne along by the rest" in impassioned collective celebration they all feel themselves to be a part of the larger truth of the timeless and potent community, which stands above the individual's limitations of mortality, self-interest, and personal weakness (Durkheim 1982: 56). "Men are more confident because they feel themselves stronger; and they really are stronger, because forces which were languishing are now reawakened in the consciousness" (Durkheim 1965: 387).

According to Durkheim, the explosion of transpersonal vitality occasioned by the ritual is expressed in breaking down the conventions of daily life and the ordinary boundaries that distinguish self and other.

> The passions released are of such an impetuosity that they can be restrained by nothing. They are so far removed from their ordinary conditions of life, and they are so thoroughly conscious of it, that they feel that they must set themselves outside of and above their ordinary morals. . . . The sexes unite contrarily to the rules governing sexual relations. Men exchange wives with each other. Sometimes even incestuous unions, which in normal times are thought abominable and are severely punished, are now contracted openly and with impunity. (Durkheim 1965: 247)

In this imagery, the engulfing flood of affect generated by group action can overcome all personal distinctions, including the most deeply ingrained taboos of sexual restrictions.[12] In his portrait of identity loss and polymorphous sexuality Durkheim again prefigures later psychoanalytic theory.

However, even in Durkheim's resolutely group-centered theory, a charismatic individual may have a place. This is because the effusion of collective participation cannot be symbolized in itself, since "men know well they are acted upon, but they do not know by whom" (Durkheim 1965: 239). Instead, the human capacity for representation is called into play to manufacture symbolic forms which can serve as foci for the vivifying collective ritual.

This symbolic object, whatever its actual form, functions to magnify the emotional impact of the group experience, since Durkheim believed that "the effect of the common consciousness is stronger when it is no longer exerted diffusely, but through the mediation of some clearly defined organ" (Durkheim 1984: 131). Because it serves as a lens through which the power of the community can be focused and amplified, the symbol is therefore endowed with a special, supernatural quality. It has, however, no such properties of its own; it is not the sun, but the moon, shining with reflected light. The true energy source, in Durkheim's view, is always society; but, because it cannot conceptualize its own brightness, society mistakenly regards the mirror in which it views itself as the source of illumination.

Sometimes, by happenstance, a person becomes a sacred symbol. Such an individual's personal qualities are irrelevant, since he or she exists solely as a sign no different from any other sacred totem. For Durkheim, then, a venerated leader is less a person than the "group incarnate and personified" (1965: 241). And because the leader is envisioned as the emanation of the group Durkheim argues that "despotism. . . is nothing more than transformed communism" (Durkheim 1984: 144).

Thus for Durkheim certain individuals may indeed be raised to great heights and worshipped as embodiments of the sacred. Indeed, according to him, this attribution is actually correct, since they both stimulate and represent the communal excitement that is the essence of the holy. But they are not innovators or revolutionaries. In fact, they succeed only insofar as they symbolize the social configuration in which they find themselves, much as traditional leaders, in Weber's formulation, are enslaved by custom. "If [society] happens to fall in love with a man and if it thinks it has found in him the principal aspirations that move it, as well as a means of satisfying them, this man will be raised above the others and, as it were, deified" (Durkheim 1965: 243).

Implicitly, then, regardless of his personal appeal, a leader will be repudiated who fails to "vibrate sympathetically" with the mood of the masses, and satisfy its desires (which are, for Durkheim, desires to ecstatically experience itself as a community). From this perspective, leaders can only be, as Michelet termed the heroes of the Revolution, "ambitious puppets" who "rather received than communicated" the communal impulse (Michelet 1967: 12).

Yet when the collective *does* represent itself in an individual, then Durkheim's picture of the crystallizing figure of the leader who coalesces and intensifies the group's collective effervescence is analogous in many respects to Weber's primordial charismatic figure, although the source of the leader's radiance is located solely in the eyes of the group, not in the person of the leader.

Durkheim recognizes that such a deified individual is not the equivalent of an inanimate sacred object. He is a being with personal desires and the potential for action, and inasmuch as he is worshipped he has the possibility of directing the group, as opposed to reflecting it. In this sense the worshipped leader is, for Durkheim, as for Weber, the prototype of the creative culture hero. But the role of the charismatic actor is never discussed explicitly in Durkheim, since for him any reference to individuals introduces the spectre of personal preference and moral incomprehensibility – the spectre Weber met with his notion of a "value-free" sociology, and with his nostalgia for a hero.

As we have seen, what Durkheim formulates instead is an explanation that subsumes individual desires and provides an experiential ethical base for all social life everywhere through the self-transcendence engendered by emotionally charged group rituals that overwhelm separate persons in the flood of collective feeling. This one intense emotion and its ritual expression gives rise to all society, and to all the moral, logical and even physical categories constructed by reason. The quandaries imposed by Hume's disintegrative philosophy are resolved by a denial of the separate self, an apotheosis of the innate morality of the group, and an assertion of the absolute and timeless value of collective participation.

But even though Durkheim envisaged collective effervescence as an eternal social phenomenon, like Weber he believed the experience of charisma to be undercut by modernity. For Durkheim, however, this was not because the soul-destroying world of technical-rational bureaucracy erodes individuality. The situation is rather the opposite: because individuals are *less* differentiated in simple "mechanical" social formations, they can more easily lose themselves in the collective seizure. In modern society, on the other hand, the complex division of labor and the dominance of an economic ethos engender an ideology of separateness and a growing distinction of roles, coupled with an increasing lack of awareness of social connectedness and interdependence. These factors make modern people feel *more* individualistic, more selfish, more detached from their fellows, and therefore less amenable to the visceral experience of essential unity and similarity that stimulates collective effervescence.

But despite this modern obstacle to charismatic communion, Durkheim affirmed that all human communities must retain the potential for charismatic experience, since without it they are mere aggregations of highly intelligent but rapacious beasts, plundering and destroying one another. Only the sharing of *communitas* in the ritual can give an inner sense of higher purpose, and this is necessary not only for the foundation of society but for individuals as well, who need a transcendent object to escape from despair and isolation.

In fact, there is implicit in Durkheim a notion that we will see become more important in later theory; that is, that the very lack of opportunity for collective effervescence characteristic of the "transitional era" of today must give modern men and women a greater desire for an escape from the self in the heat of charismatic communion, which smolders beneath the surface of society waiting to be ignited. "All that matters," Durkheim wrote, "is to feel below the moral cold which reigns on the surface of our collective life the source of warmth that our societies bear in themselves" (quoted in Bellah 1973: xlvii).[13]

Models of Irrational Attraction

In this chapter, I have outlined two very different and complex responses to the ideas about human nature offered by Hume and played out by his Utilitarian successors, and by Nietzsche. In Weber's model, the opposing paradigms of rational actor and heroic superman are placed uneasily side by side within a theory of history in which instrumental reason slowly undermines will and emotion. Charisma is posited as the final refuge of the individual creative actor in a mechanical and disenchanted world, as elusive, as appealing, and as evanescent as the inexplicable desire of a person for loss of the self in the embrace of the beloved one; and as doomed, since it must give rise to hierarchies of power, and to the deadening force of rationalization.

In Durkheim's model, the duality between "interest" and passion also remains central, but is resolved by a postulate of a distinction between the rational, rapacious individual and the moral, non-rational, emotionally compelling community, which now becomes the sole source of intense feelings. The Nietzschean belief that charisma is inherent in a potent, self-willed individual is dismissed as a necessary illusion, concretizing a relation too abstract, and too compelling, to imagine (except for sociologists). In this vision, charisma is not hierarchical, but leads instead to the affirmation of equalizing similarities in the comforting womb of the group.

Furthermore, where Weber uses the authority of the charismatic to explain action that did not fit into his individualistic and rationalistic framework, for Durkheim such action is natural, since human beings are largely unconscious, prone to the very self-loss that Weber found so inexplicable, and subject to given laws of attraction and group dynamics that are beyond individual will or intelligence.

Nevertheless, there are essential similarities between Weberian and Durkheimian images of the charismatic relation. Both agree, as I noted above, that such attraction implies a loss of personal will and identity in the subject. It is a relation that combines "massive usurpation with total consent-giving" (Glassman 1975: 624) in which self-sacrifice is facilitated because the participants have an inner sense of direct and immediate contact with the charismatic object, which subsumes them. Furthermore, in both portraits of charisma the experience of a genuinely charismatic object is regarded as deeply emotional and compelling. The visceral experience is prior to any message conveyed.

Both men begin as well with certain assumptions about human nature; especially a posited human propensity for powerful, self-transcendent experiences. Participation in collective ritual and the stimulation of intense emotions are regarded as ways to achieve ecstatic self-loss, which is often focused around the figure of an individual, who is the initiator (for Weber) or the symbol (for Durkheim) of the charismatic experience.

Both agree too that, because of its extraordinary quality, the charismatic relation stands outside of mundane self-interest. It is a creative and regenerating force likely to be favored particularly in times of social malaise and suffering, when fragmented social formations are especially in need of reinvigoration through charismatic participation. Both men concur too with the romantic belief that, although this relation of charismatic attraction and self-loss is, of necessity, transient and subject to the fatigue of erotic excess, it is nonetheless the fountainhead of hope and faith, offering the felt truth of a better world to a humanity divided by fear, hostility, and the exigencies of the struggle for survival in a harsh and isolating social world.

4

Hypnotism and Crowd Psychology: Mesmer, Le Bon, Tarde

In the last chapter we saw the development of two very distinct models of charismatic influence: one, based on Nietzschean insights, focused on the charismatic individual and his oppositional relation to rational order and history; the other, drawn from the romantic image of the collective passion of the French Revolution, directs our attention to the dynamics of the charismatic group. Both theories posit a rudimentary notion of a primal impulse to self-loss that beats at the heart of charismatic involvement, and both emphasize the importance of emotional heightening in the charismatic state. But neither has much to say about why charisma should be appealing, or about the nature of the relationship between leader and follower.

In this next chapter, I want to explore another approach to the charismatic relationship, one that springs in the first place directly from the actual experience of a charismatic bond, and was elaborated by later theorists into a "science" of crowd psychology; a science that unites the person-centered theory of Weber with the collective orientation of Durkheim within a framework of regression, and thus leads directly into the group psychology of Freud and his followers.

However, this "science" has generally had little influence on scholarship precisely because it began as an explanation of charisma by a charismatic – a man now regarded as a charlatan rather than an intellect. This individual is Franz Anton Mesmer, the inventor of mesmerism – presently known as hypnotism – who promoted his doctrine with great success in Paris in the late eighteenth century, just prior to the transformative upheaval of the French Revolution.

The Self-conscious Charismatic

Mesmer himself was an extraordinary figure – a cross between prophet and confidence trickster – a combination we shall see as typical of charismatics. The experiences he had are prototypical as well, and the effort he and his followers made to understand and operationalize hypnotic trance provide us with the wherewithal to build a more synthetic model for charismatic involvement than provided by the external analyses offered a hundred years later by Weber and Durkheim.

Mesmer was a German speaker whose French was almost incomprehensible – which added to his appealing air of mystery. He arrived in Paris in 1778 and claimed to have a special capacity to control and direct the flow of invisible energy fields he believed to be surging through the universe. He had gained this ability only after three months of aimless and ecstatic wandering in the forests in the manner of an Old Testament prophet. "O nature, I cried out in those paroxysms, what do you want of me?" Nature responded by inspiring him "to erase from his mind all ideas acquired from society, to think without using words (which Rousseau had shown to be social artifices)" (Mesmer quoted in Darnton 1968: 117). In this state of rapturous unconsciousness, Mesmer grasped intuitively the presence of the invisible energetic fluids which formed the basis of his philosophy.

This invisible energy was, he believed, a link tying together all creation in a dynamic unity. For him and his colleagues, these uniting energies were facts, experienced subjectively as sensations of intensified vitality by qualified practitioners of the new science. Furthermore, these invisible energies could be manipulated and objectively measured in the effusive convulsive trances of acolytes. By evoking these ecstatic trances the manipulators could release the blocked energy of individuals and groups, cure disease, eradicate social ills, and help bring about a new paradise in which all humanity would be in harmony with itself and nature.

Modern thought, animated by the successes of the empiricist Humean revolution and by the individualistic ethos of capitalism, does not accept the transpersonal premise of Mesmer's theory. From this perspective, human beings are not and cannot be linked by anything but interests, which are always a product of personal emotional predilections and preferences. The moral community that Mesmer promised must be an illusion, a mask for conscious manipulation to achieve personal desires.

But for those who believed, Mesmer's doctrine seemed to offer something much more. It not only explained the world, but it also offered participation in a state of rapport in which the practitioner touched and shaped the forces of life itself. According to the Comte de Montlosier, who became a convert to mesmerism despite, or perhaps because of, his scientific background, "he had found a deeper, more satisfying kind of science, a science that left room for his religious impulses without excluding his sympathies for philosophy . . . It seemed to Montlosier that mesmerism would 'change the face of the world' " (Darnton 1968: 59).

The new science, with its Messianic content and promise of enlightenment, took pre-Revolutionary France by storm. According to Darnton, mesmerism was more written about during the decade before the Revolution than any other topic. Floods of pamphlets and testimonials, along with public exhibits of curing, drew intense interest and multitudes of converts, including such later Revolutionary luminaries as Lafayette, Jean-Louis Carra, Jacques-Pierre Brissot.

The major proof of the veracity of Mesmer's revelation was in the cures he achieved by his methods, as he healed illnesses ranging from blindness to ennui. These cures were attributed to Mesmer's "magnetism"; that is, his ability to act as a node and conduit for the flow of vital energy. This magnetism was revealed in his personal intensity and vivacity, in his electrifying glance, in his exotic costume of a flamboyant lilac taffeta robe. His dramatic appearance was enhanced by the atmosphere of his indoor clinics, which were set up to give the patient a sense of being withdrawn from the mundane world into a special, cloistered, quasi-sacred environment. Soft music was played, and the lantern was damped down. The decor included strange astrological decorations and mystical signs, as well as mysterious apparatus such as tubs of iron filings, mesmerically treated water, and the iron rods used to convey the flow of energy.

In this highly charged setting, Mesmer held the patient's knees between his own and stroked the patient's body with his "magnetized" hands, concentrating on the upper abdomen, meanwhile throwing intense bolts of "fluid energy" from his eyes into the eyes of the afflicted other. Using these techniques Mesmer and his disciples could induce somnambulist trances and epileptoid fits in their clients, who awoke revitalized and very often found themselves happily cured of their ailments.[1]

Mesmer was quite aware that it was not simply his charismatic vitality and magnetic touch nor the dramatic context that was at work in his success. He believed that the amplifying dynamics of the group also had a central role, since the treatment often was more effective if a group participated. The group reinforced and magnified the flow of energy by forming "a mesmeric 'chain,' something like an electric circuit" (Darnton 1968: 8). In such circular chains, close physical contact united all participants in the charged communion of the group without regard to any differences of class or character.[2]

Mesmerism was also practiced outdoors, especially in vast open spaces where groups of people encircled a large tree, to which they were tied by "mesmerically charged" ropes, prefiguring the later mass rallies in the French Revolution which were held around Liberty Trees. In this context, the Puységur brothers, two of Mesmer's disciples, discovered a more direct way to induce mass hypnosis, putting large numbers of onlookers into trance simultaneously by the contagious power of suggestion. Once immersed in this somnambulistic condition, people believed they could see into their insides and the insides of others, communicate with spirits, predict cures, and transmit thoughts, and made other magical claims.[3]

Mesmer himself believed that such large-scale gatherings were of crucial importance not only for the health of individuals, but for the health of society as well. His concept of collective trance as a form of secular religion is found in a statement Mesmer wrote before the Revolution:

> It will be proven by the principles that form the system of influences or of animal magnetism that it is very important for man's physical and moral harmony to gather frequently in large assemblies . . . where all intentions and wills should be directed toward one and the same object, especially toward the order of nature, while singing and praying together; and that it is in these situations that the harmony that has begun to be upset in some individuals can be reestablished and health fortified. (Mesmer quoted in Darnton 1968: 147)

We can see from this how much Mesmer prefigures both Revolutionary fervor, and Durkheim's concept of collective effervescence, while his emphasis on the assertion of personal will and vitalizing emotional influence links him to the charismatic prophet evoked by Weber and Nietzsche. In his book on mesmerism, Robert Darnton notes how deeply Mesmer influenced French literature and social thought in general, touching Fourier, Saint-Simon, and Robert Owen. Gautier portrays romantic love as carried by mesmeric shafts of fluid passing between the lovers' eyes, and Balzac's Lambert goes into ecstasies like those of mesmerized somnambulists. And, of course, Mesmer's seances formed the model for later Spiritualism.

Crowd Psychology

But what is of particular interest for us is mesmerism's influence on two Frenchmen, Gustave Le Bon and Gabriel de Tarde, who wrote at the beginning of the twentieth century, and who sought to bridge the gap between the group orientation of Durkheim and the individualism of Weber by utilizing the experience of hypnotism as the framework for their theory of human motivation.

The better known of these two is Le Bon, a liberal journalist and racial theorist whose work *The Crowd: A Study of the Popular Mind* became an instant classic, inspiring much of modern social psychology, while also heavily influencing the Chicago School of sociology. More strikingly, however, was the importance of his theory of leadership for the actual practice of politics. Roosevelt met him, de Gaulle cited him, and Hitler was proud to admit that he took Le Bon as his teacher.

Tarde was a less well-known figure, but his influence has been no less far reaching. He was an academic, a statistician and penologist, and one of the original proponents of opinion polls in sociological research. He was, in a real sense, a forerunner of that vast corps of experts and media consultants who are such a part of modern political life.

The work of Le Bon and Tarde, like that of Durkheim, can be viewed as a reaction to the Revolutionary experience, and, like Durkheim, Le Bon and Tarde begin by accepting the proposition that human beings are group creatures above all. They also agree that the crowd has its own mentality that does not follow the rules of ordinary life, but imposes its own dynamic automatically on all who are drawn into it. The job of the social scientist then is to understand the dynamic of the group, which supercedes individual psychology.

But for Le Bon and Tarde the primal social group is not a moral entity, nor does it have any spontaneous form; it is instead a natural phenomenon prior to all order, mindless and shapeless, full of passion without goal, opposed to creativity and completely without meaning. The thought of the crowd member is metaphorical and condensed, exaggerated and simple; refusing all ambiguity or equivocation in favor of inchoate impulse. Because humanity is by nature a crowd creature, the crowd of necessity exerts its demeaning influence on whomever it touches. Even the most intelligent lose their moral standards when they are compulsively drawn into the group mentality. The Durkheimian perspective is thus turned upside down by Le Bon and Tarde, and immersion in the collective is seen not as the ultimate source of value, but as an unavoidable tragedy.

Like Durkheim, the crowd psychologists hypothesized that the group obeys certain natural tendencies; however, these tendencies were not toward spontaneous creation, but toward mindless repetition. They believed the primal crowd, though passive and chaotic, has the characteristic of being innately imitative; any stimulus organizes the pliable mass into a form as all the crowd members respond automatically to it. To illustrate this perspective, Tarde likens the crowd to a pond, before a stone is thrown in. The movement of history is equivalent to the expansion and eventual dying out of ripples.

Thus, where Durkheim believed gathering together and the reciprocal excitement of collective effervescence can give rise spontaneously to identity, ritual, belief – in other words, to society itself – for crowd psychologists the primal crowd is energetic, but formless and passive, awaiting any shaping influence. Human beings are portrayed as "unconscious puppets" who mechanically imitate whatever arouses them from their torpor (Tarde 1903: 77). The complexities of civilization are due simply to the overlap of multiple influences. Intellectual knowledge makes no difference to this existential condition. As Tarde asks, "if the photographic plate became conscious at a given moment of what was happening to it, would the nature of the phenomenon be essentially changed?" (1903: xiv).

In their understanding of the nature of the crowd, Tarde and Le Bon drew extensively upon the imagery of hypnotism, which they saw as the simplest case of the group condition. Following Mesmer, they argued that hypnotism is not just a special conjuring trick manifested only on stage and between individuals, but operates in everyday life, and en masse. For them, the ordinary person, insofar as he is a member of a group, is said to be "in a special state, which much resembles the state of fascination in which the hypnotised individual finds himself in the hands of the hypnotiser" (Le Bon 1952: 31). "The social like the hypnotic state is only a form of dream, a dream of command and a dream of action" (Tarde 1903: 77).[4]

The imaginative leap required to extrapolate from the experience of the mesmerized individual to envisioning society as a group of somnambulists was not difficult for the crowd psychologists. They knew from Mesmer and his disciples that the pleasurable delirium of the hypnotic trance could easily spread, and whole groups could be spontaneously and involuntarily entranced through contagion. This propensity was explained in Durkheimian fashion as a natural result of the emotional arousal and diminished critical faculties that occur automatically whenever people gather together.

The crowd psychologists validate their characterization of the somnambulistic crowd by citing parallels between the hypnotic relation and group mentality. Both, they say, are characterized by credulity and suggestibility, apparent passivity and underlying inchoate emotional intensity, shifts in identity, intoxication, blurring of personal boundaries, and so on. In both states, only a few vague and ambiguous images may be impressed into the subject's consciousness, but these images, although illogical, are nonetheless invested with heightened emotional coloring that makes them believable. Hypnotized persons, and members of crowds, were also thought to be equally capable of prodigies of strength, violence, cruelty, selflessness, and endurance of pain impossible in ordinary consciousness.

Crowd psychologists stressed as well the fact that in the mesmerized state individuals typically give up all volition, even though paradoxically they believe themselves to be acting spontaneously. This, they say, is exactly what happens in society, where people actually are slaves to imitation, even though they imagine themselves to be free agents.

The "Dream of Command"

Finally, and most crucially, both the crowd and the somnambulist require the presence of a central and inspiring figure to rouse them to action; a stone needs to be thrown, the organizing gesture made. The mobilizing example is replicated maximally, immediately, and as energetically as possible, because in mimesis form and solidity are attained. According to crowd psychology, it is only in such convulsive imitative action that human puppets gain their sense of being – their "illusion of will."

The crowd psychologists thereby assume an eternal dialectic of imitation and inspiration which obeys mechanical laws of stimulus and response.[5] The more intense the stimulus, and the more it is focused and undiluted by other competing stimuli, the more powerful it will be, and the more it will compel automatic and exact imitation, since individuals, in their primal undifferentiated group state, involuntarily respond to anything which gives them a definite form, regardless of the particular shape. Furthermore, every such compulsive stimulus also, by definition, lays claim to universality, and imitation only ceases when countered by a competing invention or idea, or by some natural constraint. So a potent charismatic relation implies a pressure toward expansion and intolerance; and the degree of commitment of the followers is in direct proportion to the intensity of the stimulus offered by the inspiring leader.

All society is said to begin with this magical and compelling assertion of will, which derives its strength from the arousing figure's expressive emotionality and his ability to convey excitement, power and absolute belief: "Is it possible to deny that volition, together with emotion and conviction, is the most contagious of psychological states? An energetic and authoritative man wields an irresistible power over feeble natures. He gives them the direction which they lack" (Tarde 1903: 198).

Starting from this central premise of the need of the masses for domination, Le Bon became famous as a new Machiavelli, who taught the leader how to meet that need. He argued that the passive crowd instinctively follows anyone who expresses intense beliefs, since this permits the crowd to take on a form. Therefore, the leader must act his part with gusto in order to appear larger than life. He must make use of emotionally charged theatricality, large gestures, dramatic illusions. By these mechanisms the leader demonstrates his fervor, focuses the crowd's attention, and stimulates the imitation and slavish worship of his disciples. It is evident that Mesmer himself is a type case of such a figure.

The leader himself, who wields this dramatic power of expression, is said to have an innate ability, and the imagery used by Le Bon to describe this charismatic spark is familiar:

> It is a faculty independent of all titles, of all authority, and possessed by a small number of persons whom it enables to exercise a veritably magnetic fascination on those around them, although they are socially their equals, and lack all ordinary means of domination. They force the acceptance of their ideas and sentiments on those about them,

and they are obeyed as is the tamer of wild beasts by the animal that could easily devour him. (Le Bon 1952: 132)

But even though the source of his fascination is mysterious, the charismatic leader nonetheless is a specific personality type. Like the epileptic prophets who are Weber's primal charismatics, he is "recruited from the ranks of those morbidly nervous, excitable, half-deranged persons who are bordering on madness" (Le Bon 1952: 118). It is not enough, however, to be feverishly emotional. The leader also is fanatically obsessed by his vision, which "has taken possession of him to such a degree that everything outside it vanishes, and that every contrary opinion appears to him an error or a superstition" (Le Bon 1952: 118). The imagery of possession is significant, since it allows the leader to feel spoken through by a higher power. In this condition of self-deification, the leader gains the single-mindedness and complete confidence needed to arouse the masses from their torpor into action.

According to crowd psychology, the content of the leader's vision is irrelevant, except that it cannot be reasonably argued. Reason offers no hope of transcendence. Rather, it destroys the vivifying dreams of the past, revealing only "the blind and silent forces of nature, which are inexorable to weakness and ignore pity" (Le Bon 1952: 110). Instead, the orator must speak the condensed, evocative language of metaphor and myth that appeal to the debased consciousness of the mob. His technique must be "to exaggerate, to affirm, to resort to repetitions, and never attempt to prove anything by reasoning" (Le Bon 1952: 51).

But the orator cannot create a world that only he lives in. He must always reflect and embody the irrational sentiments of the crowd, flattering the aspirations of the crowd members, sharing their feelings, shifting the discourse to accommodate the responses of the audience and demonstrating, above all, the ability "to divine from instant to instant the sentiments to which one's discourse is giving birth" (Le Bon 1952: 113). In other words, the leader must resonate with the mythical-cultural "genius" of the masses.

Therefore, in the dialectic of leader and follower as postulated by crowd psychology, the leader first has to mirror and magnify the followers' deepest desires in order to become the object of the crowd's imitation. The existence of previous influences means that the leader must act within a dense preset symbolic framework of ideas and beliefs.[6] But though the leader must ground his appeal in a message, appearance and emotional range that is within the cultural framework, he does not become merely a contentless symbol of that framework, as Durkheim argued.

This is because, although he represents and expresses the society to itself, the leader remains a specific person, unique and irreplaceable, with special qualities, beliefs, desires, and habits. Naturally the particular characteristics must be compatible with the demands of the mass, evoking images that are familiar and compelling. But the psychology of the group is understood to be essentially vague, mobile, and diffuse, a receptacle capable of taking any number of potential forms. Only when the collective fixes on a leader who offers a striking image from out of the infinity of images possible do the collective desires coalesce and take concrete shape. This is why, for crowd psychology and later manipulators of mass media, quirks and easily recognizable character traits are so important in the construction of a heroic leader's charismatic appeal. These individual, but replicable, aspects of the leader offer specific and obvious locations for imitation and identification by the followers.

In this perspective, the leader, by showing both his generic humanity and his (culturally acceptable) individuality in a way that is forceful and single-minded, can galvanize the amorphous, empathetic crowd to compulsive imitation and obedience. He is both a creature of the crowd, since he must mirror its innermost desires within a given cultural matrix, and also the creator of the crowd, since he brings it into being and gives it form by his every personal gesture. The creative, personal charismatic is thus reinserted into Durkheim's group-oriented model as the fundamental organizing principle. But the source of this creative energy remains a mystery, locked in the magnetic character of the obsessed leader whose passionate fantasies have the power to shape and inspire the following.

Regression and Love in Crowd Psychology

The crowd psychologists did not probe more deeply into the source of the charismatic's internal fires. Like Nietzsche and Weber, they took such individuals as outside the range of inquiry, who could be described, but not understood. Their real advance was their analogical paradigm of regression, and their idea that the group and leader are bound together not by beams of invisible energy, nor by collective effervescence, nor by contagious excitement, but by love.

The argument was that individuals who are hypnotized have regressed to an earlier, more primitive form of awareness under the stimulation of the mesmerist. By analogy, then, the crowd also is characterized by the equivalent primitive state of consciousness, and is equivalent to the mental states of other regressed categories of persons: savages, children, or women, who, according to the accepted wisdom of the era, have an undeveloped, and excessively emotional character.

For instance, in a formulation that anticipates Freud, Tarde writes that being entranced, or being immersed in the repetitious compulsions of mass society, is like being a child, subjected to the domination of parents, and especially to the overpowering influence of the father, who "is and always will be his son's first master, priest and model. Every society, even at present, begins in this way" (Tarde 1903: 78). The child's imitation of his or her parents grows over time to an identification with peers and other role models in what Tarde calls a "piling up of slumbers" (1903: 83), and it is this multiplication of "dreams of action" that makes up society.

Crowd psychology therefore conceptualizes the experience of charismatic attraction within a crude psychological matrix of human growth, and postulates that the developmental distance between child and adult, female and male, primitive and civilized, is equivalent to the gap between the crowd member and the rational individual. The crowd and the charismatic experience can thus be understood through analogies to other well-known human experiences. Gaining an understanding of the dynamics of the inner lives of children or primitive people, or the irrational mentalities of women, will allow an understanding of crowds.

The crowd psychologists felt they did not need to undertake any rigorous study to have an intuitive grasp of these regressed or unevolved mentalities. Instead their model of the irrational and the unconscious derives from the taken-for-granted worldview of their era. The infantile, the primitive, the female, the hypnotically entranced, the crowd member, were, they thought, naturally amoral, prelogical, emotional, suggestible, willful, and charged with intensely passionate but chaotic impulses. These impulses need to be channeled by parallel influences at different levels: children are constrained by the civilizing influence of the father in the family; savages by the binding chains of custom and tradition in society; women by the influence of the beloved in courtship and marriage; mesmerized subjects by the imputed magical power of the hypnotist; the crowd by the charismatic power of the great leader.

Yet all these inspiring figures have an ambivalent character: the patriarchal father, by asserting his personal will, gives the child an identity that stands against the world outside the family; the custom of the savage is originally an inspired invention of a great leader; the lover offers a dream of transcending the mundane, rule-ordered universe; the gestures of the hypnotist are compelling precisely because they encourage the somnambulist to act out his or her deepest antisocial impulses; and the charismatic offers the follower the chance to rebel against the world as it is. In fact, according to the dynamic proposed by Tarde, and echoing Weber, the very experiences which are routinized to give structure also, in their original manifestation, are oppositional and transformative.

Thus, according to the crowd psychologists, on the surface the inspiring figure at every level gives order and channels the primitive impulses, but at the same time offers an example of one who stands outside the limits of slavish repetition and custom, above the demands of social reciprocity and respect, capable of acting, living, being, and creating. Commitment to and identification with the active other offers the passive self an illusory participation in creative vitality. So the active is loved by the passive, and it is this tie of love that binds society together:

> It is a great mistake to say that populations are controlled by fear alone. On the contrary, everything points to the fact that in the beginnings of all great civilisations or, rather, of all religious or political institutions whatsoever, modern ones included, there have been unheard-of expenditures of love and of unsatisfied love at that. (Tarde 1903: 202)[7]

This means that participation in the crowd and being taken up in a charismatic movement is felt by participants to be dyadic and highly personal: "The plural is basically never more than a dual, and however large in number a corporation or a crowd may be, it too is a sort of couple in which now each individual is subject to the suggestion of all the others together ... [and] the whole group is subject to the leader's suggestion" (Tarde quoted in Moscovici 1984: 286). Each person in the crowd thus experiences the relationship to the leader as immediate and compelling, each imagines the leader's gaze directed specifically at him or her. For example, among Nazi loyalists, "a good proportion ... stress the 'unforgettable,' magical moment when Hitler looked (or they felt looked) into their eyes" (Dicks 1972: 79).

But the portrait of the love between follower and leader has a dark tone. Just as the power of the crowd is great, but debasing, the love of the follower for the leader is both intense and degrading. It is, Tarde says, an "unsatisfied love," demeaning and pathetic. It is analogous to the awed and fearful love of the child for the stern patriarchal father, the abject adulation of the primitive for the frightening witchdoctor, the submissive love of the Victorian wife for her domineering husband, the dumb veneration of the somnambulist for the hypnotist.

In fact, if crowd psychology is to be believed, the devotion of men and women has "never been bestowed on easy-going masters, but on tyrants who vigorously oppressed them" (Le Bon 1952: 54). This is because the inspiring figure is always the one who stands apart and is focused completely on an inner vision, independent of others – the one who throws the stone, who makes the gesture. Nietzsche believed that this inward aspect of the genius would isolate him from society. But the crowd psychologists argue that it is exactly the leader's self-absorption that makes him attractive, since this gives him the obsessive power to escape imitation and to embody the "dream of command" in all its fateful and compelling glory.

This imagery disturbingly affirms a deep desire on the part of the "regressed" and "effeminate" crowd to submit to domination by the active, and to adulate those who are oppressors.[8] Domination and adulation are "naturally" mixed, and it is an irrevocable law that the passive should not only obey the active, but also adore them, since through obedience the weak and empty gain an identity, and the necessary illusion of potency and will. Therefore, as a latter-day crowd psychologist puts it, members of the crowd paradoxically "have a strong sense of liberation even though they live and breathe in an atmosphere of strict adherence to tenets and commands" (Hoffer 1951: 31). And even though they are lost in slavishness, they feel immersed in love.

Mass Society: The Age of the Crowd

The crowd psychologists' picture of human society thus claims people are bound together by love, but it is the abject love of the shapeless for the shaper, and is expressed in the crowd by mindless adulation for a half-mad tyrant. In this imagery, Durkheim's theory of urgent collective participation retains its form, but has assumed a terrifying aspect, as revitalizing social "warmth" has become instead a consuming conflagration.

Even more frightening, the crowd psychologists actively affirm what Weber denied and Durkheim only intimated. Modernity, precisely because it presses against mass behavior and charismatic leadership, actually intensifies popular desire for the revelation of the leader and immersion in the mass, so that Le Bon prophesies that "the age we are about to enter will in truth be the ERA OF CROWDS" (1952: 14).

This is because the modern human being, according to Le Bon and Tarde, is cut away from old ties, declassed, atomized, and stripped of faith. Former communities are dispersed and isolated individuals are linked together only in momentary "publics" without any significant meaning or coherence. As a result of the decay of authority, the erosion of traditional categories of class and status, and the disintegration of the taken-for-granted understanding of the world, humanity has degenerated into its shapeless primal essence – "what constituted a people, a unity, a whole, becomes in the end an agglomeration of individualities lacking cohesion" (Le Bon 1952: 206).

But the resemblance to the primal crowd is not exact, since the conditions of modernity mean that the modern group is what Tarde calls a "second degree" crowd bound together not by human contact but only by a far-flung media network. Contemporary mass society is therefore not so passionate as the primal crowd because it no longer experiences the emotional intensification that springs automatically from physical propinquity. Influence is now slower, since it comes from a distance, and the multiplication of overlapping suggestions means that each single suggestion is no longer compelling. Like Durkheim, the crowd psychologists also cite social growth, with its increased division of labor and complexity, as diminishing the felt unity of the crowd.

The variety of influences and values available in modern society would also appear to make passionate commitment to any single belief or person less likely. Whim replaces interest, and fashion, rather than fanaticism, dominates the modern sensibility, which is sensation seeking, but diffuse, feeble and soon bored. The utter absence of direction and intensity means that the crowd now focuses fleetingly on immediate gratification of its caprices, while the "leaders" are themselves enslaved by the fickle tastes of the consumers, and use the public opinion polls Tarde invented to discover the fad of the moment, to which they then accommodate themselves.

Furthermore, the multiplicity of shifting values and the leveling force of democracy and capitalism favor as well increasing indifference and cynicism, as the prestige of all individuals or beliefs is undermined. Hanna Arendt states the case of crowd psychology clearly when she writes that members of the modern mass are united by "their vague apprehension that . . . the most respected, articulate and representative members of the community were fools and that all the powers that be were not so much evil as they were equally stupid and fraudulent" (1973: 315).

All of these factors of rootlessness, complexity, individualism, cynicism and detachment have been noted by our other social theorists, and cited as factors militating against charisma. Yet crowd psychology argues instead that the very circumstances of modernity which work against the rise of charismatic movements also increase people's desire for charismatic immersion, and heighten and intensify charisma when it does occur. The argument is that modern social conditions maximize the passivity and loneliness of the crowd members by minimizing the potential for participation in any vitalizing communal activity, such as the regular group rituals Durkheim found at the core of premodern society.

The inner emptiness, ennui and sense of lifelessness that result cannot be escaped by increased consumption of goods, nor by withdrawal into drugs and alcohol. Instead, modern mass man, atomized, isolated and passive, wants more than ever to identify with a force that will stimulate the most passionate involvement, the greatest sense of vitality, the most absolute beliefs. In other words, modern mass society is prepared for immersion in a charismatic movement. And then the world would change completely: "Given the power possessed at present by crowds, were a single opinion to acquire sufficient prestige to enforce its general acceptance, it would soon be endowed with so tyrannical a strength that everything would have to bend before it, and the era of free discussion would be closed for a long time" (Le Bon 1952: 153–4).

Crowd psychology thus asserts that modern humanity will not be lost in the rationalized world posited by Weber; his picture of the triumph of calculation is denied. But neither will society be reborn in spontaneous collective rituals creating new moral worlds, as Durkheim thought, since even though crowd psychology affirms the Durkheimian premise of the compelling, transpersonal, emotional character of the crowd, that character is not at all moral. Instead the modern emergence of "one great unorganized, structureless mass of furious individuals" (Arendt 1973: 315) will yield an entity united only by its infinite, inchoate desire for a shaping voice to draw it from its stupor into the feverish activity of the trance. When that voice speaks, the listening crowd will be locked, by its unreasoning love, into a universe of violence and polarization, marked by "worship of a being supposed superior, fear of the power with which the being is credited, blind submission to its commands, inability to discuss its dogmas, the desire to spread them, and a tendency to consider as enemies all by whom they are not accepted" (Le Bon 1952: 73).

In the vision of crowd psychology, Nietzsche's superman is reborn, with a more convincing theoretical base, but also in even more sinister guise, as a creature beloved by the very masses he enslaves and despises; proclaiming the destruction of all who disbelieve in his obsessions.

5

Oedipus and Narcissus: Freud's Crowd Psychology

Thus far, I have developed a picture of charismatic involvement in which the emotional intensity of the leader awakens an echoing response in the group members, uniting them in transpersonal communion. But to understand this process even the crowd psychologists rely on a mechanical model of automatic stimulus and response that is no advance from Weber or Durkheim. Leaders remain "tropical monsters" attracting by virtue of a mysterious innate power of will, while followers passively await the energetic force that is capable of giving them shape and direction.

In this imagery, charismatic involvement remains very far from our own inner experience; it is a landscape populated by blond beasts and mindless robots. It was Sigmund Freud's contribution to paint the figures in this landscape in nuanced color, and render them recognizable as human beings very like ourselves.

Freud's Model of Human Nature

Freud's theories are perhaps the most controversial of any discussed here. A great deal of this controversy is due to his assertion of the power of the libido – a vitalizing life force that has a strong resemblance to the "invisible fluids" of hypnotism – and his reliance on introspection and the cure of mental disorders to validate his theory. Freud is, in fact, in many ways a modern Mesmer, a revolutionary who used personal influence to achieve cures, and who, like Mesmer, argued that disease is caused by blockages of psychic energy. Both men also attracted a cultic following of committed loyalists, and both have been repudiated by the orthodox for creating a religious faith instead of a science. Freud himself acknowledged his debt to Mesmer, and actually began his experiments with the "talking cure" by placing his patients under hypnotic trance. And, as we shall see, his model of the relationship between leader and group is based on the relationship of the hypnotist to his subject.

But Freud was also a profound philosopher who sought to find some ground for moral meaning within the emotivist tradition. He did this, as Peter Gay (1985) remarks, by constructing what is by far the most coherent theory of emotional structure available to modern Western thought. Like Hume, he begins his task with the premise that the person's "critical faculty is not an independent function, to be respected as such, it is the tool of his emotional attitudes" (Freud 1977: 293).

However, the passions that Freud understands to be motivating reason are closer in their potency to the rages and lusts that animate Nietzschean man than they are to the equanimity of a Humean "bundle of sensations" or to the cool calculations of a Utilitarian. But even though the passions posited by Freud are powerful, they are not simply the pure and singular expression of will described by Nietzsche. Instead, he proposes a theory based on a balanced and dynamic opposition between instincts. Freud's conception of this dialectic began as an opposition between sexuality and self-preservation and progressed to a final theory of a metaphysical polarity between Eros and Thanatos, love and death, tension and equilibrium, unity and distinctiveness.[1]

Freud argues that all human experience develops within the framework of this fundamental opposition; he assumes that these impulses to merger and to separation must find expression in any social milieu. But the form of the expression will vary in every individual case, and from culture to culture, due to differences in family structure, biological makeup, and the limits and directions imposed by the social structure and environment.

Freud thus posits a dialectical model of human drives in interaction with culture that allows both a universal emotional structure and an infinite range of variety. This model replaces the chaos of personal preferences found in Hume's theory with a structured hierarchy within a social framework. Attachment and separation become the essential values, and other forms of desire are simply sublimated and repressed expressions that can be traced back to these deep impulses.

Weber's assumption that the heart can be completely molded by society is therefore rejected by Freud in favor of a theory of an eternal and irrepressible struggle between desire and the necessary constraints of culture. Freud's dialectical theory also opposes the Utilitarian reduction of emotions to greed, as well as the Nietzschean presumption of the primacy of a drive for power; on the other hand, Freud's paradigm refutes as well the Durkheimian claim for the predominance of a desire for self-loss. Instead, humanity is imagined to be existentially torn between both the will to power and the urge to selflessness – however these urges are disguised and distorted.

In this dialectical model of human nature men and women continually struggle to overcome and resolve this painful inner tension – even though any resolution must be fundamentally false to the human condition. It is this eternal struggle, and its psychic consequences, that is at the core of Freud's image of humanity, and animates as well his understanding of the impulse to self-effacing commitment by the charismatic follower, and the complementary affirmation of will by the charismatic leader. It is to this aspect of his theory I now turn.

Freud's Crowd Psychology: Love as Abasement

In most of his work, Freud's moral vision remained located in the relationship between patient and analyst, and it is his therapeutic techniques and ideas about the development of mental disease and its cure that have had the most influence on society. But his scope of thought was, as we have seen above, much larger. For him, the study of mental illness was a royal route to the study of society itself, and potentially offered a resolution for its ills. In his later life he began to develop the theory of group psychology and charismatic leadership that I will explore in the next few pages.

Freud's attitude toward both civilization and the passions was ambiguous in the extreme. Freud saw civilization as permitting human life to rise above the purely instinctive lives of animals. Yet, at the same time, like his mentor Nietzsche, Freud portrays civilization as debilitating, redirecting the vital force of natural man into sublimated and secondary channels. For Freud, as for Nietzsche, civilized man is the sick animal, but unlike Nietzsche, Freud believed this repressive sickness was necessary. Without it, the unleashed instinctive drives would yield nothing but destruction.

In particular, Freud feared that immersion in the crowd would inevitably lead to an eruption of primal passions, allowing participants to "throw off the repressions of the unconscious instinctual impulses" and to revel in "all that is evil in the human mind" (Freud 1959: 6). He agreed with Le Bon and Tarde that the group mentality is naturally a "regressed" form of consciousness, akin to the psychological states of primitives, or of hypnotized subjects, or of children, or, most fittingly, equivalent to the psychological state of the mentally ill.

Freud further accepted the crowd psychologists' idea that crowds, because they are in a "primitive" state of consciousness, very like that of the somnambulist, hunger for a hypnotic charismatic leader who will provide them with a point of absolute authority. Though he devoted most of his attention to dissecting the mentality of the follower and had little to say about the inner dynamics of the leader's character, Freud accepted as well the crowd psychologists' image of the charismatic figure as a ruthless and overweening egoist, who by his very vainglory attracts the admiration of the humble members of the herd.[2]

But even though he agreed with the general model of the group proposed by crowd psychology, Freud could not accept their simplistic premise that the bond between leader and follower consists soely of the leader's willful self-assertion and the follower's automatic and adoring imitative response. His understanding of the "regressed" forms of humanity – derived from his actual clinical study of the mentally disturbed – was far more sophisticated than this.

Freud's theory of the nature of the charismatic crowd was in fact an outgrowth of his pioneering therapeutic technique – much as the crowd psychologists' theories derived from Mesmer's actual experience of inducing hypnotic trance. In both cases the "cure" was reached not by a cognitive understanding of the source of the trauma, but by an emotional overflowing achieved within the therapeutic setting. However, while Mesmer believed he was mechanically unlocking passages for the flow of energetic fluids, Freud's work had a different aim. His clients experienced a subjective reliving of the situation that had originally given rise to the neurotic disorder. This emotionally charged reliving occurred when the analysand re-experienced repressed childhood desires by projecting them onto the analyst; the patient would then undergo a healing effusion of sexual libido – an "abreaction."

Freud discovered this process by accident when his first female patients, under the influence of hypnotic trance, unexpectedly "fell in love" with him and made sexual overtures. After he got over his shock, Freud hypothesized that the patient was taking him as a symbolic representative of an early love object that had been denied or lost. In this instance, the therapist would be adored and worshipped. By living through this unrealistic "transference," as it is called, the patient re-experienced and exorcized the trauma that had originally caused the psychic disorder.

By extension, Freud reasoned that the transference which occurs in therapy has its analogy in the follower's worship of the leader; both forms of unrealistic adulation are rooted in the universal family dynamic which the leader, and the therapist, offer to re-enact, although the analyst, seeking a cure, retains a detached distance, while the leader generally magnifies the regressive fixation of the followers' attraction to him.

Exactly what is the family dynamic at the core of transference? As we have seen, for Tarde and Le Bon, human beings acquiesce to authority because they are naturally weak, formless, and imitative; the only actor is the impassioned and obsessed leader who emerges, mysteriously, to enrapture and mold them in his image. Tarde did note the paternal nexus of domination, but for him this tie was a simple one of inevitable adoration and compulsive imitation of the powerful father by the impotent child.

Freud, on the other hand, had quite a different vision of the family, and of the bonds that lie at the heart of charisma. He begins his portrait with the famous hypothesis of the Oedipal triangle, the sexual rivalry between the young son and his father for the love of the mother/wife (a parallel rivalry was thought to occur between the little girl and her mother over the love of her father, but Freud's emphasis was on the problems of the male). Freud's fundamental assertion was that human psychological development is based on the son's thwarted sexual desire for his mother, coupled with suppression of the guilty aggression the boy feels toward the all-powerful and autonomous paternal rival.

The conflictual dynamic set up in the Oedipal conflict between sexual desire, aggression, fear of the parents' anger, and the danger of the loss of parental love, leads the child to internalize the restrictions imposed in the family. Aggression is turned away from the castrating father and against the self, as the child sets up the paternal standards as his own and inflicts self-punishment for any failure to live up to them. As Freud puts it, "a threatened external unhappiness – loss of love and punishment on the part of the external authority – has been exchanged for a permanent internal unhappiness, for the tension of the sense of guilt" (1961: 75). In this way, the child avoids the pain of conflict with the parent by punishing itself, retains intimacy by internalizing the parental image, conceals frightening anger toward parents by turning that anger inward, and still expresses aggression, albeit masochistically.

The punitive restrictions that the child incorporates as a consequence of the Oedipal conflict are termed by Freud, in his later work, the superego. This part of the psychic structure serves as the inner enforcer of social norms; it is the mechanism through which the mores of society and the family are established and internalized by way of the repressive influence of the parents, and especially the father, upon the instinctive desires of the child.[3] The resolution of these tensions through the formation of the punitive superego and the internalization of idealized norms and values has a considerable cost. It requires strict regulation of the self, constant vigilance and the self-administration of punishment for failure.

Freud then argues that this painful effort of self-restraint and self-punishment can be foregone by giving up one's freedom to the idolized patriarchal leader. In capitulating to the authority of a dominant other, the followers return to the dependency of childhood – protected by the power they attribute to the charismatic. They no longer need to struggle to control themselves; the larger-than-life leader now takes over the role of regulator, placing the disciples under the comforting protection of an external and omnipotent authority who accepts the burden of controlling and channeling their aggressive and sexual impulses, just as in the family the powerful father offered the child both a standard and a refuge (Freud 1961: 88).

For Freud then the leader is the embodiment of the child's experience of the "dreaded primal father" (Freud 1959: 59) who is believed to be superhuman, full of sexual energy, and endowed with absolute power.

In Freudian theory, this individual serves, quite literally, as the external superego of the members of the crowd, freeing the followers from the awful responsibility of self-regulation by providing them with a punishing authoritative voice which they must obey.

But the primal father offers more than a meeting of dependency needs and an opportunity to abdicate responsibility. As we have seen, Freud believed that people are troubled by deep feelings of guilt generated during the Oedipal conflict because of the son's aggressive desire to destroy and replace the father. By an absolute submission to the leader, the follower makes amends for his rivalry; he hides his aggression and desire for autonomy by bowing down low and groveling at the leader's command.

Yet the follower's deep sense of rage does not disappear, nor can the aggression and resentment that lies beneath submission be completely obliterated, despite the pleasures that self-denial offers. Following Nietzsche, Freud argues that the very servility of the crowd's obeisance masks an underlying hostility, just as excessively positive transference to the analyst always conceals deep ambivalence.[4] Rebellion inevitably seethes beneath the surface of abjection, ending eventually in revolt against the paternal tyrant and the affirmation of the equality and unity of the "band of brothers." But this Durkheimian collective must be short-lived, since guilt over the parricide leads inevitably to abasement before a new tyrant in an eternal cycle of history.

Freud argues, however, that the leader can escape, at least momentarily, from the underlying, aggressive resentment of the followers by channeling the accumulated hostility of the group outward, away from himself, and toward a despised other, who can be execrated and injured with impunity. In this way the leader allows the follower the gratification of deep aggressive desires that must ordinarily be kept sublimated and turned against the self. Instead of a difficult inner accommodation of love and hate, desire and guilt, merger and separation, the follower then is encouraged to split the external world into concrete images of good and evil – the good is the group which can be loved and merged into through the mediation of the leader, the evil can be externalized, hated and eliminated, ushering in the millennium. Freud thus gives us a theoretical framework for understanding the intolerance and violence that crowd psychology made central to its portrait of group consciousness – and which are too painfully evident in the history of modern charismatic groups.

However, there is a high price to be paid for the group unity achieved by scapegoating. As always in Freud, denial of inner tensions leads to distorted and fantastic manifestations of what has been denied. The increased suppression of difference and aggression within the group and the funneling of rage in other directions still cannot obliterate feelings of hostility, rivalry and violence among the community members; instead these repressed antagonisms are transmuted into delusional paranoid visions of penetration, treachery, disintegration and encirclement that plague the mentalities of charismatic groups.

Nonetheless, despite the problems caused by submission to the leader, Freud argues that "the group still wishes to be governed by unrestricted force; it has an extreme passion for authority" (1959: 59). Any group can only find its solidarity under the influence of the charismatic figure, the "primal father," who provides the needed authority to mute the hostility of the brothers, and denies them the sexual autonomy that would lead to jealousy.[5] Freud therefore defines the essential character of the group as "many equals, who can identify themselves with one another, and a single person superior to them all" (Freud 1959: 53).

So, we find in Freud a portrayal of human motivation and group dynamics that does credit to our own intuitions about human complexity and ambiguity. The follower is now envisioned as seeking images and relationships that offer the re-enactment of a highly charged, highly ambivalent, tie between father and child bound together in the guilt and love of the Oedipal triangle. In this paradigm, people submit to the tyrant not because they are nothing, but because what they are is too painful to be borne; they are no longer puppets, but penitents. There is, however, a serious problem with Freud's perspective – one that requires a certain reworking of his theory to bring it in line with what others have said about the inner experience of charisma.

The Narcissistic Appeal: Love as Merger

In his image of the relationship between the group and the leader Freud follows Nietzsche's radical opposition between the superman and the enfeebled masses. In this vision, only the leader is filled with vitality, while the follower, like a guilty child, joins the group to hide, not to exult. So, if Freud offers us a more complex view of charisma, he also gives us one in which the leader's intoxication literally feeds upon the energies of the followers, dampening, rather than igniting, the fires of their enthusiasm.

The problem arises in the paradoxical fact that for Freud, as for the crowd psychologists, the leader is not only feared, respected, and held in awe; he is also, despite his tyranny, an object of passionate adulatory love, like the love felt in transference for the analyst, or the lover's adoration of the beloved. For the crowd psychologists, this was again a manifestation of the love of the weak for the strong. Freud's understanding of love was more nuanced because of his awareness of ambivalence, but he too generally portrayed the love of the follower for the leader as a relation of meek devotion to another person regarded as vastly superior to the self. As he writes, "a person in love is humble.

A person who loves has, so to speak, forfeited part of his narcissism" (1957: 98).

According to Freud, love at all levels of experience has an equally demeaning and debilitating quality. For instance, men's love for women is pictured as a way to expiate male Oedipal guilt; therefore men habitually fall in love with narcissistic, self-involved women who do not return their ardor (Freud 1957: 88–9).

This image of love as a diminishment of the self is strictly parallel to Freud's understanding of the servile adoration felt by the follower for the demanding, selfish leader who, as a modern Freudian writes, "will seek out others because they will maximize his gratification although he will expend very little love on them and will try to use and exploit them ruthlessly" (Slater 1977: 121–2). The follower, like the lover, worshipfully offers abject adoration to the self-absorbed and vastly superior beloved. It is this general model of love, which much resembles that of the medieval courtly tradition, that allows Michels to characterize the great leader as a "cold coquette" (1949: 126).

But this image of love as deference is far from the ecstatic picture of charismatic involvement offered by Durkheim, or even the image of emotional excitation we have seen in Weber. And Freud too has another view of love that permits us to understand the exhilaration and expansion typical of charisma, although we do not find this view expressed in his discussion of the crowd and the leader; we only discover it when he speaks of romantic love, and specifically when he extols sexual intercourse with the loved one as "our most intense experience of an overwhelming sensation of pleasure" (Freud 1961: 29); a sensation that provides humanity with a lived model for happiness.

What is important for Freud in this form of transcendent sexuality is not solely the physical convulsion and the immediate gratification of instinctual need, but also the ecstatic loss of boundaries of the self – which he writes about much as Durkheim writes of immersion in the group, as an escape from the inevitable human experience of difference and separateness:

> At the height of being in love the boundary between ego and object threatens to melt away. Against all evidence of his senses, a man who is in love declares that "I" and "you" are one, and is prepared to behave as if it were a fact. (Freud 1961: 13)

> The highest phase of development of which object-libido is capable is seen in the state of being in love, when the subject seems to give up his whole personality in favour of an object-cathexis. (Freud 1957: 76)

Although Freud exults in the expansive and intoxicating self-loss of dyadic love, in his discourse on the group the emphasis remains on guilt, anxiety and repressed aggression. Yet Freud is clear that the two experiences emerge from the same psychic matrix, sharing with hypnotic trance the characteristic loss of personal autonomy in the service of another (Freud 1959: 47). But the brutal primal father of Freud's crowd psychology seems to have nothing about him to provoke ecstatic states of boundless love, even though Freud specifically portrays him as the equivalent of the beloved one in romantic attachment. This equivalence works only when love is imagined in every case as abject self-abasement, but not when love is conceived and experienced as ecstatic and empowering rapture.

In order to resolve this apparent contradiction, we have to return to Freud's late understanding of human nature in which the inner life of human beings is imagined to consist of a dialectical tension between fundamental, if entangled, psychic needs for attachment and separation which must find expression, even if in disguised or distorted form. The elements of this dialectic are always in interaction, but the need for attachment, it seems, has priority. This is because there is a developmental movement of all human beings away from a state of complete empathetic merger with the loving, responsive mother, and toward greater autonomy and personal distinctiveness. For Freud, the infant's primordial fusion with the mother was the only unambivalent human relationship, and formed the model for all the paradises of human imagination (Freud 1959: 33).

But the individual ordinarily must lose this original unambivalent unity, since the mother is not completely responsive, and since the process of maturation and the pleasures of muscularity and autonomy require separation and differentiation. It is, however, nostalgically remembered, and momentarily recaptured in Freud's portrait of the ecstatic union of sexual love. By analogy, the resurgence of this same primal, rapturous and selfless communion accounts for the ecstatic component of charismatic immersion which Freud's Oedipal theory of the group dynamic cannot explain.

Freud's own work, and that of his disciples, gives a theoretical base to this claim that charismatic involvement is, in its ecstatic aspect, a recapitulation of an infantile state of merger rather than a submission to the Oedipal father. According to Freud, there are certain types of mental disorders (he calls them paraphrenia) that arise from difficulties in the infantile "narcissistic" phase of development in which the child's self is fused with the mother. These mental disorders, which include modern categories of schizophrenia and paranoia, are clearly distinguishable from the transference neuroses rooted in Oedipal rivalry, and involve much more serious regression in which the self is blurred and fragmented; anything which requires an awareness of personal identity, including the development of a superego and the experience of the Oedipal conflict, becomes impossible to achieve. "Object love," Freud's term for mature love of another individual, is out of the question, since all others are not experienced as separate and independent entities, but instead are merged with the self, or are despised as externalized projections of inner aggressive rage.

Freud had little clinical experience with people suffering from these serious disorders. Since they did not have developed selves, they therefore could not experience transference, and could not be cured by his methods. However, in terms of theory, Freud recognized the great importance of narcissistic symptoms, and believed study of them could lead to the discovery of the characteristics of primary process thought beneath ordinary rational awareness. What he found in his research – and what has been borne out by later workers – was a strange, subjective universe in which time has no meaning, space is permeable, thoughts can be intercepted, the world is populated by vivid forces, and the ordinary rules of logic do not hold; an inner world where powerful emotional impulses dominate, where feelings of omnipotent grandiosity are augmented by paranoid fears and rage, and by cognitive processes of splitting and projection.[6]

In other words, Freud and his disciples discovered within the paraphrenic a mental universe of the unconscious that has much in common with the non-rational beliefs and the intense desire for self-loss and fusion that our other social theorists have pictured as characteristic of charismatic states. The polarization of the world into good and evil and the projection of hostility outward that were central to Freud's nuanced vision of neurosis, and, by analogy, to his understanding of the group, had an even more central place in the mentality of narcissistically disordered individuals, expressed and enacted in violent forms in which the motive force was not ambivalence and repressed guilt, but unending, destructive rage against frustrations that limit and deny the possibility of self-loss through merger.

Pursuing the parallels between the charismatic crowd and the paraphrenic state allows us to overturn Freud's image of the group depleted by energy flowing out to be invested in the idealized object – in this case, the beloved leader. Instead, in narcissistic disorders – as in love, or hypnotic trance – the self of the subject is actually enmeshed and lost in the self of a potent object. In Freud's terminology, this process is one of identification – a recapitulation of the earliest form of tie in which the boundaries of the self are blurred, and the object and ego fuse together (1959: 37).[7] In this imagery, the beloved object "infects us with the significance of *our* own lives if we give in to it" (E. Becker 1973: 157). Therefore, the charismatic follower, far from being enfeebled and humble, actually feels vitalized and grandiose precisely because his or her self is merged in identificatory fusion with the charismatic leader.[8]

This euphoria is the same effect Durkheim and the crowd psychologists have characterized as the essence of charismatic involvement; that is, the invigoration paradoxically felt by members of charismatic groups as they lose themselves in worship of the leader. And it is also the imagery of the rapture of the loss of self in the intoxication of romantic love, as Freud envisioned love in his later work. Freud's presentation of love between individuals thus provides a base for a new theoretical understanding of the group. Instead of love conceived as analogous to a depleting, anxious transference neurosis, Freud begins to construe the ecstasy of lovers in terms of boundary loss, fusion, and the identity transformation connected to the experience of primary narcissism.[9] And, by extension, so too do the followers feel joyous expansion in their fused identification with the leader.

But while Freud was willing to accept, and even to praise, the ecstatic character of romantic love, which is a parallel experience to charisma, he could not bring himself to allow a similar value to immersion in the crowd. He refused to follow the logic of his own reasoning about the crowd phenomenon and its similarity to the ecstatic component of eroticism, and retained instead a model of mass behavior based on repression and Oedipal guilt – a model in which followership is enfeebling and unattractive rather than vitalizing.

Freud also tried to escape from the consequences of his logic by arguing that the attraction of immersion in the group would be repressed as society became more rationalized, just as in personal histories individuals progress from the infantile merger with the mother, to greater autonomy and love of differentiated others, and finally to identification with abstract norms and values of the culture.

But Freud was too intellectually honest to leave it at that. Like Durkheim and the crowd psychologists, his premises led him to affirm that the primal desire for self-loss remains latent and powerful, since people always wish to escape from the existential pain of separation via an experience of narcissistic fusion. Ordinarily, this self-destructive impulse is held in check and channeled into acceptable forms by the intrapsychic mechanisms of defense and repression and by the limits imposed by the social configuration.

In times of crisis, however, the sense of identity that is generated by participation in a secure, strong social world is challenged, leaving the individual suffering from a crippling sense of shame and impotence, coupled with rage at the unfairness of the situation. Freud and his followers believed that under such conditions the masses are prone to merger with the posturing charismatic figure who is himself constructing a fantasy world of power and control, whose inner state mirrors that of the society at large, and who offers external objects upon whom rage can be vented, as well as presenting himself as the object for absolute love and merger.

Freud also believed, like Tarde and Le Bon, that the rationalization of society may actually exaggerate the human yearning for self-loss in the passionate mob gathered around the charismatic. This is because the ever greater restrictions of civilized life and bureaucratic organization of necessity increasingly frustrate instinctual demands – in particular the demand for ecstatic experiences of merger. Heightened repression means that charisma, which satisfies the desire for self-loss, will be revealed in an excessive and convulsive manner since, according to Freudian theory, "that which is repressed *becomes and/or remains* infantile and antisocial" (Eagle 1987: 208). Therefore, the repressive conditions of civilization imply that the desire for charisma increases in reaction to social sanctions against it, and that in modern circumstances charisma will take radical forms when it does appear.

More than many of his followers, Freud thus foresaw the danger of modern rationalization and individualism; he knew the enervation and alienation implicit in this process, and feared that the deep human desire for self-loss in the vital maelstrom of the crowd, if repressed too long, might take extreme forms – especially when the system itself lost its legitimacy, and the fragile constraints of rules and norms were dissolved.

6

Charisma as Mental Illness or as Resocialization

We have now outlined a few of the more important concepts of the nature of charismatic involvement. Some are fundamentally positive in their evaluation of charisma: Nietzsche admired the passionate superman; Weber saw the epileptic prophet as the fount of creativity; Durkheim believed collective effervescence to be the source of all morality. On the other hand, the crowd psychologists' image of the mesmerist's domination over the entranced mass was one of enslavement to violent prerational forces, while Freud saw dangerous primitive emotions of sexual desire and projected rage at the core of group leadership. In this chapter I want to compare two modern ideologies of charismatic experience that grow out of these moral positions – a psychological view that emphasizes the pathology of charismatic leadership versus a sociological discourse that ascribes a positive value to charismatic groups.

Mental Illness and the Charismatic Leader

We have seen in the last chapter that Freud never connected the psychology of the crowd with infantile problems of identity and merger. He continued throughout his life to believe that the crowd is bound together primarily by Oedipal guilt and repression under the domination of a punitive, patriarchal, superego figure. This perspective has been maintained by many psychoanalysts who portray the charismatic as a neurotic type.[1] They postulate specifically that charismatic figures will tend to have emotionally distant but authoritarian fathers and close relationships to their mothers – an Oedipal configuration that theoretically should give the child an unreal and grandiose image of the paternal figure as well as an exceptionally strong desire to replace the father and capture the mother's love (Wolfenstein 1967, 1969). According to Erik Erikson, who is perhaps the best known spokesman of this paradigm, this means that the great man "grows up almost with an obligation (beset with guilt) to surpass and to originate at all cost" (Erikson 1970: 64).

According to this theory, because of his drivenness and his unrealistic image of the father, the son transposes his struggle with the paternal figure to the political sphere where his symbolic re-enactment of rebellion against and subsequent transformation into the patriarch "becomes a liberating event for each member of the awe-stricken audience" (Erikson 1970: 64; see also Wolfenstein 1969). This is because the audience is afflicted by similar Oedipal conflicts, though of lesser intensity. As the leader publicly overcomes the patriarch to take the throne himself, he gains the approval of the onlookers, who can participate in his rebellion, but at a safe distance.

The idea of charismatic leadership proposed in this paradigm evidently springs from the same Oedipal matrix discovered by Freud, though the emphasis has changed from a focus on domination to a focus on the revolt that domination engenders. Like Freud, Erikson and his disciples assume that patriarchal leaders and their rebel sons are separate and powerful individuals enacting personal neurotic conflicts. They become leaders because their fantasies happen to run parallel with those of the group. The researcher unmasks the childhood traumas that have formed the character of the leader, and reveals how these traumas are publicly displayed in a way that elicits approval and participation from the audience.

But, despite the brilliant work that has been done by the Eriksonians, and despite Erikson's own subtle awareness of cultural differences in the way the leader presents his trauma to the public, the Eriksonian school's emphasis on the leader's autonomy does not take sufficient account of the degree to which the leader's character is actually transformed by interaction with his followers. In particular, this perspective does not allow for the ecstatic merger of leader and follower which seems so central a part of the charismatic experience (Mazlich 1981).

As we have seen, another image of charisma is expressed, albeit only cursorily, by Freud when he writes that the essential character of the leader is not his aggression nor his sexual desire, but his unwillingness to accept the distinctiveness and separateness of others. Freud says this type of leader is in a state of "narcissistic complacency," which strongly resembles the supposed narcissism of the infant. Theorists who have taken up this line of approach (influenced by Melanie Klein and the object-relations paradigm of infantile mentality, or by Heinz Kohut's model of primal narcissism and identity) no longer portray the leader as a rivalling, hypermasculine individual aggressively seeking sexual conquest, but as someone recapitulating infantile experiences of merger and narcissistic unity.

Because the group and leader are imagined as functioning on a level of primal identity formation, Wilfred Bion, one of the most influential theorists in this school, writes that although "groups would, in Freud's view, approximate to neurotic patterns of behavior . . . in my view they

would approximate to patterns of psychotic behavior" (1961: 181).
From this point of view, then, the charismatic is no longer an Oedipally
fixated neurotic, but a far more seriously pathological individual; a
paranoid or schizophrenic scarred by an intense and ambivalent
relationship with an unresponsive mother and an absent or passive
father.[2] Such individuals never develop an autonomous self, but have
a fragmented and fragile identity, full of rage and fear, marked by an
inability to accept any difference or distance, maintained largely by
grandiose fantasies of omnipotence and domination. This type of leader
is a pre-Oedipal figure whose sexuality is not phallic, but, like the
sexuality of an infant, is "exemplified in a way that suggests ...
polymorphous perversity" (Little 1984: 113; Schiffer 1973).[3]

Charismatic individuals may find refuge from inner disintegration
and recompense for the injuries done in infancy by denying the
limitations of reality and the necessary separation between self and
surround, constructing instead a total world which they can completely
encompass. This accounts for the extreme logic of the systems they
imagine, in which "everything follows comprehensibly and even
compulsorily once the first premise is accepted" (Arendt 73: 457-8).
In this magic world, love is given without being earned or reciprocated,
while the universe itself is charged with the raging energies of the id
that surge so close beneath the surface of the charismatic's personality.
As the novelist Richard Hughes writes, for such a person, " 'men' were
merely him-mimicking 'things,' in the same category as other tools and
stones. Always and unalterably his 'I' must blacken the whole vault
from pole to pole" as the fear of emptiness and rage at solitude is
projected outward in increasingly paranoid delusions (Hughes 1961:
266-7; see Bion 1961, Devereux 1955, Halperin 1983, Chasseguet-
Smirgel 1976, Kohut 1985, for similar images of the leader's character).

But although the leader allows his followers no autonomy, at the
same time he needs them to confirm the reality of his imagined world
and to act "as a regulator of [the leader's] self esteem" (Kohut 1985:
202). The charismatic leader must reach out to his audience in the
effort to combat his sense of inner vacuity, he must ignite them with
his fervor, and bring them into his imagined world of absolute power.
He can accomplish this because of the very injury he seeks to escape –
the underlying fluidity and instability of his personal identity, which
permits him to empathetically discern the motivations of others. As
Heinz Kohut puts it, "narcissistic leader figures ... experience the social
surroundings as a part of themselves." They therefore can "discover
... small or dormant motivations in others" which correspond to their
own deep needs for power and narcissistic expansion. This uncanny
ability to ferret out nuances of narcissistic desire in others is used by
the charismatic to manipulate his audience into collusion with his
fantasies. "He melts them into his personality so to speak and brings

them and their actions under his control as if they were his limbs, his thoughts, and his actions" (Kohut 1985: 54).

Thus, where Freud proposed that the relationship between leader and follower, though conflictual and mentally regressed, could at least be resolved by working through the transference and liberating the sexual energy of the Oedipal conflict, these later theorists have a more dismal picture of group life – one in which collective effervescence and the emotionally vitalizing charismatic are viewed as equivalent to the most extreme forms of mental disorder – the delusional psychoses of paranoids and the fragmented worlds of schizophrenics.

The claim made by Bion and his colleagues that the charismatic figure is actually a full-blown psychotic seems on the surface to be far-fetched – an artifact of his experimental model.[4] A true clinical psychosis would have little appeal for any following, as the delusional world of the paranoid schizophrenic is far too obviously deranged to compete with ordinary life except in the most chaotic circumstances (though, as we shall see, modern charismatics do indeed have a strong tendency to actually become clinically psychotic under the tension of maintaining leadership).

But since Bion's pioneering work, others have done research on narcissistic disorders, and have discovered a range of less disintegrated personality types who are more likely to take the role of charismatic leaders. In fact, one category of narcissistic disorder has been suggested by Robert Waite (1977) to have a particular resemblance to the image of the charismatic leader. This is the "borderline" personality, a narcissistic personality disorder that is difficult to define precisely because it is characterized by an incredible capacity to alter self-representation:

> We can devise a scheme using the central role of the ego as the axis of a continuum along which are located the psychoses, borderline states, transference neuroses, and conflict-free capacities. Movement along this axis is a regressive or a progressive shift that could take place, for example due to successful psychotherapy, the vicissitudes of life, organic states, and so on. *The amazing capacity of borderline patients is to have a tremendous range and flexibility of movement along the ego axis.* (Chessick 1979: 534 – emphasis in the original)

In other words, the borderline individual can shift rapidly from exceptional emotional expressions associated with deeply regressive abreactions and near-psychotic fugues to states of relative normality. These shifts of intensity and expression may be partially involuntary, but, like Weber's prototypical epileptoid shaman, the borderline also has learned a degree of control over his or her volatile emotions. People of this character type therefore exhibit what Otto Kernberg calls "a chameleon-like quality" of constant role playing and fluid changes in identity. By acting capable of doing anything and being anybody the borderline individual tries to persuade both himself and his audience of his power and stability; the aim is to give an impression of complete self-confidence (Kernberg 1967: 677).

The borderline thus offers both to the world, and to himself, a grandiose but highly flexible and extremely fragile self-presentation designed to stave off pervasive inner fears of disintegration. Furthermore, in the borderline syndrome the individual has an uncanny ability to enact intense emotional states and yet remain detached, since the performer is never fully committed to the emotions displayed, because the underlying identity from which the emotional states spring is only provisionally integrated.

The borderline is characterized as well by a great desire and ability to empathetically merge with others while simultaneously revealing an absence of any compassion or respect for the rights of those around him. It is a paradoxical condition, made possible because the borderline feels the other to be an emanation of himself, and is therefore exceptionally responsive to the other's emotional nuances if they support his or her fantasy, but not if the other asserts difference or autonomy. Borderlines exhibit too the tendencies toward paranoia, primary process thinking, polarized morality, and uncontrollable rage that indicate narcissistic injury.

The Regressed Follower

One can easily see that a dominating relationship with the adoring and imitative crowd would meet the needs of the borderline personality for empowerment and merger, but what do the followers discover that leads them to accept and to revel in the leader's authority? In Freud's basic model, the leader as punishing patriarchal superego apparently offers the follower only the monkish pleasures of self-flagellation and guilt, and Erikson's anti-authoritarian rebel is really only a new patriarch on the rise. Either may evoke respect and awe, and guilty self-abnegation, but neither character inspires love.

However, the altered paradigm I have attempted to formulate in the last few pages implies that the charismatic leader and follower are actually mutually enmeshed, each inspiring the other to escape from the human dilemma of solitude. As Christopher Lasch writes, the follower is trying "to dissolve the tension between the desire for union and the fact of separation ... by imagining an ecstatic and painless reunion with the mother". The defensive assertion of absolute independence by the charismatic leader aims to dissolve the same existential problem, but by the opposite route of "imagining a state of complete self-sufficiency and by denying any need for external objects at all" (Lasch 1984: 177). The paths converge in the charismatic experience as the follower and leader fuse together in the group, each fulfilling the fantasy of the other.

From this perspective, the leader's psyche is imagined as one which fits with and serves to amplify the mental state of the crowd, since the leader is prone to enacting exactly the experiences of pre–Oedipal fusion that the crowd members long for. Leader and follower thus are locked in a loop of mutual reinforcement, as the leader's effort to live out his infantile fantasy of merger makes him the object around whom the group can coalesce and recapture their own "narcissistic complacency." When this occurs, the leader is drawn into a vortex, as the crowd's adulation validates his fantasies and magnifies his emotional volatility.

In this theory, the leader is not a Nietzschean autonomous individual, but rather is someone who, more than others, "is able to sink his identity in the herd" (Bion 1961: 89). In enacting his own disintegrative fantasies, the leader infects those around him, tempting them into merger in the group he has catalyzed. Through identification with the leader, the followers too can escape the boundaries of character and civilized morality, and partake of the protean range of emotions and intense psychic states that he manifests. This identificatory experience is the source of the follower's love for the leader; a transcendent love in which the boundaries of self are lost.

In the case of this psychological version of charisma, then, we can see that the individual's willingness to die in the service of the group is not a self-sacrifice, since the crowd member and the leader are pictured as regressed to a condition prior to the development of a separate ego. Leader and follower are entangled in an empathetic communion within the collective, so that physical death no longer has its sting.

It is imagery that is close to the rapturous vision of Durkheim. But the rhythm of participation proposed by Durkheim is now amplified not simply by spontaneous effervescence within the group but by the inflaming, magnifying power of the charismatic leader, whose fragmented self, understood through a psychoanalytic model, gives him access to the raw emotional electricity of the unconscious; an electricity that can excite the group into coalescing and arouse a similar emotional intensity in the followers.

In this paradigm the leader's vitality and selflessness are not benign; they are a result of damage, and in mirroring and incorporating the masses he seeks reparation and revenge – an infinite and terrible task that is taken up by the crowd surrounding him. Along with the transcendence of death and the ecstatic feelings of selfless love that accompany charismatic relations come processes of violence, coercion, delusion and paranoia. So the group and the leader are envisioned not as healthy, but as fundamentally diseased.

It is assumed, then, from this psychodynamic point of view, that not only are charismatics more or less psychotic, but those who succumb to the charismatics' blandishments have also reverted to an infantile, dependent state of mind far removed from a rational, civilized mentality. It is only one more step to claim, as many psychologists do, that those who join charismatic groups are predisposed to do so because they already are mentally unbalanced. For instance, it is argued that people with fragmented or distorted identities will find charismatic groups especially appealing because their anxiety over separation leads to a strong need to find "a merger experience and self-object which will fulfill the longings for self-cohesion in the seeker" (Kriegman and Solomon 1985a: 254; see also Olsson 1983); while others argue that "conversion and mystical states can be employed to resolve a variety of conflicts involving both oedipal and preoedipal strivings, and sexual as well as aggressive urges" (Deutsch 1983: 120).[5]

Like that of Freud, and the crowd psychologists, this approach takes its paradigm of sanity and moral behavior from the rationalistic standards of bourgeois society. The business of psychiatric practitioners is to adapt patients to the "ordinary misery" (as Freud put it) of daily life in this environment. People who joint groups which offer ecstatic collective experiences are "regressed" and "infantile," if not psychotic, in contrast to the "adult" who manifests autonomy, ego integrity and enterprising, self-aggrandizing individualism – a moral stance congruent with a Utilitarian model of human nature. But where the Utilitarians came to this model by reducing passion to calculation, psychology comes to it from the opposite direction, admitting the chaotic intensity of passion, but invoking the admittedly feeble power of rationality as the only possible way to channel and repress the flood of desire that lies beneath the surface of the human psyche.

Freud himself was always deeply ambivalent about the costs of rationalization and civilized constraint, which he felt implied an inevitable lessening of human pleasure and an increasing degree of neurotic repression. But many of his successors have a far more negative view of the charismatic group and a more positive view of rationalization. This evaluation is perhaps born out of the experience of Hitlerism, which undoubtedly awakened in many theorists a deep fear of the eruption of uncontrollable emotions in a collective context. Bion, for instance, argues powerfully for the absolute value of "task groups" which doggedly pursue an instrumental end. Contrary to Utilitarians, he favors such pragmatic instrumentality not because technical reason has any positive value in itself, but because he regards it as the only way to prevent the dangerous disintegration of a group into a psychotic mass. Instrumental reason – which was the object of such tortured ambivalence on Weber's part and such detestation on Nietzsche's – is thus praised by Bion as a necessary prophylactic against the very effervescence Durkheim took as the ultimate human value.

As a preventative against the emotional intensity of the collective, however, practical reason does not seem very effective; the alternative it offers is unlikely to be inspiring to people desirous of escaping from their existential condition of suffering and isolation. And even if pragmatism is accepted as an ultimate value we still have the problem of deciding exactly what is practical; a problem solved generally by judging practicality on the grounds of efficiency in gaining a desired end. Without a meaningful *telos* this end must be nothing more than the gratification of personal preferences; and these preferences, according to Hume's inexorable logic, are themselves derived from emotions.

So we are obliged to return again to pleasure as a validation even of civilized, instrumental rationality. And it seems, from the data and the logic proposed by psychoanalysts, that the exciting and vital immersion in the group is a pleasure that is superior to all save the embrace of the beloved. The moral opprobrium in which these theorists hold charisma is therefore not grounded in their material, but is instead an artifact of a desire to uphold the civilized world and its values, without any way of justifying them.

Sociological Perspectives: The Rationality of Charisma

Weber would have understood the negative valuation of charisma by therapists as a consequence of rationalization, and would have drawn a contrast with less complex social worlds in which charismatic participation may have been held in far greater general esteem and may have appeared far less threatening and absolute. In other words, Weber would argue that it is not charisma itself, but the social configuration in which it occurs, that determines the way it will be experienced and evaluated.

This alternative view is held by most sociological analysts, who agree that it is primarily the social milieu that colors the way in which charisma is portrayed. They paint a picture of charismatic involvement that contrasts on almost every point with that of psychology. Where modern psychologists tend to focus on leaders, and emphasize their disturbed personalities, sociologists have little to say about the characteristics of leaders, but are concerned instead with the followers and their surroundings. And where psychology sees pathology among followers, sociologists are concerned to show the followers are no more psychologically disturbed than anyone else. "Although socially isolated persons may find fellowship and security in a sect and sect preachers occasionally precipitate a psychosis in persons under severe emotional stress, there is no evidence that sect membership is an indication of poor mental health" (Yinger 1946: 88).

And indeed, the data from many studies of the members of various cult-like charismatic groups support this statement, though the material may be skewed by the investigators' antipsychological biases. Nonetheless, it is generally conceded that even in groups as extreme as the Peoples Temple the participants did not seem to be more unbalanced or to have more traumatic family histories than a random sampling of the society at large. Nor are recruits into charismatic groups necessarily products of overt deprivation or disorganization processes that might have broken down their sanity (Hine 1974).

Some theorists have even argued that membership in a modern charismatic group is very often a useful and quite normal transitional interlude in an environment where there are no rites to mark the passage of adolescents from family into society. These groups, then, are thought to serve as "a rehearsal for separation, practice for growing up" (Levine 1984: 26). And, in fact, the vast majority of members "graduate" of their own accord from the totalistic environment of the commune, repudiating the excesses of the group, but recalling the warmth and security of participation with continued affection.[6]

It follows then that simply because the members of a group act in a way which their culture defines as deviant does not mean the people participating are necessarily mentally deranged. Instead, deviance means only that the members are operating according to a belief system that is at odds with accepted cultural values. They are denounced by the mainstream because the group is a threat to the taken-for-granted worldview. The imputation of "insanity" to cultists is therefore explained by sociologists as an effort by society to avoid confronting social critique.

So, in opposition to psychological arguments which seek to discover pathologies behind charismatic membership, interactionist sociological theory avoids making any negative value judgements about the mentality of charismatics and their devotees, focusing on the structure of the group itself, its pattern of recruitment, its ideology and its contradictions, the mechanisms used to gain commitment, and the maintenance and evolution of the group within a given social context. The orientation is pragmatic, and emphasizes the strategies used to promote the group's interests in the "marketplace" of alternative religions.

In terms of the inner lives of the members, the general understanding is that collectives resocialize participants through a number of technical methods (Kanter 1972). From this perspective, new ways of living, of whatever content, are gradually learned within the encompassing personal network of the group. In this process, personal reality is redefined when malleable individuals change identity in order to fit the mold of their group context. The behavior and mental state of charismatic group members is therefore presented sociologically as a product of education within an isolated and reinforcing environment, analogous to the way the larger mainstream culture fits people into roles within its overarching framework. Sociologically speaking, any claim that the members in charismatic groups are pathological because their thoughts have been changed is mistaken, since *every* collective forms and alters the thoughts and actions of the participants.

Given this premise, any apparent irrationality is considered to be the result of the observer's unawareness of the assumptions operating within the group. Usually, these assumptions are thought to be quite conscious, and involve maximization of a valued good, so that problems of understanding the charismatic mental state are in principle no different than the difficulty the modern banker would have in understanding the "uneconomic" generosity of the nobleman of the Renaissance. The nobleman, like the banker, is seeking to maximize what is valuable to him – though for the nobleman the valued commodity is status-honor, not money. Similarly, in the charismatic group it is asserted that people are acting in order to get "what they want." For Weberians, "what people want" is coherent meaning, and the job of the analyst is to discover the meaning system of the group. This done, action within the commune will make sense.

In a more Durkheimian vein, other sociologists downplay meaning – as well as pathology – and argue that reasonable people participate in charismatic groups simply because the group offers "what people want" in the form of community, as "social implosion" draws members into ever more rewarding, intimate and inclusive relationships (Bainbridge 1978). This intimacy facilitates the group member's withdrawal from external influences and permits greater deviance from the social norm in the pursuit of the communal experience (see Lofland and Stark 1965 for the classic statement of this perspective).

Underlying this model of commitment is the Durkheimian idea that people naturally wish to participate in communal life. Furthermore, sociology often implies that such community is hard to find in modern society, which is characterized as favoring isolation and afflicted with problems of meaninglessness and anomie. Within this alienating situation, people will tend to gravitate to alternative groups that do offer a sense of collective participation, in spite of the apparent irrationality of their ideologies. This sociological model thus argues that anyone afflicted by the conditions of modernity might join a charismatic group under appropriate conditions, and does us the service of rendering the experience of charisma less foreign.

This paradigm also places the actual fact of being a part of the charismatic community at the center of its theory, thereby balancing an overly leader-centered psychological viewpoint. Moreover, it is assumed that this communal experience is essentially healthy, and that modern society, insofar as it disallows community, is diseased – again reversing the psychological concept of charisma.

But if many psychological explanations err by assuming that charismatics and their followers must be insane, these sociological approaches have shifted too far in the direction of a dull rationality. In these accounts, the ecstatic and passionate character of the leader, which was so important to Weber and Nietzsche, is left aside almost completely. Any discussion of leadership focuses solely upon the leader's message and its contradictions, not upon the person himself. Nor do we get any sense of the excitement of participation in an ecstatic group. Instead, a football team or management consortium that has developed a sense of camaraderie and loyalty is not distinguishable analytically from a charismatic group except in the structure of the organization and the method of recruitment. And even the emotional content of charismatic participation is a pallid image – "the nurturant atmosphere, coupled with the security of a communal group" (Bromley and Shupe 1981: 123) – that is obviously very far indeed from Durkheim's powerful vision of rapturous, erotic communion in the collective.

Classic social theory and our own common-sense understanding of charisma make it evident that charismatic groups and their leaders offer something rather beyond the homey and sensible picture given by a sociological theory that claims people "choose" to participate in a group because they like the comforting atmosphere it promotes. We can see that this stretches the notion of rational choice beyond its boundaries if we think of the real, subjective experience of charismatic groups where members feel lost in total love, and are capable of dying, or killing, for the sake of the group.

This aspect of charisma is captured far better by the psychoanalytic portraits of groups bound together by compelling motives of unconscious drives toward self-loss, by shared group regression and the satisfaction of powerful emotional impulses, all awakened by the leader's highly charged capacity to stir up deep identificatory states of merger in the hearts of those around him.

We have then two opposing modern approaches to charisma: one, derived from psychoanalysis, gives credit to its intensity and transcendent quality, but is judgemental and places too much emphasis on the personal character of the leader; the second perspective recognizes the importance of the group and the desirability of communal participation, but removes passion from the experience, ignores leadership, and downplays the unconscious drives that underlie the charismatic tie. Each offers us part of the charismatic experience – but not the whole.

In a real sense, these efforts recapitulate a familiar moral tension that derives from the fundamental premises of emotivism. Among psychologists, Nietzsche's apotheosis of the passionate characteristics of the charismatic has been transmuted, through the mediation of Weber,

Freud, Le Bon and Tarde, into an outright horror of the charismatic advent and a panicked clinging to instrumental, pragmatic reason as the only protection against a descent into the vortex of unconstrained desire. The psychologists, led by their premises to a reliance on emotion as the final arbiter of value, attempt to deny it in favor of repression.

On the other hand, the sociological orientation has retained a Durkheimian faith in the moral goodness of the communal experience, or, at least, a concurrence with Weber's more intellectual idea that subjective participation in the social world is the only thing that can give life its felt significance. But if psychology has recoiled from its own insights into the emotional roots of group life, sociology has reacted in a different way; not by repudiation of emotion, but by making collective emotions tame. People in charismatic groups are imagined to be consciously seeking coherence, rather like mathematicians constructing a theorem, or else they are looking for a warm club-house atmosphere. This is obviously not only far from the psychotic imagery of group consciousness proposed by Bion, but also far from the erotic frenzy of charisma as imagined by Durkheim and Weber. So, charismatic involvement is either given its full weight, and fearfully repudiated, or else eviscerated so that the corpse may be safely embraced.

7

Synthetic Theories of Charisma

In the last chapter I sketched in exaggerated chiaroscuro the divergent moral evaluations of charismatic involvement typically made by some contemporary sociologists and psychologists. In this chapter, I want to consider several efforts to develop a more synthetic model of charisma. These theories begin by accepting the existential tension between development of autonomous personal identity and an opposing tendency – psychological or physiological – for self-loss in states of merger. They argue that certain kinds of external pressures may act to undercut and blur personal identity while simultaneously enhancing the likelihood of immersion in a charismatic group. But even though these theories try to link external and internal dynamics in a way that modern psychological and sociological theories do not, in moral emphasis they are all descendants of crowd psychology, viewing charismatic involvement in an unrelentingly negative light.

"Thought Reform"

One such synthetic theory was articulated by Robert J. Lifton in his influential work on "thought reform" in China (1961). In his work, Lifton argues that the systematic use of techniques for the destruction of personal identity within a totalistic communal structure precedes and fosters merger in the charismatic group. This merger holds at least for as long as the input lasts, and in some cases for much longer.

As illustration of his thesis, Lifton analyzed thought reform (popularly known as brainwashing), which used a number of identity-challenging coercive techniques to gain the loyalty of opponents to the Chinese communist regime. The procedures included alternating organized torture and humiliation with leniency and offers of friendship, repeated breaks in routine, continuous demands for confession and for public revelation and re-evaluation of one's past and present inner state, the stimulation of guilt, and intensive peer group pressure to cooperate and participate. This constant bombardment often led the unwilling prisoners toward inner sensations of identity disintegration, regression to childhood states of dependency, and dramatic personality transformations couched in the terms of death of the old individualistic ego and rebirth as a new "collective" self.

According to Lifton, the victim of successful thought reform becomes closely equivalent to the crowd member imagined by Le Bon and Tarde. Like a somnambulist, he is lost in adulation of the charismatic leader and prone to absolute moral visions marked by a strong polarity of good and evil; his thought becomes constricted and mythical; dependency on and merger within the group is deep, while personal privacy and difference are denied in a discourse of confession, self-purging, and absolute loyalty. In this case, the end result often was strong loyalty to the government of China, and to Mao Tse Tung.

But the process is not simply one of avoidance of pain. According to Lifton, the disintegrative experience of thought reform can also "offer a man an intense peak experience: a sense of transcending all that is ordinary and prosaic, of freeing himself from the encumbrances of human ambivalence, of entering a sphere of truth, reality, trust, and sincerity beyond any he had ever known or even imagined" (1961: 435). This ecstatic component gives thought reform a powerful appeal despite its coercive character; even as the victims' personalities dissolve under the unrelenting pressure placed upon them by their tormentors, they paradoxically feel the extraordinary communion we have found to be essential to charismatic involvement.

Lifton pictures the psychology of this state in a way very like the model of narcissistic merging posited by psychoanalytic theorists. It is seen as analogous to the pleasurable experience of the child fused with the parent, and Lifton links it with "the ever-present human quest for the omnipotent guide ... that will bring ultimate solidarity to all men and eliminate the terror of death and nothingness" (Lifton 1961: 436). Lifton's argument, then, is that the human psyche has certain qualities that are a consequence of infantile desires for fusion and dependency, imagined in mythic terms of the death of the ego and rebirth as a member of the transcendent collective under the leadership of the charismatic figure.

But Lifton does not understand this state as pure psychotic regression. It is instead portrayed as "a new form of adult embeddedness, originating in patterns of security-seeking carried over from childhood, but with qualities of ideas and aspirations that are specifically adult" (Lifton 1961: 437). All human beings have an innate potential for self-loss in such forms of adult embeddedness – a potential that can be activated through specific identity-altering mechanisms of coercion and exhortation in a closed group environment.

Many have disputed Lifton's argument, claiming that it is inappropriate to compare voluntary groups with those in which membership is coerced, but this misses Lifton's point; he believes the rewards of charismatic immersion touch upon a deep and ineradicable part of human nature that is usually buried beneath the calming, identity-maintaining facade of ordinary interaction. Coercion simply rips that facade away, accentuating the desire for an escape from the isolated self in the arms of the welcoming charismatic community. Similar conditions occur during "periods of cultural crisis and of rapid historical change" (Lifton 1961: 437), when objective threats to the self replicate the disintegrative environment of the prison camp. In these stressful periods, many people are likely to participate quite voluntarily in totalistic groups that offer a refuge from confusion within a new, transcendent, group identity.

Bettelheim (1943) made a parallel argument in his discussion of the characteristics of Nazi concentration camp victims. In the camps, identity-challenging techniques were systematically employed, including arbitrary punishment, the rigid enforcement of meaningless rules, extreme torture and humiliation, group responsibility, treatment of the inmates as children, and the forbidding of any autonomous action. The hapless victims of these terrible pressures on personal identity often asserted, against all evidence, that the top officers of the camp were really good and kind; and sometimes demonstrated their loyalty to and identification with their oppressors by wearing cast-off Gestapo uniforms. Infantile dependency, moral polarization, intensification of feeling, identification with Gestapo values, and idealization of the Gestapo leaders, were all generated among these tormented souls – a familiar and terrible constellation.

Bettelheim, like Lifton, argues that this response is merely an extreme example of a general case. He warns that such abject responses will occur as well within state systems if citizens are placed under similar self-destructive conditions of fear, indeterminacy, and physical and mental anguish.[1] That the self has been broken by the same person who stands as an authoritative model is irrelevant; the shattered identity will cling with love to whomever is offered as an object for attachment, permitting the follower even a minimal "illusion of will" by his gestures of command and offer of participation in charismatic communion.

Physiological Theories of Trance and Charismatic Involvement

Other theorists have built a model of charisma very similar to Lifton's, but from a non-psychoanalytic perspective. They argue instead that immersion in a charismatic group is primarily a mechanical result of physical and mental inputs that automatically stimulate trance-like dissociation and hypersuggestibility in the acolytes, leading them to submit themselves utterly to the commands of the leader. This perspective gains its credibility by systematically collecting evidence about the content of trance states that the crowd psychologists took as the paradigm for charismatic involvement and then positing a scientific explanation based on brain neurology.

Of course, the scientific study of abnormal forms of consciousness poses great difficulties. William James was one of the first investigators of such phenomena, and he put the challenge clearly:

> Our normal waking consciousness ... is but one special type of consciousness, whilst all about it, parted from it by the flimsiest of screens, there lie potential forms of consciousness entirely different. . . . No account of the universe in its totality can be final which leaves these other forms of consciousness quite disregarded. How to regard them is the question – for they are so discontinuous with ordinary consciousness. (1929: 378–9)

Despite the difficulties, Arthur Ludwig and others have developed typologies of altered states of consciousness (ASCs), focusing primarily on the attributes these altered states share, and on the way they are brought about. This research utilizes both objective tests and personal reports of people who have entered altered states in experimental or natural settings, and places them within a systematic comparative framework.[2]

What was discovered from this exercise is that ASCs involve something very like the Freudian image of "primary process" thinking in which cause and effect blur, incongruity and ambiguity predominate, and the inchoate desires of the unconscious come to the fore in all their passionate intensity. Ordinary rationality is set aside in favor of highly charged metaphors and fantasies. There is also a subjective sense of timelessness, accompanied by schizoid-like mental disintegration and an obliteration of the boundaries between self and surround. Under these conditions, as S. A. Luria writes, there is a feeling that a powerful impersonal "It" has overwhelmed the individual "I."

Paradoxically, as the limits of rational consciousness and individual identity are superseded, the person in trance, like the charismatic follower, may have a feeling of power and revelation. In this state of what Oliver Sacks has called "deceptive euphoria," the universe may suddenly seem to be intuitively graspable; the self, as it dissolves, experiences a sensation of omnipotence. For example, Maya Deren describes her own trance experiences as "accompanied by a sense of an explosion upward and outward ... possession is the ultimate self-realization to the point of self-transcendence" (1953: 321).

But although those who have been entranced may feel grandiose expansion, at the same time they are likely to be hypersuggestible, responding uncritically to the instructions and cues of an authority figure. Arthur Ludwig and other theorists relate this characteristic suggestibility to the predominance of highly charged primary process thought in the ASC. In this state, the individual is filled with overflowing emotional intensity while simultaneously the structures of ordinary thought are undermined. As Arthur Deikman puts it: "the undoing of automatic perceptual and cognitive structures permits a gain in sensory intensity and richness at the expense of abstract categorization and differentiation" (1972: 36). In this condition of psychic deconstruction reality suddenly seems, as William James says, more "utterly utter" and the individual feels himself lost in merger with a world shimmering with energetic life.

Yet, since euphoric expansion coincides with the disintegration of boundaries of personal identity and the effacement of ordinary categories of thought, self and surround lack shape and purpose. Panic lies not far beneath the surface of the entranced condition, as the sense of expansive limitlessness conceals a potential collapse into a frightening void where the self vanishes forever. The leader rescues the somnambulist from this danger, giving the chaotic world substance and direction by the pure assertion of will. The self, having been lost in fusion, is restored and renewed as the authority figure constructs an identity, and a world, by his commands. Radical shifts in value orientations are then possible, as these commands are experienced as emanating from a new, transcendental core of being. This perspective obviously is in complete accord with that of the crowd psychologists.[3]

Studies also show that long-term immersion in such altered states of consciousness correlates with a consistent personality change. As one researcher writes: "With the diminution of conscious control or inhibitions, there is often a marked change in emotional expression. . . . sudden and unexpected displays of more primitive and intense emotion than shown during normal waking consciousness may appear" (Ludwig 1972: 16). In other words, those who have had been accustomed to an altered state, whether because of disease,[4] or psychosis, or hypnosis, or initiation into a cult, or other training, may acquire an emotional tone that is remarkably vivid and expressive. "These changes indicate a distinct behavioral syndrome involving a deepening of affective response with the preservation of intellectual function" (Winkelman 1986: 185).

The reader will recognize that this research, which is essentially descriptive, replicates much of the imagery of earlier theory. Weber's picture of the leader as vividly emotional is validated in the expressive capacities of those who have had long-term participation in an ASC. It appears as well that an altered state of consciousness, like the paradigmatic hypnotic trance as understood by Tarde and Le Bon, is a condition of inchoate excitability, in which the passive subject awaits the shaping oracular voice. Furthermore, the portrait of group mentality drawn by Durkheim and identity theorists also runs parallel with the experience of the ASC, as in both instances individuals lose their personal boundaries and simultaneously feel a surging sense of heightened vitality.

But in this case, the theory as to why all this should occur pivots on a notion of humans not as social products, nor as psychological entities, but as physical beings. The cause of immersion in the ASC is taken to be a mechanical result of an interruption in the ordinary flow of input into the psyche, either through overstimulation (such as drumming, dancing, chanting, hyperventilating, or torture), or understimulation (solitude, darkness, immobility). Extreme mental concentration is also conducive to the experience of ASCs, as is the cultivation of a state of passivity. Psychotropic drugs can cause altered states, as can physical fatigue, hunger, thirst, disease, and so on.

Arthur Deikman calls this entrancing process "deautomatization," since it requires a breaking down of the ordinarily ordered structures of consciousness that pattern our perceptions. Our consciousness, he says, usually consists of highly stereotyped "automatic" ways of understanding and acting; sensory and emotional input are limited and organized by the brain in order to allow efficient action. We live with blinders on to force us to focus on where we are going. But the techniques and conditions cited above, and many others, have the potential to neurologically disrupt this channeling "until the self is no longer experienced as a separate object and customary perceptual and cognitive distinctions are no longer applicable" (Deikman 1972: 34).[5] This leads to "a state of parasympathetic dominance" in which more primitive and "non-logical" parts of the brain are in command, much as occurs in temporal lobe epilepsy when disinhibition of the temporal lobe allows brain activity in the older, emotional seat of the brain to dominate (Winkelman 1986: 174).

According to this view, disintegrative techniques serve to "keep the parts of the mind – the connections inside the central nervous system – divided in function, in action, and in their connection with the outer world ... the longer it goes on, the further apart all of this gets to be – like the chronic schizophrenic" (Clark quoted in Appel 1983: 134). The follower's state of mind, like schizophrenia, is reckoned to be a physical phenomenon, which can be understood by the study of brain chemistry.

But even though the emphasis here is on the physiological changes in the brain induced by specific techniques, this mode of approach, like Lifton's and Bettelheim's, does call attention to the relationship between external social-psychological influences and the subjective state of the follower. In all these perspectives, the systematic disruption of "normal" consciousness leads automatically to a highly regressive condition analogous to a narcissistic personality disorder or a prolonged hypnotic trance, in which the individual is prone to self-loss in a charismatic group. The physiological evidence does not contradict the more psychological and social paradigms; it corroborates them by showing the physical mechanisms through which intense commitment can be engendered.

These theorists all regard the state of self-loss with horror as the essence of dehumanization, while personal autonomy is given the highest possible value. Considering the extreme cases used as illustrations – concentration camps, cults and prisons – this negative view of charisma and group merger is understandable, but it is harder to justify when we see people joining charismatic groups voluntarily – as Lifton and Bettelheim say is likely to happen when social conditions threaten identity.

Modernity and "Other-directedness"

The identity-threatening milieu that favors charisma is usually thought to be a result of some kind of catastrophic threat or cultural collapse which leaves people desperate for leadership. But many recent thinkers have raised the possibility that present-day social mechanisms, even when running "as usual," may in fact strongly press individuals toward charismatic involvement.

The earliest examples of this tradition of thought derive primarily from the painful struggle to understand the German experience with Hitler, and include Erich Fromm's (1941) analysis of the Nazi followers' "flight from freedom" in a chaotic and identity-challenging environment, Wilhelm Reich's (1970) seminal effort to relate sexual repression to the psychology of Fascism, Alexander Mitscherlich's (1969) concept of "society without the father," the dissection of the "authoritarian personality" by Theodor Adorno and his colleagues (1950) and Bertram Schaffner's (1948) effort to relate German family structure to Nazi participation. Some of this material will be used later, in a discussion of Hitler.

The German experience, however, can be dismissed as highly unusual, the product of just the sort of extraordinary cultural crisis that is thought to precede charisma. But we can find as well theoretical perspectives that imply a similar propensity toward charismatic involvement throughout modern society. These theories begin with the contemporary ideology of radical individualism – derived from Utilitarianism – which affirms human beings to be islands separate from the rest of the social universe (for example, Bellah et al. 1985). Within this ethos it is impossible to make a moral statement about the positive value of community, since people can only speak of action as self-interested and derived from personal preference. This is, of course, the emotivist position in its purest form.

According to many social theorists, the emotivist premise corresponds to the general conditions of modern social organization, including increased technical diversity of the work force, the continued decomposition of integrated local communities and the deepening isolation and alienation of individuals, who find themselves lost in a proliferation of fragmented roles. In this environment, work is more specialized, less interconnected with the world at large, less personally satisfying. People are unaware of how they fit in a larger pattern, and feel themselves set afloat in an uncertain and perilous world where meaning is hard to discern and secure commitment unlikely. Society itself is perceived as "lacking authentic institutional or symbolic form" (Lifton 1970: 52). This amorphous and anxious state is exaggerated by the proliferation of media images that undermine all taken-for-granted beliefs, replacing them with ephemeral fashions. Certainty is replaced by cynicism, boredom and alienation.

Without any accepted moral guidelines the freedom of choice granted by this fluid, highly competitive society can lead to a tremendous anxiety about making "correct" decisions. Persons are obliged to pay cautious attention to the choices of others, since accommodation to and imitation of the decisions of others will validate the value of one's own decisions, and ratify one's position in a confusing and dangerous world without clear boundaries or status markers. Reliance on personal preferences in the absence of value hierarchies thus can imply nervous conformity to the preferences of others – a kind of "social radar" that David Riesman and his colleagues famously characterized as "other-directedness" (1962).

According to this argument, the anxious lack of confidence in the validity of one's own desires is accentuated by the increasing preponderance of vast corporate structures which demand conformity from their members and a willingness to adapt immediately to circumstances. Adaptation means one must be quick to change appearance and to put on appropriate protective coloration; one must also be mobile, willing to move quickly to a new location, able to establish new, if shallow, emotional ties immediately. Most important, it means that one's inner life must be flexible, so that morality becomes situational. One must be alert to nuance, and always prepared to shift direction with the prevailing wind. From this point of view, in modern society the ideologically regent self is becoming ever more and more self-consciously pliable, more "Protean" (to use Lifton's phrase).

In this fluid and competitive context "Protean man . . . has constant need of a meaningful inner formulation of self and world, in which his actions, and even his impulses, have some kind of 'fit' with the 'outside' as he perceives it" (Lifton 1970: 54–5).[6] Even pleasurable inner sensations, the ultimate motivation for action and judgement according to the emotivist ethic, are rendered problematic, since they too are matters of anxious comparison, to be measured in relation to the achievements of others, who may have a faster car, a more ostentatious ring, more and better orgasms.

As uncertainty reaches into the core of the individual's way of experiencing, the modern, "other-directed" person is portrayed in much of contemporary social theory as a bad actor, without an inner self at all. This thin character is supposedly manufactured completely by the world around him, caught up in a confusing social context of multiple roles, hyperaware yet distrusting of the audience, self-consciously manufacturing the appearance of appropriate feelings in order to maintain a precarious social front, while in actuality nearly paralyzed internally by pervasive anxiety about putting a foot wrong: "Behind many masks and many characters, each performer tends to wear a single look, a naked unsocialized look, a look of concentration, a look of one who is privately engaged in a difficult, treacherous task" (Goffman 1959: 235).

The compensation for this pressure and tension is a materialistic ideology of possessive individualism that promises happiness and validates personal worth solely through the competitive acquisition, display, and endless consumption of ever expanding amounts of material goods and services. But the reward itself increases tension, since there is no end to accumulation, and anxious comparison with others is continuous.

So, from this perspective, modern culture is marked by an apparent paradox: "an absolutely autonomous self, and a self determined completely by the social situation" (Bellah et al. 1985: 80). The paradox, however, is only on the surface, since absolute autonomy, without any base for hierarchizing preferences, leads, as these theorists argue, to absolute conformity in an era in which the self is floating without moorings, and can find only physical sensation and material possessions as a moral peg upon which to hang a highly contingent identity.

But the disintegrative effects of the loss of tradition, the division of labor, the absence of meaning, and the impossibility of grounding identity do not mean that the search for charismatic communion ceases. On the contrary, from a Durkheimian perspective, modern solipsism acts to push individuals toward immersion in a charismatic group. Psychologically, this is because "man cannot live without attachment to some object which transcends and survives him" (Durkheim 1966: 210). Structurally, it is because "bureaucratic political organization . . . produces the concomitant longing for charismatic leadership in those individuals alienated by the structure of bureaucracy itself" and because in the modern world, rent by futility, alienation, and anxiety, "the cohesion problems . . . are so complex that pressures toward some kind of irrational unification figure or symbol become almost necessary if anomie and social conflict are to be reduced to manageable levels" (Glassman 1975: 633, 636).

The more ambivalent psychoanalytic perspective also rests on the faith that a social formation not permitting expression of "the fundamental pattern of separation (anxiety, aggression) followed by union" (Roheim 1970: 43) will find the repressed aspect erupting in some form. If modern society seems to prohibit communion, then in reaction alienated individuals must possess an "unappeasable appetite" for emotional experiences with which to fill an inner void (Lasch 1979: 72). It follows that charismatic movements, or their equivalents, will appear to sate that hunger.

Reasoning from these premises leads to an argument that the desire for experiences of merger and attachment will actually *increase* incrementally as these pleasures are ever more restricted by rootless and isolating modern conditions. When the self is devalued and stripped of identity markers and ties with others, and yet simultaneously affirmed as the sole validation for any action, then the intensity and inner certainty offered by a charismatic revelation and immersion in a communal group of devotees will be highly attractive. This form of heightened interaction offers just what the social formation lacks – a feeling of communion, ecstatic self-loss, transcendence, faith.

The "Culture of Narcissism"

A more specific argument in favor of the contemporary desire for charismatic self-loss is implicit in the psychoanalytically influenced theories of Christopher Lasch (1978), who made the "culture of narcissism" a standard shorthand for characterizing modernity. His argument begins with the sociological image of contemporary life I outlined above – an image of competitiveness, complexity, personal isolation and social fluidity. The character type that is supposedly developed in this context Lasch describes as similar to that of a patient with a narcissistic identity disorder; a fragmented and enraged self engaged in a convulsive search for pleasure and stimulation to compensate for a lost sense of vitality and meaning.

Lasch is not alone in his formulation. Equivalent arguments, differing in technical detail and analytic expertise, have been made by a number of other theorists, both within and without the psychoanalytic community, starting from a post-Freudian model of the contradictory relationship between modern social formations and basic identity needs. For instance, Simcox-Reiner (1979) claims that the absence of support networks in modern society leads to anxieties about identity and to borderline and narcissistic personalities seeking salvation in fused relationships. Heinz Kohut (1977) argues in a similar vein that the modern isolation of the nuclear family, coupled with the intrusion of the marketplace into family life and the subsequent erosion of familial emotional ties, tends to increase the number of narcissistic pathologies derived from a lack of empathetic communion within the household. These theories that link modernity with disorders of the core identity are borne out in practice, as many psychotherapists concur that their patients are more and more likely to be persons suffering from narcissistic pathologies.[7]

From this perspective the psychological problem of today is not one of Oedipal conflict, but one of the absence of an identity, with people seeking to fill the inner vacuum left by inadequate parental care and a lack of emotional support. This modern personality type is generally regarded as the psychological expression of a social world in which alienation, ennui, and anomie prevail.

Attempts by individuals to escape this enervated condition through drugs or sex or the consumption of material goods do not provide real satisfaction, since the basic desire is to recapture the security and ecstasy of moments of primal fusion. As one psychologist puts it in an essay on narcissistic personality types: "When they are not in a relationship in which they are partially fused to or merged with another person, they feel empty, fragmented, alone, and uncertain about who they are and who the other person is" (Adler 1979: 644–5). Such individuals will ceaselessly search for others with whom to identify, and through whom they can find the powerful sensation of boundary loss without the fear of complete disintegration.

Although not usually carried in the direction of understanding social movements, it is evident that the "culture of narcissism" argument logically implies an inclination by the narcissistically damaged to submit to a charismatic leader who will facilitate an empowering, ecstatic merger in the group. As we know from psychological theories of the group, the character of a charismatic follower resembles nothing so much as a person with exactly the personality disorder outlined by Lasch and Kohut as typical of modern men and women. And the leader such individuals will find most entrancing is exactly the volatile borderline psychotic who embodies and enacts their own deepest fantasies of fusion, intensity and rage. So, according to this paradigm, modern society is characterized, it would seem, by the widespread appearance of personality types whose feelings of inner deadness impel them to charismatic relations.

Starting from another, more orthodox, Freudian perspective, but ending in the same place, Gutman (1973) has explicitly linked modernity and the rise of charismatic leaders. He begins with the modern challenge to the veracity of traditional values. As external standards are undermined all forms of authority are delegitimized, even by the authority figures themselves. Parents look to their children for love and meaning because they are uncertain of their own values, and so of themselves. The child's aggression can therefore not be converted into the internal controlling power of the moralistic, punitive superego, but must be channeled by an external source.

This process coincides with a resurgence of mythical thought, and a tendency to boundary loss in worship of charismatic leaders who offer themselves as substitute superegos who can turn aggression outward. "When the internal autocrat of the superego disappears, it is reborn externally. . . . It becomes the coercive power of the priest, the prince, the sorcerer – and the 'group' " (Gutman 1973: 615). Thus both identity theorists and more traditional psychoanalysts come to the same point – arguing for an elective affinity between modern social life and a personality structure with strong tendencies toward charismatic immersion.

We have then two synthetic pictures of conditions that lead to charismatic involvement – one in which an alienated modern society and a "culture of narcissism" combine to make people likely to accept charismatic immersion; the other a portrait of techniques for "thought reform" that disrupt personal identity and prepare individuals for self-loss. Neither assumes that members of charismatic groups are necessarily pathologically traumatized, as the psychological model does, nor do they consider the charismatic cult to be simply an alternative form of rational action, as the sociological model does. Instead, human beings are envisioned as susceptible to the disintegrative effects of certain techniques and social conditions that act to challenge personal identity, promote engulfment by the group, and favor ecstatic adulation of the formative leader.

These dark fables are not mutually contradictory. In fact, they mesh. If Lasch and other theorists are right in their claim that alienating modern social conditions may produce anxious and uncertain narcissistic personalities, and if it is correct that narcissists are searching for self-loss and merger in order to redress their injuries and vent their rage, it follows that these malleable individuals will be particularly susceptible to voluntary indoctrination into charismatic groups by the "brainwashing" techniques discovered by Lifton, Bettelheim, and the physiologists of trance. In fact, modernity itself, in its radical challenge to the grounds of selfhood, may be seen as analogous to the pressures applied in "thought reform."

Escapes from Modernity

If we take this portrait of modernity seriously, the future appears to consist of greater and greater pressures on individuals, increasing loneliness, solipsistic ideologies, heightened competition and anxiety. Many more or less utopian escapes from this unhappy situation have been proposed. But these escapes take no account of emotional structure, and do not recognize the potential for charismatic leadership in their imaginary utopias. They operate instead within an understanding of human psychology that is rationalistic and individualistic.

For instance, Marxists imagine a revolution against individualism and greed and in favor of community, affirming the equality of all. But history shows that the ideology and enactment of equality does not militate against a cult of personality. In fact, egalitarian revolutionary movements enjoin the merger of the individual within the mass while simultaneously requiring worship of the charismatic central figure who embodies the group's revolutionary fervor. Even Lenin, who opposed the cult of personality, nonetheless was the object of such a cult, and remains so in his sacred tomb (see Tumarkin 1983).

Perhaps instead, as a number of neo-conservative thinkers who find modern moral vacuity disturbing suggest, traditional normative values can be resuscitated, and people can be brought out of the anomic slough of relativism to find the old familiar lights of faith and trust burning once again (for example, Sandel 1982). But for these theorists establishing traditional bonds is based on a re-establishment of an ethical consensus, when in fact the morally disintegrative reality of competitive individualism allows no ideological armature to support such a revival.

Furthermore, the academic appeal for a reaffirmation of traditional values assumes that these values are primarily a matter of education and consociation. This may be true for intellectuals (though it probably is not true even then), but the evidence shows that widespread revivalist movements draw their strength not from ideas or nostalgia, but from the emotional intensity generated by a charismatic figure. And a prophet who demands a return to a millennial past is no less radical than a prophet with a vision of the transformed future; both require the dissolution of the status quo, both demand an undermining of the comforting values and intellectual consensus that neo-conservatives hold so dear.

Or one can adopt a Sartrean existentialist position, and undertake a quest for an authentic ontological identity beneath social conditioning; finding communion within the self and thereby negating the appeal of merger within the group. But if followed seriously the quest for subjective authenticity has a propensity for driving its adherents into a corner from which only innate personal preference can be called upon to give shape to identity. From this position the compelling emotional intensity of a charismatic and the group becomes peremptorily appealing, since these relations provide the illusion of will and a subjective intensity of feeling that allows an escape from solipsistic emptiness. Thus, the search for the authentic self can lead to a more personalized form of tyranny, as we shall see later in some of our cases.

Another possibility lies in recent "postmodernist" efforts to reinterpret modernity. The argument is that the erosion of traditional values and the fluidity and normative relativism of modern society mean we have the potential for a self-aware, personal creation of our own value systems. Social structure becomes an enabling mechanism, providing a multitude of roles which are both models and protective covers for the creative construction of new selves in interaction with other equally innovative and playful actors.

There are a number of problems with this optimistic vision of the postmodern individual as creative actor: for instance, it rests on highly questionable assumptions that roles are freely chosen, and that there is no underlying tension between role and emotional need. But here I wish to draw attention only to the implicit claim that free individuals, charmed by their capacity to try roles on and take them off, like children toying with disguises, will naturally enjoy a life of constant, pleasurable self-transformation.

Instead, the paradigms we have drawn indicate that the emotionally distancing, role-playing quality of modern life is actually conducive to charismatic relations, since it involves a devaluation of the integrity and stability of personal markers of the self. As these markers are stripped away an individual can indeed become anyone, but only because he or she has already become no-one, and is therefore susceptible to identification with the group and the leader who can give the Protean, shapeless individual a new transpersonal identity. So it seems that a postmodernist play ethic is more a precondition of than a defense against charismatic involvement, and in fact we will discover this very play ethic utilized by modern charismatic figures as a method for precipitating self-loss in the group.

All escapes from contemporary alienation, then, seem to lead in the same direction – toward charismatic involvement as the dialectical counterpoint to the ethic of possessive individualism. A final alternative is to build a moral system based precisely upon the paradigms of emotional desire and charismatic involvement I have drawn above, finding value in the emotional intensity of the charismatic leader, envisioned as a beacon igniting the inert masses who without him are merely empty shadows in the dark, without form or character. As we have seen, this is the position notoriously taken by Friedrich Nietzsche.

This image of the group and the leader resonates with that drawn by the crowd psychologists, and Freud, as well as by Lifton, Bettelheim, Bion, Kohut and the other synthetic theorists we have discussed in this chapter. All have been obliged to accept the Nietzschean vision of the power of the charismatic and the desire of the masses for a force to mold them. But they refuse to take Nietzsche's lead and celebrate the charismatic's inevitable apotheosis.

Yet the image of modernity and of human personality that is accepted by these theorists means that the compulsion to immersion in charismatic relations must have an inexorable appeal to members of modern society. Utopian ideologies which claim to offer escapes from the conditions of modernity offer no exit from the charismatic's appeal, nor does decrying the immorality of charisma give any refuge from being overwhelmed in the adoring mob. At the same time, the experience itself has been denuded of the positive value attributed to it by Weber and Durkheim, leaving us with a tragic vision of individual impotence in the face of the appeal of the charismatic leader who embodies the regressed consciousness of the group.

Reprise

What I have described in this second part of the book is a theoretical movement that begins with Hume's original elevation of emotion over reason and works through subsequent attempts to construct some moral theory out of this radical assertion. As we have seen, Hume's demystified view of "people as they really are" was supposed to dissolve all forms of demagoguery by denying the validity of systematic thought. But at the same time, Hume gave us a vision in which it is impossible to justify any action over any other, save on the shifting basis of personal preferences that lack all structure and hierarchy.

I have sketched out the various responses to this challenge: the Utilitarians' efforts to establish a moral economy of emotion by reducing desire to the calculating "calm passion" of greed; Nietzsche's counter-argument that if passion is all, then strong passions are to be worshipped – anything less is the whimpering of the envious and feeble; Weber's tragic evolutionary perspective that placed expressive charismatic supermen at the origin of history, but relegated them to the periphery in rationalized modern bureaucracies; Durkheim's brilliant transformative theory that turned away from individual feeling and toward socially generated emotion as the source of morality; and the crowd psychologists, who accepted Durkheim's basic premises, but reversed his values, so that the crowd became diabolical and rationality regained a new place as a bulwark against the raging power of the mob.

Finally, I discussed a psychoanalytic paradigm deriving from Freud that seeks to establish what Hume and all the other theorists lack; a dialectical structure of human desire. Freud's postulate of an existential tension between deep impulses toward attachment and separation permits us to construct a new moral theory that begins not with a welter of incommensurate personal passions, but with a connection between the expression of fundamental desires and the constraints of the social world. From this point of view, human beings must find a way to manifest their contradictory yearnings, but the form these desires take is shaped by social pressure and may be revealed in ways that are dark indeed. One of these manifestations is charismatic involvement, where impulses toward merger are met in the effervescent collective emotions aroused by expressive charismatic figures.

Freud himself found the crowd repulsive, and feared the charismatic leader and the fusion he offers. Yet, on the other hand, he believed in the positive value of merger in the embrace of the beloved; a self-transcendent moment that is analogical to the self-loss participants discover in the group. His view of the crowd and charisma thus had an ambivalence absent in other theorists; the experience of self-loss was deeply appealing and revitalizing, yet also dangerous and potentially destructive.

But all of the positive aspects of charisma that lie beneath the surface in Freud, and are overt in Durkheim, Weber and Nietzsche, have been lost in modern social psychological theory, which has been traumatized by the direction mass movements have taken in the contemporary era, so that charisma has become synonymous with evil. These theorists fearfully point out to us how technical measures and social conditions precipitate self-loss in charismatic involvement. Yet, as in crowd psychology, we are left only with frightening assertions of the ineradicable power of group emotions, and without any refuge from them, since these emotions seem to be favored by the very grounding conditions of our contemporary existence. Instead of demagogues disappearing, as Hume hoped, they now look to be inevitable. According to Alasdair MacIntyre: "The Nietzschean stance turns out not to be a mode of escape from or an alternative to the conceptual scheme of liberal individualist modernity, but rather one more representative moment in its internal unfolding. And we may therefore expect liberal individualist societies to breed 'great men' from time to time. Alas!" (1981: 241). Is this indeed the future? What will it be like, and what alternatives are possible?

To answer these questions, we need to begin by looking at the actual processes of charismatic involvement, placing each advent in historical context, and entering into the world of the participants by listening attentively to their own accounts, not to the abstractions of theory. This is the task of the next part of this book.

Part III

Practice

8

The "Possessed Servant": Adolf Hitler and the Nazi Party

Nothing is anchored anymore, nothing is rooted in our spiritual life anymore. Everything is superficial, fleeing past us. Restlessness and hate mark the thinking of our people. The whole of life is being completely torn apart.

Hitler quoted in Waite 1977

The Charismatic Milieu in Germany

The negative image of the charismatic context and process that is characteristic of most modern social theory is derived, in large measure, from the history of Hitler and the Nazi Party.[1] Germany prior to Hitler was a test case for the disintegrative effects of modernization that were so feared by the crowd psychologists and their followers. The crumbling of traditional ties was especially agonizing in turn-of-the-century Germany because there was no strong national identity with which to replace them. Unlike the other European states, Germany had emerged from feudalism relatively recently, and the degree of cultural provincialism and antagonism remained considerable. While rural society was turned inward, urban sophisticates looked out from Germany to European culture for their models of behavior and action, so that Germany lacked a sense of cultural coherence. Differences in religion exacerbated regional and rural–urban divisions, as Protestants and Catholics cherished memories of centuries of animosity. These rending distinctions were added to and intensified by the class antagonisms that accompanied Germany's rapid industrialization.

Erik Erikson (1985) has argued that the anxiety generated by the German lack of social cohesion led, in reaction, to a popular belief in an authoritarian dictator who could bind the society together. This deep-seated German desire for an absolute leader has also been related to a number of other factors, cultural, ideological and structural, including the heritage of the authoritarian German family structure, the feudal past and the romanticized link between lord and fief, the German lack of experience with pluralistic democracy, the salvationist religious tradition, and the personalizing of political relations corresponding to a social ethos that still looked to the village *Gemeinschaft* as the ideal community.[2] Whatever the causal factors, it is clear that the popular yearning for a dictator to provide the country with spiritual unity and continuity was heightened by the increasing fragmentation and internal conflict of Germany at the turn of the century. In this context, liberal concepts of democratic pluralism were never able to achieve the same sort of central place in German society that they did in England, or even in France.

German anxiety was also added to by the nation's inability, due largely to its own clumsy policies, to participate to any great extent in the colonial endeavor. As a result, many Germans considered themselves surrounded by enemies and unfairly excluded from their proper position on the world stage. A fear of encirclement, accompanied by a general sense of resentment and paranoia, pervaded German consciousness long before Hitler came to power.

After World War I, conditions in Germany worsened; social fragmentation and internal hostility undermined traditional roles and status positions, strikes swept the country, and roving armies of freebooters spread chaos. Meanwhile, the navy rioted and Munich was ruled by Communists, then by rightists, and the dispiriting atmosphere of continued economic crisis continued as rampant inflation all but wiped out the middle class, who elsewhere in Europe provided the base for inculcation of pragmatic and anticharismatic liberal values.

Even more disturbing for Germans, perhaps, was the sense of humiliation and betrayal left by the country's unexpected and ruinous defeat. The "stab in the back" theory soon gained popular acceptance as a way of explaining the country's misfortunes. As one returning soldier recalled: "Shame reddened our cheeks and anger constricted our throats. Clearly there were people at work intent on turning things upside down. Heroism had become cowardice, truth a lie, loyalty was rewarded with dastardliness" (quoted in Abel 1938: 27).

There was as well a widespread consensus that the Weimar Republic was a political failure, run by special interests who were uninterested in governing for the benefit of Germany as a whole. And, in fact, the plebiscitary nature of the Weimar electoral process, with its undiluted proportional representation, did encourage legislative logjams and endless manipulations for coalitions, so that the parliament was often immobilized and ineffectual.

In this trying time, a sense of despair prevailed among many Germans. As one activist wrote in 1923: "Our history has gone astray. Nothing of ours is succeeding in the world. Nothing today; nothing yesterday. . . . Something has gone wrong with everything. And when we try to set anything aright, it breaks to pieces in our hands" (quoted in Waite 1952: 263).

For a vast majority of Germans, the rifts in society seemed insurmountable, the traditional world appeared to have collapsed, the government had lost its mandate, and all expectations were disappointed. Clearly, this unhappy moment of fragmentation provided an ambience – a cultic milieu – that favored the appearance of charismatic leaders who could give the crowd a new shape and intensity, and who could provide channels for the expression of the rage and frustration generated by the disintegration of society and of the markers of personal identity.

Pre-Nazi Charismatic Groups

But in spite of favorable conditions, no particular leader in the post-war period could gain enough of a following to master Germany. This did not, however, indicate an absence of charisma; on the contrary, the impasse was due in part precisely to a proliferation of rival charismatic figures heading up a cornucopia of revitalizing religious-military-political-mystical organizations. There was, in fact, a kind of boiling over of charismatic collectives – a cultic efflorescence that culminated eventually in National Socialism.

Important precursors for Hitler were the Youth Organizations that sprang up like mushrooms throughout Germany in the wake of the war, espousing almost every form of belief and practice imaginable, from homosexuality to vegetarianism, from socialist atheism to *volk*ish nationalism. Under all this seeming variety, however, we see some of the typical features of charismatic commitment, beginning with an unconditional repudiation of all traditional values:

> They thought that parental religion was largely sham, politics boastful and trivial, economics unscrupulous and deceitful, education stereotyped and lifeless, art trashy and sentimental, literature spurious and commercialized, the drama tawdry and mechanical . . . family life repressive and insincere, and the relations of the sexes, in marriage and without, shot through with hypocrisy. (H. Becker 1946: 51)

Instead of the depreciated values offered by tradition, the alienated youth proposed an emotional mysticism, a worship of nature, a return to the felt authenticity of the body, and, most especially, the apotheosis of action, "action simply for the sake of action itself" (Waite 1952: 19). These groups were, in emotional tone, not far removed from the Durkheimian model of the early community, united by shared participation in the communion of group rituals which, in the absence of other values, were all that remained for the youth to believe in.

The gathering of the disaffected young had, moreover, another characteristic aside from the exuberant sharing in collective rituals. This was a general consensus on the necessity of personal leadership, both within the group, and in the nation. Only a great leader, they felt, could bring the order and commitment the era required. But since ideology had proven to be corrupt this commitment could only spring from the leader's expressed power to move and inspire the souls of the followers by his emotional intensity.

Ideally, the leader should feel this vitalizing power flowering within himself and reveal it spontaneously, inflaming the followers to action. The longing for the mystical and inchoate act that would galvanize the followers is, of course, strictly parallel with the crowd psychologist's theoretical understanding of the leader as the creative agent, who arouses the dormant crowd into imitation by his gesture.

But the Youth Organizations were not alone in their yearning for communion in the group, magical action, and emotionally compelling charismatic leadership. The same desires motivated the members of the Free Corps, the ex-soldiers whose independent armies fought against leftists in Germany as well as in the Baltic region, and who later became the mainstay of Hitler's storm-troopers, the SA, in the early years of his rise to power. Like the youth, these freebooters, who called themselves "wanderers out of the void," (a term Hitler also used to describe himself) saw the post-war world as empty, and traditional values as debased. Like the youth, they felt themselves to be rootless and alienated in a Germany where all they had fought for was apparently turned upside down.

But the Free Corps men had a more positive ideal of community as well, one that offered a substitute for the corrupt civilian world which they now utterly rejected. As one writes, "we soldiers of the front had never known the fabulous comfortable road; nor did we feel any longing for it. Fighting had become our life purpose and goal" (quoted in Abel 1938: 45). These men were in fact brought together by a profound desire to recapture the transformative "front experience" they had undergone as storm-troopers in the trenches.[3]

Operating under the constant threat of death, and repeatedly undergoing the heightened emotional experience of attack and violence, many storm-troopers had found in the intensification of battle a kind of mystical ecstasy. This feeling is clear in ex-storm-trooper Ernst Junger's apotheosis of the front, taken from a hugely popular book published shortly after the war:

> The condition of the holy man, of great poets and of great love, is also granted to those of great courage. . . . [Participation in battle] is an intoxication beyond all intoxication, an unleashing that breaks all bonds. It is a frenzy without caution and limits, comparable only to the forces of nature. There the individual is like a raging storm, the tossing sea and the roaring thunder. He has melted into everything. He rests at the dark door of death like a bullet that has reached its

goal. And the purple waves dash over him. For a long time he has no awareness of transition. It is as if a wave slipped back into the flowing sea. (quoted in Herf 1984: 74)

The communion the youth groups sought had thus been realized by the storm-troopers momentarily and under extraordinary and terrible circumstances in a way that Durkheim may have never pictured, but which is nonetheless analogous to his image of collective effervescence.

Once again the "band of brothers" yearned for subordination to an absolute leader, since for the storm-troopers "the only thing that counted was the will of their own Führer" (Waite 1952: 111). The authority of this superior officer was not due to the formal hierarchy that predominated in the regular army. On the contrary, the officer was first of all one of the men, participating personally in all their trials and pleasures; he fought beside his soldiers in battle, shared danger with them, ate with them, and was called the familiar "du" by them. He shared as well the social background of the men, since, unlike the officers of the regular army, storm-trooper officers were usually recruited out of the ranks. The extent of the officers' involvement can be gauged by the fact that they were unmarried, since it was felt that their loyalty should be directed only toward their soldiers.[4]

We have then a group of men, bound together by the transformative experience of battle, and devoted to a leader who was held in reverence which, as a semiofficial history put it, "was above all of a spiritual nature. . . . to them he was not their commanding officer; he was their Leader! And they were his comrades!" (quoted in Waite 1952: 27). We do not need to assume pathology to understand these soldiers' devotion to their leader. Under the extraordinary circumstances of battle the glorified commander provided a point of stability and identification for the men in the disintegrating chaos of the battlefield, where obedience to orders and participation in the group offered not only refuge but also a new, and transcendent, communal identity. Living out the charismatic drama of immolation and rebirth in the holy community, the soldiers, inspired by their leader, dared to confront death, and either died horribly, or, miraculously and against all odds, survived and were transformed. Furthermore, they were given enemies to be killed, and comrades to be loved. The fact that the soldiers had no real choice about what they were undergoing makes no difference for the felt validity and potency of the experience.

All battlefield soldiers have similar transcendent moments of greater or lesser intensity, which accounts for the nostalgia for war felt by many ex-combatants. But in Germany the unsettled environment of the post-war world kept the front soldiers from being reabsorbed by the softening influences of family, friends and work, as they were elsewhere in Europe; instead they were unemployed and full of resentment at what seemed an unjust defeat. For them the heightened sensations and mystical communion of army life seemed infinitely preferable to the corruption of civilian existence. So, in the opening provided by social collapse, the Free Corps arose, with an ideology summed up by Ernst Von Salomon, a Free Corps activist, in the following words:

> "What do we believe in?" you ask. Nothing besides action. Nothing besides the possibility of action. Nothing besides the feasibility of action ... We were cut off from the world of *bürgerlich* norms ... The bonds were broken and we were free. ... We were a band of fighters drunk with all the passions of the world; full of lust, exultant in action. What we wanted, we did not know. And what we knew, we did not want! (quoted in Waite 1952: 269)

But when they joined the Nazi Party many of these "wanderers in the void" did indeed find what they did not know they wanted. In the fellowship of the group they discovered the same discipline, absolute charismatic leadership, heightened emotional intensity, immediate action, and manly comradeship that they had experienced in the battlefield. As one devotee wrote: "What fellowship there was among the men who left their wives, families and parents, preferring the sacred sign of the swastika to their means of livelihood! ... What joy and honor to be allowed to fight side by side with such comrades!" (quoted in Abel 1938: 145–6).

Hitler's Rise to Power

But as we have seen, Hitler and his party did not immediately gain the loyalty of the charismatically predisposed. In the confused cultic milieu of the twenties, the multitude of opposed charismatic action groups and other political factions canceled one another out, leaving a space in which the Weimar Republic seemed to be slowly evolving into an established and functioning plebiscitary democracy.

After 1924 this process accelerated as a degree of prosperity and stability returned and the era of putsches came to an end. The new stability precipitated a shift in power distribution, signaled by the electoral success of the Social Democrats in 1928 and the apparent triumph of liberal reform. Had this trend continued, Hitler might very well have remained another of the multitude of marginal right-wing fanatics howling in the dark.

Nonetheless, even in this period of relative stability and liberal democratic triumph, Hitler built up his power base. Many of the disaffected had been attracted to him after the abortive beer-hall putsch in 1923, not so much for his participation in the failed coup, but for his bravura speeches during the trial, which were widely reported in the press. After his release from prison he gave up the idea of a coup and focused his attention on getting absolute control of the party apparatus, and on gaining greater public approval. With this shift in emphasis, Hitler came into his own, reveling in his immense capacity to inspire a mass audience through techniques I will discuss in the next section.

But despite Hitler's success as an orator and propagandist, it was the great depression of 1929 that really spelled the death of the Republic and provided the proper ground for Hitler's rise. Germany was once again plunged into chaos; great numbers of the population were suddenly unemployed, inflation was rampant, and all the progress that had been made seemed to slip away in a moment, leaving, as one German wrote in his diary, "a frightful feeling of uneasiness, of pressure, of isolation – a frightful weakness, a frightful anxiety affecting existence itself" (quoted in Weinstein 1980: 64).

In the wake of the Depression, polarization in parliament again increased, and the government was completely deadlocked between left and right elements. Playing on a widespread fear of communism, the conservative forces rallied behind the symbolic figure of Hindenburg to dismantle the parliamentary apparatus. But Hindenburg too was unable to act, and in desperation yielded to the advice of conservative mentors, appointing Hitler as the presidential chancellor. Hitler had been given his opportunity, and he took it with alacrity, gaining more and more power, first as presidential chancellor, then as independent ruler, and finally achieving absolute domination over all countervailing forces by the establishment of his private armies of the SS and Gestapo. And Germany greeted him as its saviour.

The Nazi propaganda machine stressed the inevitability of Hitler's rise, and it is, of course, dangerous to place too much reliance on these self-interested accounts of the suddenness of Hitler's success or the absoluteness of Hitler's hold over Germany. Historical studies now reveal that his seizure of power in 1933 was actually less abrupt, and less total, than was portrayed. Many believe that if the Left had been able to act forcefully, or if the Junkers had seen that Hitler would not be their puppet, or if the military had opposed him, Hitler might have been stopped before he precipitated catastrophe. And even at the height of his authority Hitler was not able to act completely autonomously. His euthanasia program, for instance, was curtailed by popular protest, as were his efforts to undermine the Protestant churches.

Historians and political scientists confronted with the frightening fact of Hitler naturally wish to demystify him and his movement, and so stress the fact that many contingent variables combined to allow him to gain and hold power: economic, political, ideological, and cultural influences are cited, depending on the investigator's own theoretical perspective. The Nazi era has been explained as a transitional moment, a Jacobean period in the painful process of German social transformation and modernization (Dahrendorf 1967). Or the Nazis have been portrayed as the culminating tragedy of a nihilistic strain in German thought, so that 1945 becomes "year zero."

My way of looking at the Hitler movement does not deny any of these perspectives. But what is important for my purpose is not "what might have been," nor the internal maneuverings for position that consolidated Hitler's position, nor even the causes and consequences of Nazism. The historical and ideological background, the class conflicts, the contradictions of state structure, the struggles for power by various interest groups, and the complex chains of fortuitous or necessary events that led to National Socialism have been well analyzed by any number of writers, but do not touch on the experience of being *in* the movement. To get at this extraordinary experience, which is the essence of charisma, we need to look at the subjective states of those who participated, and who believed in Hitler's charisma; only in this way can we gain any insight into this moment in history, which, no matter how often and how convincingly it is logically derived from previous conditions, nonetheless seems so far outside our rational understanding.

To grasp the inner reality of National Socialism we must begin by realizing that Hitler arrived and remained in power because people of many class and status positions supported him wholeheartedly. Especially after 1933 "the wave of acclamation for Hitler was infectious . . . the adulation expressed by millions was the norm," and those not swept away were isolated (Kershaw 1987: 57).[5] The outpouring of belief in Hitler was manifested in spontaneous poems and testimonials sent from all over Germany which proclaimed the Führer to be a miraculous, messianic figure. As one of the faithful put it, "Hitler was given by fate to the Germany nation as our savior, bringing light into darkness" (quoted in Abel 1938: 244).

Nor was veneration of Hitler as saviour confined only to the rank and file. According to Ian Kershaw, "the undiluted 'Hitler myth' – the fully fledged cult of the 'superman' Leader in all its glorification – embraced the Nazi elite almost in its entirety" (1987: 263). For example, Himmler's doctor reports that his employer "regarded Hitler's orders as the binding decisions . . . from a world transcending this one. They even possessed a divine power" (Kersten 1957: 298).

This faith followed the pattern of charisma; it focused on Hitler as a *person*, and all relationships and authority in the Party were thought to emanate from him. As the Party theorist Rosenberg said, "with us the Führer and the idea are one and the same . . . he embodies the idea and he alone knows its ultimate goal" (quoted in Fest 1974: 279). In what was called "the Leader Principle," the Party, the state, the ideology, and the future were comingled and incarnated in Hitler: the Nazi Movement became the Hitler movement; the Nazi salute, "Heil Hitler," became the national greeting. This process reached its apogee when Hess told the great Party rally in 1934 that "Adolf Hitler is Germany, and Germany is Adolf Hitler." And in return, Hitler declared: "I know that everything you are, you are through me, and everything I am, I am through you alone!" (quoted in Fest 1974: 445, 159).

Hitler was obviously held in awe as the deified embodiment of the spirit of the Party and the nation, but along with awe was adoration and identification. For instance, Goebbels confided to his secret diary in 1926, when he and Hitler were at odds: "My heart aches so much ... I have been deprived of my inner self. I am only half." And later, "Adolf Hitler I love you, because you are great and pure at the same time" (quoted in Nyomarkay 1967: 13). The image of Hitler as beloved was conveyed to and believed by the people as well, especially in the early phases of his rule, when his seemingly miraculous successes overcame all skepticism and gave Germans a new sense of power and purpose. Thus in 1935 Goebbels could write with accuracy that "the entire people loves him, because it feels safe in his hands like a child in the arms of its mother" (quoted in Kershaw 1987: 73).[6]

The adoring cult surrounding Hitler was enacted symbolically in the great Party ritual convocations, where tens of thousands of participants marched, joined together by a common faith, cemented in the performance of the great gathering and in Hitler's benediction. In Durkheimian fashion, these ritual occasions were standardized into a new liturgical calender, with a massive celebration of Hitler's birthday as the Spring Festival, All Saints' Day replaced by commemoration of the beer-hall putsch, and so on. There were sacred objects as well, notably a venerated flag that had allegedly been soaked in the blood of the martyrs of the beer-hall putsch. All new Nazi banners were touched to this sacred flag in order to partake of the mystical powers flowing from it. At the same time, parade grounds became sacred spaces, rallies became religious processions, and a whole panoply of shrines and pilgrimage centers acted to sacralize the Nazi world around the catalyzing figure of the Führer.[7]

The religious character of Hitler's aestheticization of politics is clear not only in ritual, but also in the Nazi ideology, which aimed at the creation of a revitalized universe in which men, under Hitler's mystical inspiration, would be elevated to gods as the forces of evil were exterminated forever. In this polarizing eschatology Hitler made the Jew the concrete symbol of what must be destroyed. "Two worlds face one another – the men of God and the men of Satan! The Jew is the anti-man, the creature of another god." The cataclysmic battle between these two forces is, Hitler said, "in truth the critical battle for the fate of the world" (quoted in Rauschning 1940: 241, 238).[8] The centrality of this fantasy for the Nazi movement is clear when we note that the cosmic battle took precedence over military logistics, as resources were channeled away from hard-pressed German armies at the close of the war and devoted instead to speeding the extermination of the hated Jews.

It is quite appropriate, then, to argue that Nazism was, as Robert Waite writes, a new religion "complete with Messiah, a holy book, a cross, the trappings of religious pageantry, a priesthood of black-robed and anointed elite, excommunication and death for heretics, and the millennial promise of the Thousand Year Reich" (1977: 343).

The Techniques of Frenzy

The Nazi faith, beneath its rationalization and ideology, had a living god, and this was its essence. It was not enough for Hitler to offer his followers an eschatological explanation of a world out of joint, nor even for him to proclaim a solution that would change the world as it is into the world as it should be. Issues, ideas and beliefs were not at the center of Hitler's appeal, and in his speeches Hitler was hardly original, mining the stock stereotypes promulgated by many radical nationalistic groups – the "stab in the back," the need for strong leadership, the betrayal by the Jews.

What he offered went beyond these standard cultural forms: it was an experience that gave the follower a sensation of merger with the collective under the Führer's guidance, and therefore a taste of the promised land in the present, that inspired the listeners to convert to the Nazi faith. This extraordinary moment was achieved in the mass rallies that Hitler made the centerpiece of all of his political campaigns.

Again and again the reports of followers at every level verify that conversion to Nazism came above all from actually hearing Hitler speak. There, pressed among the cheering throngs, the crowd members felt the transcendent presence and passion of the man about whom they had read and heard so much. Statements by some devotees give the flavor of this participatory experience:

> I felt as though he were addressing me personally. My heart grew light, something in my breast arose. I felt as if bit by bit something within me were being rebuilt. (a convert quoted in Abel 1938: 212)

> The intense will of the man, the passion of his sincerity, seemed to flow from him into me. I experienced an exaltation that could be likened only to religious conversion. (Ludecke 1937: 14)

Even those who did not convert were moved by the emotional communion established between Hitler and his audience. Percy Schramm writes that the personal impact of Hitler was like "a kind of psychological force radiating from him like a magnetic field. It could be so intense as to be almost physically tangible" (1971: 35).

How exactly was this effect achieved? Hitler himself believed that much of his power to compel was due to the atmosphere of the crowd which he gathered around him: "At a mass meeting thought is eliminated. . . . what you tell the people in the mass, in a receptive state of fanatic devotion, will remain like words received under an hypnotic influence, ineradicable, and impervious to every reasonable explanation" (Hitler quoted in Rauschning 1940: 212). In the turmoil and enthusiasm of the mass meeting Hitler – who was an avid follower of Le Bon – thought that personal beliefs of individuals, already weakly held, would be submerged by the overwhelming power of the collective he could arouse through his speech. This power "burned into the small, wretched individual the proud conviction that, paltry worm that he was, he was nevertheless a part of a great dragon" (Hitler quoted in Fest 1974: 326).

In order to attain the necessary deindividualizing mass consciousness, Hitler relied on a number of techniques, planned with the principles of crowd psychology in mind, to facilitate the loss of personal identity and the intensification of emotion that favor the emergence of the mass mentality:

> I order everyone to attend the meetings, where they become part of the mass whether they like it or not, "intellectuals" and bourgeois as well as workers. . . . And remember this: the bigger the crowd, the more easily it is swayed. Also, the more you mingle the classes – peasants, workers, black-coated workers – the more surely will you achieve the typical mass character. (Hitler quoted in Rauschning 1940: 212)

Every precaution was taken to ensure that the rally met its goal of dissolving the individual into the inchoate group. Official Party guidelines mandated that a room where a rally was going to take place should always be too small, so that people should be pressed together and have a sensation of heightened density and excitement. At least a third of the audience must be Party members, who could infect the rest of the audience with their enthusiasm. They should be tieless in order to show working-class solidarity, and should not reveal their Party affiliation to newcomers. Women, whom Hitler saw as his most fervent and emotional supporters, should be in the front, where they would be most likely to become emotionally involved and spread their zeal to others through the mechanism of contagion.

Hitler himself spent a great deal of time meticulously planning his performances, ensuring the quality of sound in a particular auditorium was high, overseeing the lighting effects, and so on. For him "the chief concerns of the politician were matters of staging" (Fest 1974: 51), and the dramatic surroundings were skillfully constructed for spectacular effect. Hitler spoke only at night; and in the great meetings, encircled by red banners, facing the orderly rows of onlookers, beneath the vaulting canopy of spotlights, he achieved grandiose masterpieces of crowd manipulation where the audience was both a prop, and a participant, in a cosmic magical theatre.[9]

The crucial aspect of the performance was of course the speech itself, which was equally ritualistic and dramatically conceived. Before Hitler's arrival, hours of march music built up suspense, as speaker after speaker eulogized the great man. Then he appeared suddenly, without introduction, radiating purpose and energy as he rapidly strode onto the stage and faced the roaring audience. His speech followed a standard format that, in his early years, began with a vigorous attack on the corruption of the present.

About fifteen minutes into the speech, however, something magical would occur, which "can only be described in the primitive old figure of speech: the spirit enters into him" (Fest 1974: 327). In this fevered state, Hitler enacted a reciprocal dialectic with his audience: "His figure shoots up and down on the platform; his arms saw the air in gestures that, though they are poor miming and do not illustrate what is said, do excellently convey the speaker's emotions, and infect the listeners with them" (Heiden 1935: 79).

Via virulent expessions of execration, fierceness, and contempt, Hitler "communicated to his listeners an excitement that in turn provided fresh impetus to his voice" (Fest 1974: 328). The performance built to "an orgasm of words" (Hanfstaengl 1957: 72), as crowd and orator reached a climax together in an exultant exhortation of unity. Hitler himself saw this relationship in sexual terms, and remarked that "by feeling the reaction of the audience, one must know exactly when the moment has come to throw the last flaming javelin which sets the crowd afire" (quoted in Waite 1977: 53).[10]

Note that in these rallies passion coincides with careful preparation and awareness of theatrical effects. Hitler proudly called himself "the greatest actor in Europe" (Fest 1974: 517), and he was indubitably correct. His staginess extended to every aspect of his daily life, since he had to always maintain his image of Wagnerian demigod, with whip, leather coat, and German shepherd in tow. Hyperaware of his position, and acutely sensitive to any possibility of ridicule, Hitler was a man of excruciating self-consciousness who, as Joachim Fest writes, was so "fearful . . . of a frank emotion that he held his hand before his face whenever he laughed" (1974: 517).

Yet we must not be deluded into believing that Hitler was merely a fraud.[11] Beneath his self-conscious theatricality, Hitler felt himself to be a prophet whose feelings and thoughts derived from a higher source;

a "possessed servant" (E. Weber 1965: 27) who goes "the way Providence dictates with the assurance of a sleepwalker" (Hitler quoted in Bullock 1962: 375). As he told Otto Wagener, "I'm now and then aware that it is not *I* who is speaking, but that something speaks through me" (quoted in H. Turner 1985: 150). Like the shaman who must enter a trance to inspire his congregation, Hitler – the possessing force of the Party – felt himself to be a possessed somnambulist.[12]

In dramatically enacting his state of possession, Hitler displayed a remarkable capacity for empathy that allowed him to be attuned, as he said, to "the vital laws and the feelings of the mass" and gave him the ability to mirror their desires. As Otto Strasser wrote:

> Hitler responds to the vibration of the human heart with the delicacy of a seismograph, or perhaps of a wireless receiving set, enabling him, with a certainty with which no conscious gift could endow him, to act as a loudspeaker proclaiming the most secret desires, the least admissible instincts, the sufferings, and personal revolts of a whole nation. (quoted in Bullock 1962: 373)

Nor did Hitler need to be before a crowd to impress himself upon his listeners. It is clear from the reports of his followers that when wooing a potential convert, Hitler had an ability to respond with an equally sensitive intuition of the listener's own hidden wishes: "Within a short time he had a clear image of the secret yearnings and emotions of his partner. The pendulum of conversation would start to beat faster, and the person would be hypnotized into believing that there lay in Hitler immense depths of sympathy and understanding" (Hanfstaengl 1957: 282).

Hitler's extraordinary capacity for rapport went along with a remarkable depth and range of emotional expression, so that when he emerged from his habitual stupor to talk he often displayed an evanescent shape-changing fluidity which is, as we shall see, characteristic of other charismatics as well:

> In the course of a conversation he would quite often show the most variegated sides of his personality. . . . At intervals of a few minutes he would show himself detached, sincere, suffering or triumphant. (Fest 1974: 519)

> The swiftness of the transition from one mood to another was startling; one moment his eyes would be filled with tears and pleading, the next blazing with fury, or glazed with the faraway look of the visionary. (Bullock 1962: 377)

In particular, Hitler was an artist of paroxysms of rage in which he would suddenly appear "to lose all control of himself," trembling and literally swollen with anger, drumming on the wall and shrieking out abuse. Then just as abruptly he would return to normality, calmly smoothing his hair and resuming conversation (Bullock 1962: 376). This frenzied performance evoked fear and a "shudder of awe" in his followers.

Certainly this capacity for rage and emotional fluidity also has a theatrical quality, and "we can assume that in such situations he did not lose control and that he was exploiting his own emotions just as purposefully as he did those of others" (Fest 1974: 518–19). But again it would be wrong to emphasize only the falsity of Hitler's paroxysms, just as it would be mistaken to reduce Hitler's capacity to inspire the masses to clever propaganda and dramatic lighting.

Instead, Hitler is evidently marked by the same extraordinary combination of calculation and conviction we will find to be typical of charismatic performance in general, as an actor-like simulation of the outer appearance of emotional intensity serves as a technique for achieving the real excitement of the inner state – an excitement which then could overwhelm both the performer and his audience.[13] Clearly, Hitler was a virtuoso of ecstasy, who inspired fear, but also evoked love, by offering his followers participation in his own disintegrative, but controlled, abreactive frenzy.

Hitler's Character

What sort of man has this capacity in the modern world? In part the ability to be both in and out of ecstatic intoxication must have to do with the performer's personal background. Much has been written of Hitler's family life, and of the effect of this family background on his personality – all of which is suggestive, but not conclusive.[14]

Whatever the family dynamic that lies at its root, it is evident that Hitler's personality was marked by extremes, great emotional intensity, and deep contradictions. For instance, his sexuality was portrayed by Nazi propaganda and by Hitler himself as completely sublimated for the sake of the Party, but in private he may have been engaged in voyeuristic, sadistic and masochistic relations. Some theorists conjecture that participation in Hitler's perverse sexual activities may have impelled several young women, including his beloved niece Geli Raubal, to commit suicide.

Whatever his sexual life, it is certain that Hitler was prey to terrible anxiety and fears of fragmentation; he admitted himself to be plagued by "tormenting self-deception" and "obsessed by frightful nervous apprehension" (Hitler quoted in Waite 1977: 38, 47). Despite his power, he felt threatened, isolated, and pathetic – "if only I had someone to take care of me!" (Hitler quoted in Waite 1977: 48) – and is reported to have had hallucinations of demonic apparitions.[15]

Hitler, like other charismatics we will discuss, was both worried and fascinated by mortality. He continually warned his colleagues that "he did not have 'much time left,' would 'soon leave here,' or would 'live only a few years' " (Fest 1974: 535). Accompanying his crippling fear and self-pity came a deep rage revealed in his cruelty, his love of war, his pleasure in torturing his enemies, his obsession with blood and decapitation, his portrayal of himself as a wolf, and his dehumanization and hatred of the Jews, whom he sought to extirpate.

In all, Hitler was a Protean figure, full of intensity, hard to grasp, in whom contradictions were barely contained: he made legislation to ensure the painless death of lobsters and was tender to children and animals, yet could be inhumanly cruel or terrifyingly enraged; his lethargy alternated with periods of intense hyperactivity; he was a would-be artist whose dreams of creation were contradicted by fantasies of annihilation; a pragmatist prey to unrealistic delusions; a soldier of real courage unmanned by pervasive fear; a companion of charm or utter gaucherie; an austere man with profligate habits – all indicating for the psychoanalytically inclined a serious, near psychotic condition.

Yet Hitler's inner anxieties, fears of collapse and feelings of alienation were hidden by a front of absolute confidence, grandiosity and utter control. "I never make a mistake. Every one of my words is historic" (Hitler quoted in Fest 1974: 285). He liked to claim that he was motivated solely by an icy logic that emanated from a higher source. His daily routine was "disciplined to the point of unnatural rigidity" (Fest 1974: 518), while his personal habits were characterized by compulsive cleanliness, paranoia about his smell and bowels, phobias about being polluted, and complete vegetarianism, a constellation obviously indicative of a tremendous effort to maintain coherent boundaries of the self against the pressure of overwhelming instinctive impulses.

In particular, Hitler resembles the "borderline" personality, who is marked, as we have noted, by exactly these deep contradictions of identity, and by the same inner rage, paranoid splitting of the world, surface grandiosity and inner sense of emptiness and self-deception. This hypothesis is supported when we note that Hitler had the borderline's capacity to play a variety of roles with conviction, and yet retain detachment, and displayed as well the borderline's uncanny capacity to detect emotional nuances in others and empathetically reflect them back to themselves (see Waite 1977 for an extended version of this argument). And we know that Hitler's childhood does resemble that of the prototypical narcissistically disturbed individual, in which the family dynamic is full of intensive stresses and problematic parent–child relationships that distort the child's core identity.

But this labeling cannot really be explanatory in itself; it simply provides us with a shorthand way to conceptualize the character of the charismatic. It is not explanatory because we know that many persons are burdened with similarly unhappy and conflicted childhoods, and may react with various sorts of deviation and pathology, or they may not – nor do the pathologies which appear necessarily go in the direction of charismatic leadership. We can say, nonetheless, that personal background probably does form an enabling condition for Hitler's manifestation of charisma.

But even given a psychic predisposition, it is clearly reductionist to assume that Hitler's personality (or anyone's) is merely a reflection of childhood traumas. Instead, we see a long-term process, similar to that undergone by other charismatic figures, that began when Hitler underwent a prolonged experience of involuntary "deautomatization" of perceptions as his already shakey psychic structure was broken down under stress. There followed a revelation of his mission and a gradual rebuilding of a new charismatic personality through emotional re-enactment of the precipitating situation, as the traumatic event was controlled and revealed in a cathartic public performance.

This transformative process commenced after he left home as a young man and resided in Vienna for some years, hoping to make a career as an artist.[16] But his rejection by the Viennese art academy was a devastating blow to Hitler's identity, which was already disturbed by his family background. According to his childhood friend, during this period it seemed "that Adolf had become unbalanced. He would fly into a temper at the slightest thing.... I did not know to what this present mood of deep depression was due.... He was at odds with the world" (August Kubizek quoted in Waite 1977: 190).

Hitler withdrew in humiliation from his more successful friends and found refuge in the anonymous world of the slum boarding house. There he experienced considerable real poverty, and also found himself lonely, aimless, and filled with rage. An orphan, an outsider, rejected by the art academy in which he had put all his hopes, without family, vocation or friends; shy, hesitant, faltering, possibly sexually deviant, and driven by inner feelings of hatred, envy and resentment, Hitler was close to a complete mental breakdown. He lived a peripheral life of misery and grandiose dreams, gradually giving his inner conflicts form through a virulent philosophy of anti-Semitism as promoted by the mystical Germanen Orden and other visionary cults that proliferated in the intellectual underworld of that era.

This period of withdrawal and self-reconstruction might have ended in eventual psychotic breakdown or in a new identity as a racist crank and cult follower if Hitler had not been psychologically reborn during his heroic service in the front line during World War I. Hitler literally found his home in no man's land (Fest 1974: 70). There he discovered the community, the commitment, and the meaning that had evaded him up to this point. Later he told Hermann Rauschning heatedly that "war is life. Any struggle is war. War is the origin of all things" (quoted in Rauschning 1940: 7).

Hitler's love of war is evident in his relentless pursuit of it, and in the fact that his millennial vision was obviously modeled after his own front experience. In his philosophy "the leader was the army officer lifted to superhuman heights" (Fest 1974: 103), loyalty and unthinking discipline were the cardinal virtues, the unity of the community was all-encompassing, and the "new men" of Nazism displayed above all the storm-trooper's qualities of heroism, fearlessness, ruthlessness and self-sacrifice.

But Hitler's new-found stability, based on his experience of the transformative communion of the Front, was again challenged by the humiliation and chaos of German defeat. His response marked the turning point in his life, and in German history. Earlier, Hitler had been temporarily blinded at Ypres, but had recovered. When he heard the news of the armistice, he felt himself collapsing back into blindness. "Everything began to go black again before my eyes. . . . I had not cried since the day I had stood at the grave of my mother" (Hitler quoted in Waite 1977: 204). One need not be a psychoanalyst to see that the defeat of Germany had thrown Hitler into a condition of fragmentation and symbolic death, connected to the earlier deep trauma of the loss of his mother.

But Hitler did not distintegrate. His experiences had altered him, so that at this hopeless moment he received the call that reformulated his identity. Voices, like those which inspired Joan of Arc, told him to rescue the motherland from the Jews. His blindness miraculously vanished as Hitler suddenly knew himself to be the saviour of his adopted nation. Henceforth, he and Germany were, he felt, mystically merged, and he could act from his inner feelings with absolute certainty.[17]

But even though he had gained a sense of identification with universal powers, Hitler had not yet learned how to reveal his vision. It was only when he spontaneously expressed his feelings in public speech that his transformation was complete. Conveying his passion to an audience, he discovered in practice that he could ignite his listeners, and himself, by revealing "what before I had simply felt within me, without in any way knowing it" (Hitler quoted in Fest 1974: 120). He had learned to exorcise his inner demons in the outer world, and to spontaneously infect the audience with the ardor of his own "deceptive euphoria."

In his speech, Hitler re-enacted for his audience his own violent drama of suffering, fragmentation, loss and eventual redemption through the assertion of a grandiose identity, and the projection of all evil outward; a re-enactment that resonated with the traumatic history of the society at large. The message he brought was one of polarization and rage offered with extreme fervency and commitment by a man who felt himself to be participating in the realm of the gods.

In responding to Hitler's magnetic performance the audience members discovered themselves revitalized and powerful, merged in an active collective, and filled with devotion and awe for the man who had brought them together. Through him they could not only see a vision of the future, they could partake of ecstasy in the present; he united them and gave them enemies to hate and comrades to love; above all, his intensity reformed their disintegrating world. As a convert put it, "we all gained something of this energy. . . . We remained firm when everything wavered about us" (quoted in Abel 1938: 299).

Institutionalized Chaos: The Rule of the Irrational

The success of National Socialism brought with it problems for Hitler's maintenance of his charismatic power. In the early days of struggle by "a handful of obscure men in a defeated country" (Ludecke 1937: 72), loyalty and unity were fairly easily maintained, since the Nazis were pulled together by their shared sacrifices, their absolute faith in Hitler, and the warmth of the collective. As Norbert Elias writes, the objective circumstance of such a fledgling charismatic movement "entails the minimization, though not the disappearance, of internal tensions, and the concerted outward pressure of all members into the area to be penetrated" (Elias 1983: 124).

It is an ironic truth that political success actually undermines charismatic unity. This is because the hidden purpose of the charismatic group is not to "succeed," but to experience itself. The collective experience is intensified under the pressure of external threats. Failure also solidifies the group in a different way, since the faithless fall by the wayside, leaving only the core who are united in their defiance of accepted reality and their continued affirmation of group values despite all evidence to the contrary (see Festinger et al. 1956 for an example).[18]

But when a charismatic movement gains power, as the Nazis did in Germany, it expands into the world at large. It becomes the status quo and acquires fair-weather converts who have not undergone the binding effects of struggle and oppression. These converts, while enthusiastic, are likely to fall away in periods of stress. Furthermore, the inner tensions among the group members, concealed when the project was unlikely and the world was hostile, can now come to the fore. There is no longer the goal of gaining power to give unity, no longer opposition to incite solidarity. Ideological purity and self-sacrifice are corrupted by the spoils of victory (for an early statement of this process, see Khaldun 1981).

Nonetheless, after his victory, Hitler refused to compromise with rationalized order and institutionalization, and managed to continue a charismatic movement even within the framework of government.[19] He achieved this in part by keeping himself at the center of all decision-making, while simultaneously refusing to articulate any specific policies whatsoever. "You could never pin him down, say that he was this thing or that thing, everything was floating, without roots, intangible and mediumistic" (Hanfstaengl 1957: 129). His entourage were therefore never sure of what their leader really wanted, and they spent great effort trying to intuit his inner desires, thereby increasing his psychic centrality in their lives and enhancing their dependence on him.

In this charismatic universe "headquarters was a collection of little Hitlers who bowed to the big Hitler but were apt to ignore or mistrust each other. . . . It was every man for himself – for the Party's sake" (Ludecke 1937: 75). Power and influence came not from efficiency, nor from the rational following of rules, nor from position in a bureaucratic structure, but solely from gaining Hitler's whimsical favor. This too increased his power, since he was not simply the head of a hierarchy, but the expression and embodiment of the movement itself. As the final arbiter, the one who could unite the opposing forces through his own intrinsic authority, Hitler served as the keystone of the whole unwieldy edifice of Nazism; without him, it would collapse into its disparate components (see Nyomarkay 1967 for an expansion on this theme).

There was thus a self-ratifying cycle, wherein the emphasis on Hitler's charismatic leadership increased his importance as the sole possible mediator of the intensive rivalry occasioned by his very elevation. In such a world, the only cohesion and safety comes from absolute loyalty, regardless of the content of the orders. "What may seem to you advantageous may, from a higher point of view, be injurious. My first demand from you, therefore, is blind obedience" (Hitler quoted in Rauschning 1940: 145).[20]

The way Hitler enacted his role as leader also increased his charisma in another way, since the Führer's distance from daily affairs and his role as mediator kept him apart from the perceived corruption and incompetence of the Nazi Party. His aloof stance not only protected his stature, but increased it, since the people looked to their great leader as their salvation from the injustices and cruelties imposed by his minions – "If only Hitler knew . . ." The Nazi Party could therefore lose popular support, as indeed it did during the war years, while approval of Hitler remained impressively high right until the end.

Hitler pursued similar policies in the society at large, confusing distinctions in an effort to turn all of Germany into a gigantic and permanent mass meeting, awaiting his galvanizing appearance. He stated his plan clearly to Rauschning:

There will be no license, no free space, in which the individual belongs to himself. . . . The day of individual happiness has passed. Instead we shall feel a collective happiness. Can there be any greater happiness than a National Socialist meeting in which speakers and audience feel as one? It is the happiness of sharing. Only the early Christian communities could have felt it with equal intensity. They, too, sacrificed their personal happiness for the higher happiness of the community. (Hitler quoted in Rauschning 1940: 191–2)

The result of this policy was a social configuration with an amorphous and internally conflicted structure (Neumann 1942).[21] Within the government, Hitler created multiple bureaus and parallel institutions with purposely unclear and competing spheres of influence. Incapable of following routine, without well-ordered lines of authority, dependent completely on Hitler's changeable inclinations, the bureaucracy was in the process of gradually being reduced to utter shapelessness.

A parallel pattern occurred in the military, as Hitler used his power to create alternative branches of the service, undercutting the traditional lines of authority while simultaneously asserting his own transcendental inspiration as the final justification for all action. At lower levels technical rationality was more or less retained, though it could be overridden at any moment by an order from above. But Hitler aimed to dismantle even this aspect of rational order when the millennium arrived.[22]

In daily life as well post-war atomization had not totally broken German community and culture. Individuals were members of hunting groups, unions, cultural organizations, sporting clubs, and other groups that offered a sense of identity, activity and belonging that potentially opposed merger in an undifferentiated mass (see Allen 1984 for local examples). But when Hitler took power, he sought to eradicate even these small-scale local institutions. All independent organizations were forced into the Nazi net in an effort to denude the society of any remnants of autonomy.

Aside from policies aimed at the incorporation of all distinctive organizations into the amorphous state, Hitler also sought to retain his charismatic influence through initiating war. A Germany surrounded by enemies and struggling for dominance reiterated the experience of the Party in its efforts to gain power – and recapitulated Hitler's psychic state, in which he had to continually remake the world to fend off his own inner demons. This strategy, while in keeping with Hitler's cosmic plan, and with his polarizing personality structure, also functioned to increase group consciousness and loyalty among Germans who might waver.[23]

The Formation of the "New Man"

A final policy for maintaining Hitler's charisma deserves special attention. This was the effort, through intensive training and education programs, to construct a "new man" who would live solely to worship Hitler. As we shall see, the techniques used are prototypical of the "brainwashing" techniques outlined by Lifton and others, which also aimed to dissolve personal identity in order to promote immersion in a charismatic group. But in the German case, the "victims" were proud to request the privilege of being indoctrinated.

The paradigm for the new men were the strictly trained SS, the "high priests" of the Nazi cult, who replaced the freewheeling SA. The SS were all volunteers, selected by a combination of Himmler's mystical intuition and a rigorous vetting of the applicants' physical and racial characteristics. Where the old loyalists had been bound together by the intense experience of shared struggle, the SS were united by artificial deprivations and the planned infusion of a deep sense of community under the overarching, absolute leadership of the Führer.

This was achieved by a number of specific methods. In the first place, the recruits were obliged to go through a long and arduous initiation period of a year of training, labor service, two years in the army, and then final initiation. Considerable sacrifices were demanded of the recruits, including an oath of poverty, just as the original Nazis had to make sacrifices in their pursuit of the millennium. These sacrifices had the effect of making commitment to the group more important, since so much was given up to join. Furthermore, many volunteers were rejected, increasing the value of the goal. Only the truly worthy could become SS, the propaganda said; the impure and weak would be found out and returned to the hoi polloi. In this way Hitler and Himmler recreated the sense of solidarity and elitism that the early fighters had gained through struggle against odds.

In the indoctrination training itself, the recruits were subjected to a demanding and exhausting regimen of physically excruciating drills and a continual round of demeaning insults and violence. The combination of extreme fatigue, pain and humiliation helped break down the men's connection with their past and to erode any sense of independence. This is, of course, standard procedure for initiation into any total institution which aims at identity transformation (for similar patterns in communes, see Kanter 1972; for mental institutions, Goffman 1968).

Spying was encouraged, and slight infractions led to expulsion, increasing the men's sense of precariousness and their focus on the group leaders. Expressions of emotion were forbidden and self-denial was demanded, increasingly devaluing the individual and emphasizing the importance of the group. In this vein, exercises such as killing animals by hand and suffering agonizing ordeals served to replicate the front experience that had hardened the original Nazi followers, and trained the recruits to depreciate their own feelings while eradicating any empathy they might feel for Jews and others who were to be exterminated.

In the evening the recruits were given intensive instruction in doctrine, and especially in their sacred role as purifiers of the earth. Ideologically, the whole process of indoctrination and membership was grounded within an eclectic blend of mysticism and gnostic doctrine aimed at devaluing the self, undermining all traditional values, and impressing the recruits with a sense of their grand purpose. Within this framework the intellect was totally denied in favor of "cadaver obedience" to the sacred order, modeled after the absolute obedience given by the Sufi disciple to his teacher. Elaborate rituals, similar to Catholic and Masonic practices, intensified the self-abnegatory collective experience.

Immersion in the collective was increased by isolation; the SS had its own courts and judges completely apart from the military and civilian hierarchy, SS men were never stationed near their family homes, they were regularly transferred, they were never given street duty, and they were discouraged from outside contact. They were also set off from the rest of the world by their distinctive black uniforms and by the aura of mystery and danger that was cultivated around them. The emphasis was on shedding the old self and taking on a new, and total, identity as a member of the SS. This was symbolized when the men were given Teutonic names to replace their Christian ones.

Within this completely involving world even the most intimate personal relations were put into the SS framework, to ensure that loyalty to the group would be maintained. Himmler had final say over any marriage, and had the right to question the men about details of their sexual lives. Elaborate rules limited possible marriage partners, and the SS also encouraged the men to father illegitimate children. The reason given was racial improvement, but the covert function was to undercut the sexual bonding of marriage and increase group solidarity.

Ideally, recruitment into the SS meant that one joined the elite group of "supermen" who were bound together indissolubly in an intensely affective community, without individual characteristics, cut away from any ties of morality, somnambulistically yearning to be formed by the word of the Führer. The end result, as Himmler proudly told an SS audience, was a cadre capable of "the highest form of activity . . . which can sacrifice all pride, all honours, all that we hold dear" (quoted in Dicks 1972: 62). In the place of these outmoded individualistic values were inculcated "loyalty, which comes from the heart; obedience, which never asks why; and camaraderie, which means all for one and one for all" (Himmler quoted in Nyomarkay 1967: 140). Thus Goebbels could make his famous comment that the Nazi program was written on the faces of the marching storm-troopers.

To a large extent, the indoctrination achieved its ends. While participating in the program, "one got so that one lost all criticism; one just lived in this life; one was simply an SS man. One lost the thin thread to the parents. There was no other thought than 'cadaver obedience' " (quoted in Sklar 1977: 98). The ultimate success of the training process is evidenced by the fact that Hitler entrusted the SS with the working out of his final plan for extermination of the Jews and other impure races.

Some special indoctrination was required to harden the men for this duty, but the pattern followed was not unlike that of ordinary SS schooling. The trainer, an officer named Eicke, first gave the men their badges, the skull and crossbones, and they were told to be proud of the great trust their Führer had placed in them. Then the training began. It consisted of the following:

> the worst excesses of barrack square bashing as well as insult and humiliation. . . . Next they would be paraded to see "official" flogging and torture of prisoners, and were watched for signs of compassion or revulsion . . . And then when he had terrified, exhausted and shown them his pitiless hate and devotion to his Führer's cause, he would become all "comradely" and spend the evenings plying them with beer. . . . They called him "Papa Eicke," a great scout. (Dicks 1972: 55)

The combination is a potent one. The sense of being specially selected is coupled with violence and humiliation to the self, which reduces the value of the individual and reinforces the power and glory of the group. This is followed by training in dehumanization and the permitted expression of hatred toward a helpless other, and then by intensified camaraderie under a leader portrayed as a representative of the sacred Führer who inspires and embodies the mystical force of the nation itself. Under these conditions it is, then, hardly surprising that the SS, believing themselves to be agents of God on earth, isolated within an all-encompassing and absolute social configuration, indoctrinated to believe their victims were antihuman, united by powerful bonds of collective solidarity, could be motivated to cooperate in genocide.

In this environment, these distorted men became the tools for enacting Hitler's, and Germany's, darkest fantasies – fantasies that led eventually to the defeat of Germany, and to Hitler's own suicide. The fantasies themselves sprang from a conjunction between the social environment of the society, and the tormented inner life of Hitler, who inspired his audience with his vision because of his ability to enter into immediate revelations which "transform[ed] despondency into intoxication," and made "weakness aware of its strength" (Fest 1974: 764).

The Hitler movement answered Nietzsche's prayers for a "superman," Weber's yearning for a "new prophet," and Durkheim's call for the revitalizing intoxication of "collective effervescence." But Hitler's revelation seemed to give the lie forever to these positive evaluations of charismatic experience. Hitler's charisma claimed permanence and total power for its paranoid avatar; it led to a self-annihilating and genocidal quest for absolute purity where all ambivalences could be denied, where steely hardness and ruthless cruelty would be the norm. In this world, the SS would be the first representatives of the new man, committing mass murder en route to paradise. It was a future that frightened even Hitler. "I have seen the vision of the new man – fearless and formidable. I shrank from him!" (Hitler quoted in Rauschning 1940: 248). In that shrinking in horror from his own monstrous creation, Hitler reveals his humanity – but the creation itself is a human creation, another answer to what Milan Kundera has called the terrible "anthropological question;" that is, "what is man capable of?"

Obviously, he is capable of far more extreme behavior than we would like to admit. As Heinz Kohut writes, "it's so easy to say that the Nazis were beasts and that Germany then regressed to untamed callousness and animal-like passions. The trouble is that Nazi Germany is understandable" (Kohut 1985: 251). In the next two chapters we will look at other extreme charismatic groups, but within a more familiar context, to see how understandable they are, and how much closer they can lead us to answering this ultimate "anthropological question."

9

"Love is My Judge": Charles Manson and the Family

We're going to find ourselves, know our souls, understand our
hearts and learn from our children. We are going to cast aside our
remaining egos, rid ourselves of all the crap our parents threw
down on us, quit reflecting our mothers every time we open our
mouths. Be ourselves. We will have no leaders, no followers, just
our individual selves. Individuals so strong with each other that all
of us will be one.
    Charles Manson on his hopes for the Family, quoted in Emmons
                                                              1988

The destruction wrought by the Hitler movement was the most traumatic
event of this century. We can distance ourselves from this catastrophe
by remarking on the special history of the Germans, on their tendency
toward authoritarianism, on the fragility of their institutions, on the
social contradictions that were unresolved, the tensions of class conflict,
and so forth. The Nazi advent thus becomes explicable by its special
antecedents, or as an unfortunate interlude in a teleological process. Or
we can simply see Hitler as the emergence of the destructive principle
on earth, no more comprehensible than a bolt of lightening or, as Weber
would have it, an epileptic fit.

But a comparative approach that focuses on the subjective experience
of charisma does not allow such an escape. In the next chapters, we
will discuss two groups in the United States which coalesced around
charismatic leaders regarded by the followers with the same awe and
overwhelming love evoked by Hitler among the Germans. And, like the
Hitler movement, these cultic groups also tended to spiral toward
paranoia, violence, grandiosity, and collapse.[1]

By considering these extraordinary manifestations within our own
cultural context and memory, we can bring the experience of charisma
uncomfortably close, since the data oblige us to acknowledge that the
charismatic experience does not attract only people whose lives are very
unlike our own, or the downtrodden, or desperate neurotics unable to
cope with reality. On the contrary, in America (and, to a lesser extent,
in Europe) charismatic leaders in the last generation have very often

found their acolytes among intelligent, well-educated, privileged, caring and concerned members of the society.[2] As one convert wrote, the media's "invention of our 'bizarre personalities' is done in an effort to isolate us from the people.... We could be *anyone's* daughter, son, husband, wife, lover, neighbor or friend" (Tania, a.k.a. Patty Hearst, quoted in McLellan and Avery 1977: 527). How can this propensity toward charismatic involvement be understood?

The Cultic Milieu in America

In one sense, we can see participation in charismatic groups as part of an American tradition. Clearly, in comparison with Europe, North America has long been a fertile ground for the flowering of obscure religious "cults," which can appear within orthodox religion as a result of a personal, transforming revelation, but may also begin outside organized church structure, crystallized by a prophetic message, and grow, rigidify, and perhaps form their own orthodoxy or, in most instances, die out.

No doubt, as de Tocqueville noted, the tendency in the United States toward cultic revelation is at least partially a product of the constitutional separation between church and state that allows all religions an equal footing under the law. As a result, religion has never been discredited, as it was in France by the Revolution, nor made simply one more aspect of class identity, as in England.

The laissez-faire attitude of the United States government toward religion correlates with an acceptance of pluralism, voluntarism and inspiration, so that, as David Martin writes, American religion is free to "take on as many images as there are social faces.... The element of subjective choice in the denominational model, as rephrased by Americanism, can become a universal stress on feeling and spontaneity and eventually an emphasis on genuineness" (1978: 30). The concern with authenticity and emotion in religious expression is also connected to the Puritan ideology of personal responsibility and inner grace as the road to salvation – a belief that, as Hume noted, can press converts to demonstrations of enthusiasm to validate their saved status both to others, and to themselves.

But attributing the modern cultic efflorescence in America solely to "American exceptionalism" masks the fact that the United States is characterized by social patterns thought to be prototypical of modernity: an absence of traditional class and social groups, a lack of given models for judging and legitimating one's actions, a polity of extreme fluidity and pluralism, an ethos of egalitarianism and free choice based on personal preference, and a high level of urbanization, industrialization and specialization.[3] Even S.M. Lipset, a strong proponent of American distinctiveness, writes "It may be argued that the entire Western world has been moving in the American direction in their patterns of class relationships, family structure, and "other-directedness," and that America, which was democratic and equalitarian before industrialization, has merely led the way in these patterns" (Lipset 1963: 130).

If the United States is truly providing "one of mankind's possible futures" (Martin 1978: 32), it is also suffering from the problems endemic to that future: alienation, a sense of fragmentation and an absence of intimacy in a world "where atomization has become the most prevalent social mode" (Martin 1978: 88). And according to synthetic sociological theory, these conditions should favor charismatic movements as compensation, not only in America, but everywhere that social change has undercut old ties. So we then have a double-pronged rationale for the growth of cults in America; one derived from special characteristics of American history, the other from more general circumstances of modern life.[4]

But why should charismatic cults have been prevalent in the sixties and seventies, and why were the members in these cults drawn from a white, middle-class, affluent, usually college-educated background that hardly made them seem favorable candidates for radical experiments in collective transformation?

In part, it is clear the cultic involvement of middle-class youth in the sixties was a consequence of social and psychological conditions that led them to feel detached from the grounding values of the society.[5] A rash of assassinations of popular political leaders, the demoralization and political radicalization occasioned by an interminable war, continued racial injustice and riots, all reflected and helped precipitate a general sense of social malaise among educated and idealistic young people that was a precondition to later charismatic immersion.

But American youth were drawn to charismatic cults not only out of disillusionment with the present. They also had the modern faith that the important world is in the future, and the future is to be newly created by the young. The devaluation of history coincides with a growing division between the often outdated skills of the parents and the newly acquired and more advanced technical knowledge of the children; a divergence expressed in an expectation that the youngsters of the educated middle class would naturally surpass their elders. This denigration of tradition and the high evaluation of the potential and ability of the educated young enhanced their willingness to try experimental life styles, and to dare charismatic groups that offered transcendent values at the apparently low cost of disavowing all ties to a useless past.

The commitment of many middle-class American young people to charismatic groups shows us that the appeal of charisma is not only to the desperate and downtrodden who find in charismatic involvement

an escape from intolerable conditions. It is evident that the willingness
to risk the self in a charismatic movement can take a more positive
form among those who have confidence in themselves and their potential,
but who find the world they live in to be suffocatingly safe, morally
corrupt, or simply dull. They are ready to give up that world not
because of desperation or marginality, but because of an adventurous
urge to live more vividly and fully:

> I've always felt that I've been given the best of everything that life
> can offer. . . . Yet I still feel – well, incomplete. (an est trainee quoted
> in Wallis 1984: 54)

> I had no goal in mind, but I was seeking something substantial. I
> didn't feel really fulfilled. I felt there was something missing. I wanted
> to be more than I was. (a convert to the Unification Church, quoted
> in Bromley and Shupe 1981: 83)

The stimulus for joining the group among these persons was the
alluring vitality and warmth offered by the collective, which made
ordinary life seem pale and without feeling: "I remember very specifically
my first reactions in going to my first meeting of all the people, which
was one of an absolute whirlwind of energy, stimulation, intensity!
Dynamic! All of the things you'd wish. Extraordinarily intense!" (a
convert to the Process, quoted in Bainbridge 1978: 38).

Another factor that propelled people toward cults was the altered
state of consciousness induced by the psychedelic drugs that the youth
culture used to escape from the tedium of the daily round. Hallucinogens
induce a trance-like state in which ordinary sensory and cognitive input
is "deautomatized" and feelings of the loss of individuality and the
sensation of participating in a larger cosmic entity are created: "Drugs
open up many new doors and avenues for exploration. Life becomes
pliable, bendable. The realities one may have sheltered so long suddenly
bend and you see the illusion of this life. . . . Psychedelics get people
back to where they were before social conditioning" (converts to Guru
Maharaj Ji, quoted in Downton 1979: 109–10).

Shared drug experiences provided profound, but transient, moments
of heightened consciousness and almost telepathic feelings of self-
transcendence and fusion. The very real dangers of a "bad trip" also
served to unite the sojourners together as survivors who had taken
ultimate gambles in search of ultimate goals; a unity that was
enhanced by a self-proclaimed and publicly displayed deviance from the
mainstream. Of course, many found in the drug experience merely an
interlude; but others discovered in it a very desirable imaginary future.

The content of that future, however, was by no means clear from
the drug trip itself, which shook up preconceptions, stirred the emotions,
and challenged boundaries of the self, yet provided no form to maintain

the experience or make sense of it. Those most affected by hallucinogens were left with a feeling of vacancy when the drug wore off, neither attached to the old world and the old self, nor participating in anything which could approximate the intensity of the psychedelic state.

Like the storm-troopers who yearned for a re-enactment of their mystical "front experience," what many drug-users wanted was to retain the drugged, oceanic feeling of crossing the boundaries of the self. "Once one begins to see that mankind has no true limits, only self-defined limits, then the search for reality and unity begins" (a convert to Guru Maharaj Ji, quoted in Downton 1979: 109). This search for a reality beyond "self-defined limits" brought the seekers to leaders who could give them a direction, and a new, and more compelling, reality within the powerful, mystical, charismatic collective.[6]

Detachment and alienation from the cultural mainstream, a sense of boredom and enervation, the confidence to attempt new life styles, and the search for pleasure in disintegrative experiences of drug use, all were legitimized by a value system that took as its ideology the injunction to "do your own thing" and to "be in the moment."[7] Within this framework, it was assumed "that all persons can know with certainty what is good by means of direct experience and intuition. They can simply look at and see their own feelings, whether on drugs, making love, or sitting alone in an empty room" (Tipton 1982: 17).

This is, of course, the emotivist premise of mainstream culture taken to its logical end. The hippy counterculture's ideological radicalism lay exactly in its complete acceptance of the solipsistic implications of modern morality, an acceptance which allowed it to contemptuously dismiss as hypocrisy all attempts by the mainstream to claim for itself any objective values. In place of the rejected morals, broken connections, and fragmented identities offered by the world, the counterculture looked instead for the strongest possible feelings which could in themselves validate action and commitment. And, as we have seen, charismatic immersion offers just such a potently motivating 'pure' inner pleasure, and so became especially appealing. The search for validating personal sensations of existential being thus often led exactly to the subordination of the self.

There is, however, another route into charismatic commitment that is less common in America, but that we have seen already in the Hitler movement. This pathway begins not with an individualistic ethic but with a communal ideology of identification with the masses and an absolute rejection of mainstream self-centeredness. From within this ideological framework (whether left or right) all competing attachments to family, kin, friends, and even to one's own identity are attacked in an overheated atmosphere of continual debate and challenge. As a communiqué of the Symbionese Liberation Army puts it: "We must deal with all the conditions outside ourselves which oppress and enslave us, and we must deal with the enemy within" (quoted in McLellan and Avery 1977: 522).

American radical political groups following this self-denying ideological line were cemented together by dramatic and dangerous political actions that cut them away from the outside world they believed to be completely corrupt. At the same time, the rewards of group consciousness and of submission to the leader were offered – just as crowd psychology had postulated: "We DO have a leader that loves the people, and lives and fights for the people. This example helps to make a love among comrades that gives attention, appreciation, care and protection – from each brother and sister to the other" (communiqué of the Symbionese Liberation Army, in McLellan and Avery 1977: 522).

Thus, even though following ideologies diametrically opposed to those of the hippy communes, American political groups of the sixties and seventies often also ended as charismatic cults. For instance, Lyndon Larouche elicited unthinking devotion in a fashion completely analogous to other charismatic leaders. The Internationalist sect of Toronto revered and imitated their founder, Hardial Bains, to the degree that his stilted English became the standard form of discourse among the initiates (O'Toole 1975). And the Symbionese Liberation Army coalesced around the "Fifth Prophet" for whom they were willing to sacrifice their lives.

We have then a picture of a cultic milieu in sixties America encompassing young people who oppose their wealthy but troubled society and who have the self-confidence to try to build instead their own worlds, in which equality, unity, emotional expressiveness and creativity will be fostered. Whether motivated in the first place by desire to find the true self idden behind conditioning, or the desire to lose the self in service to the masses, the idealists of the counterculture, mystical or political, believed that they would realize a utopia of complete freedom, coupled with total acceptance; an unlikely combination made possible by mutual love: "The idea of the commune is beautiful: people living together in a non-possessive way, neither possessing things nor possessing persons; people living together, creating together, celebrating together, and still allowing each one his own space" (Bhagwan Shree Rajneesh, quoted in Fitzgerald 1986: 54).

Yet the result of these hopeful experiments was often far from the proclaimed liberated ideal. Instead, in his extensive survey of American communal groups over the sixties and seventies Benjamin Zablocki concluded that "there is a tendency in all communes, however, both now and in former times, to gravitate to increasing authoritarianism as a function of time. And the form this authoritarianism invariably takes is charismatic" (1980: 46–7).

It is evident, then, that the cultic milieu I have outlined here, operating within the specific conditions of the sixties and seventies and within the general framework of American culture, inspired by the hippy version of emotivism or by a radically oppositional ideology of massification, had an affinity with the rise of charismatic figures. Those who sought freedom either for themselves or for "the people" often found themselves in chains, chains they appeared to love, so that in one not unusual case "Devotees reported experiencing ecstasy when hit by the guru. It was commonly felt that the guru's favorites were those who submitted most completely to him" (Deutsch 1980: 1,571).

In order to see how this ecstatic self-abnegation occurred, let me turn now to a close investigation of one of the best documented and most excessive of these destructive cults – the Family, led by Charles Manson.

"Outlaw from Birth": Charles Manson

Manson was the founder and head of a loosely organized cadre of about 35 young people who pursued their leader's millennial vision in Southern California from 1967 until late 1969. This vision, built around a message of absolute love and earthly perfection, ended in the bizarre and bloody murders of at least ten people, including the actress Sharon Tate. In a celebrated court case Manson was convicted of persuading his following to commit these murders in the hopes of initiating an apocalyptic destruction of the bourgeois world. He is presently serving a life sentence for his crimes.

The members of the group who surrounded Manson were white, middle-class dropouts, alienated from "straight" society, hostile to their parents, adrift in the floating countercultural world of Southern California. As Manson said, "most of the people at the ranch that you call The Family were just people that you did not want, people that were alongside the road, that their parents had kicked them out or they did not want to go to Juvenile Hall" (quoted in Schreck 1988: 39). At first, Manson was simply one among the many gurus in the area catering to this floating clientele, and the Manson Family was "virtually indistinguishable" from other rural communes included in a survey of countercultural groups (Zablocki 1980: 327).

Manson himself had quite a different personal history from his followers. He was not only older (born in 1934), he was also from a lower-class background; a product of poverty, illegitimacy, and familial chaos. He was raised by a variety of people, including his fanatically religious and overbearingly authoritarian grandmother. His ambivalence toward his promiscuous mother, who continually abandoned and then reclaimed him, was deep and corrosive.[8] As Manson tells his biographer, Nuel Emmons, "I was an outlaw from birth. . . . Rejection, more than love and acceptance, has been a part of my life since birth" (Emmons 1988: 24).[9]

Manson learned early to fear betrayal in love. He was a habitual runaway who was first incarcerated at age 13. Then, in a school for boys, he was subjected to sadistic sexual humiliation by the guards and older inmates, so that he welcomed his later stay at age 16 in federal prison. There, for the first time, he met men who had been respected in the outer world, and he resolved to become a successful criminal himself. But he was not a very adept thief, and was back in jail at 21, abandoned by his new wife and even more embittered at the world. Released again at 23, he tried to make a living as a pimp, but was again arrested and sentenced to ten years in prison.

Left alone by everyone he knew in the outside world, Manson retreated into the protective jail environment, where he found himself a new identity as a "good con." When his term was up, he asked if he could stay in prison. "I saw myself as a man sleeping in sleazy rooms and wondering how I was going to pay the next night's rent or find food for myself the following day" (Manson quoted in Emmons 1988: 77). His reluctance is understandable, since in his short periods of freedom Manson had known nothing but fear and betrayal at the outermost margins of society.

But the burgeoning counterculture of San Francisco accepted Manson. No-one was interested in his past, and his ability to play the guitar won him friends. Living was easy, poverty was no longer cause for humiliation; plenty of people were sleeping on the streets and sharing crashpads. Mind-expanding drugs were everywhere, and in 1967 Manson took LSD at a concert of the Grateful Dead where, like so many others, he "experienced rebirth." As he tells Emmons, he didn't corrupt the kids, they corrupted him – they were his teachers. And he learned quickly, adopting the hippy life style, buying a van, taking advantage of the free love ethic, playing his guitar on street corners. He began to feel himself a participant in a new world. "For the first time in my thirty three years, I was current with fads and lifestyles" (Manson quoted in Emmons 1988: 101).

Manson thought he had something to give back to his teachers, especially since he saw similarities between their experiences of alienation and his own disintegrative and chaotic background. As he says, "I had been under that, on the under road, on the backside of what's happening, in other words, in the darkness" (Manson interviewed by Kennedy 1985). His history of personal rejection and inner redemption was a drama that found resonance in the lives of the young people who listened to him: " 'The way out of a room is not through the door,' he said, laughing. 'Just don't want out and you're free.' Then he unfolded a tale of the 20 years he's spent behind bars, of the struggle and the giving up and the loving of himself" (Lynette "Squeaky" Fromme, a member of the Family, quoted in *Time* 1975: 12). His listeners discovered in him and in his journey through rejection and suffering to a spiritual rebirth an example for themselves, just as Hitler gave his followers an image of escape and transcendence forged out of his own personal struggle.

Becoming Family: Indoctrination and Ideology

But aside from his myth of the conquest over alienation, Manson had a specific message to give that he had culled from his experiences and his training, and that was well suited to his listeners. The message that Manson enunciated is a familiar one in hippy ideology, and has a genealogy we can trace back to gnosticism and medieval cults such as the Brethren of the Free Spirit, or even to Eastern mythology (see Zaehner 1974).

Manson himself was probably unaware of all of this background. Instead, his eclectic brew of ideology was taken partly from Scientology, which he studied while in prison. There he also read avidly on hypnotism and psychotherapy, especially Eric Berne's book *Transactional Analysis* (1978) where he found the idea of a pure child mind. He was inspired too by Robert Heinlein's novel *Stranger in a Strange Land* (1968), which was about a telepathic Martian with an insatiable sexual drive who attracted a fanatical following. The first child born into the Family was named Valentine after the hero of this novel. Ed Sanders (1971) also claims that Manson was an initiate of the Process, a dualistic and highly theatrical cult group active at the time.[10] It is possible too that he was influenced by local neo-Nazi satanic organizations such as the Ordo Temple – this Fascist influence may be the specific source of Manson's polarizing emphasis on the separation of "kinds" and his insistence on the inferiority and debased character of blacks.

Whatever the textual origins of his faith, the basic creed was one that resonated with his own unhappy life and with the antinomialist ethic of the hippy counterculture; it was a message that called for denying the influence of society and the family, living absolutely in the present, avoiding reliance on others, violent hatred of "oppressors," and disintegration of the ego in the search for a perfected and authentic presocial self. In this search "no sense makes sense"; distinctions of all types were blurred, including the distinction between life and death. The task of validation was thrown back on the experiencing self, which also proved, on reflection, to be unreal: "Everything you see is an illusion, a figment of your imagination. You create the world you live in. You are what you see. Get outside yourself and look back at yourself, and you will see that even you are an illusion. There is really only One, and we are all part of that One" (Manson quoted in Atkins 1977: 132).

Manson claimed that membership in the Family would allow the convert to overcome all divisive, individual differences through participation in a transcendent realm of absolute community. At the same time, as in Nazism, outsiders were excluded and vilified, and a racist ideology was elaborated.

In order to achieve the state of spontaneous immediacy, the followers "first had to become individually nothing, undergo a psychological and spiritual death that burned out any independent personality within us and left only a blank, *dead* head" (Watson 1978: 72). Manson called this process "deprogramming," and it required removing all the "false masks" obscuring the underlying, felt unity. He justified the use of psychological manipulation as a way of discovering the underlying feelings that were the sole possible source of value.

The actual deconditioning processes consciously challenged and undercut social mores and connections with the outside world while simultaneously offering intense, collective emotional experiences orchestrated by and focused upon Manson. One of Manson's basic techniques for achieving this end was to encourage converts to live out whatever was "hanging them up." This often involved sexual acting out of fantasies, frequently in a group context. During communal dinners, people would discuss their fantasies, and "if it was at all feasible, the rest of us would try to see to it that every suggestion was acknowledged and every desire fulfilled" (Manson quoted in Emmons 1988: 150–1). Manson also sometimes simulated an act of incest to "free" a potential convert: "Make love with me and imagine that you're making love to your father. You must break free from the past. You must live now. There is no past. The past is gone. There's no tomorrow. There is *now*. You've got to break free from your father. Now" (Manson quoted in Atkins 1977: 8).

Manson had had some practical experience in the "world of darkness" which had prepared him for his role as sexual guru. In particular, in prison he had learned pimp techniques for establishing loving compliance through the use of fear, intimidation and sexual excitation.[11] But it was only after his "rebirth" in California that he became aware of an ability to detach himself from his own sexual desires in order to control his sexual partner. Sex, he discovered, "is a mind trip" (quoted in Emmons 1988: 97), and Manson expressed his new power over his mind through his capacity to make his lovers "die to themselves" under his sexual domination.

Manson used his detachment to maintain control during the sexual orgies he organized and orchestrated among the inner circle: "He'd set it all up in a beautiful way like he was creating a masterpiece in sculpture, but instead of clay he was using warm bodies" (a Manson convert in Bugliosi 1974: 237). In these orgies, the Family members felt themselves bonded together under their leader's masterful direction.

Fusion was also furthered and symbolized by conscious policies against any differentiation within the group. Clothing was shared, personal history was denied, and clocks were forbidden. "The Family lived in the present, the moment and its fancies, not questioning where we'd come from, who we'd been" (Watson 1978: 61). The only history was Manson's past, which became the myth of the group. And only he kept his real name; all the others were given nicknames to indicate removal from the world of the past.

Mind-altering drugs – especially LSD – were also used to break down the Family's separate identities and to undermine their grasp on ordinary reality. "Things that had always seemed real were revealed as empty shells, while fantasies were suddenly substantial, powerful." In place of the "empty shell" was their leader's vision of the undifferentiated One, with himself at the center. "The time came when we could look into each other's faces and see our own features, when we could be sitting together and suddenly all think the same thought. It was if we shared one common brain" (Watson 1978: 71, 73). Manson himself was immersed in the same group dynamic: "We shared more than simply doing things together. We looked at things through the same eyes, thought as one, lived as one. We were all one" (Manson quoted in Emmons 1988: 114).

Separate identities were challenged as well by the practice of changing roles constantly, so that "if one day one suddenly . . . took on a new personality, then you just rode with it" (Watson 1978: 68, 61). In the Family, then, "everybody was just playing a part, you know, like most people get stuck in one part, but like we were just playing different parts every day . . . just like a bunch of little kids playing" (Manson quoted in Schreck 1988: 63). This mechanism for dissolving personality – which sounds discouragingly like the ideologies of contemporary "postmodern" aesthetic theories – was legitimized as aiding members to realization of the absence of any permanent ego. "Look at it like a movie on TV and face the serial of thought and then change channels and walk on a different street" (Manson quoted in Schreck 1988: 26).

Also helping to disintegrate identity was the practice of cutting all personal ties, both with those outside the group, and with those inside. For instance, Manson decided who should have sex together and made sure that no stable dyads formed. Children were not to be raised by their mothers, but by the community. Any bonds converts still had with parents were to be utilized to extort money, since the parents were "pigs" and should be exploited.

Once converts had been fused into the group, Manson held their loyalty with a self-conscious combination of private flattery and public humiliation, keeping the devotees continually uncertain of his real feelings about them, continually struggling to make "Charlie" love them more, continually proving themselves to him by subordinating themselves ever more completely, continually rivalling with their competitors for his attention, yet bound together by shared adoration for him. And, like Hitler, he kept his orders and relationships vague and often contradictory, forcing the followers to intuit his desires and thus to focus increasingly on him. "There was a hug here, a smile there, with no dependable pattern. But he had me hooked" (Atkins 1977: 89).

The solidarity of the group and Manson's influence was increased as well by the isolation Manson sought as he moved the family further and further from urban centers:[12] "You can convince anybody of anything if you just push it at them all of the time. They may not believe it 100 percent, but they will still draw opinions from it, especially if they have no other information to draw their opinions from" (Manson quoted in Bugliosi 1974: 483–4). However, Manson's desire for isolation was not simply to maintain influence over his group. It was also a deeply felt need on his part to get away from the complexities, restrictions, and demands posed by the mundane world: "The farther I got from civilization the better I liked it. . . . There were no fences or boundaries. The only restrictions that existed were the mental and physical limitations of the person who lived there. . . . We could be like the first born on earth. Society's rules and demands didn't reach way out here" (Manson quoted in Emmons 1988: 153–5).

But despite the distractions offered by civilization, Manson's indoctrination techniques and the ideology that supported them were extremely successful at merging converts deeply into the Family, where they were filled with a sense of absolute pleasure. As Tex Watson writes:

> It was love that flowed through your body like thick syrup in your veins, warming wherever it went, making you so "one" with the person you were with that you'd have laid down your own life for him or her, and it wouldn't have mattered because you were so "one" that the distinctions between the two of you hardly existed anymore. (Watson 1978: 53).

The Unprogrammed Man: Manson as Charismatic

Manson himself has always denied his status as a charismatic figure. According to him, the Family members did only what they wished, and any attribution of charisma to him is actually a creation of the media catering to the projected fears of a threatened society which is "trying to make me your executioner" (Manson in Rivera 1988: 27). These fears, Manson said, led him to be "convicted of witchcraft in the Twentieth Century" (Manson quoted in Schrenck 1988: 26):

> I was a half-assed nothing who hardly knew how to read or write, never read a book all the way through in my life, didn't know anything except jails, couldn't hold on to my wives, was a lousy pimp, got caught every time I stole, wasn't a good enough musician

to hit the market, didn't know what to do with money even if I had it and resented every aspect of family life. But a week after Sadie's story, I was a charismatic cult leader with a family, a genius who could program people into doing whatever I asked of them. (Manson quoted in Emmons 1988: 222).

There is a disturbing amount of truth to this. Certainly, Charles Manson was and remains the favorite devil of the media, who made him a household word and who still interview him regularly, trotting him out as a titillating captive exemplar of evil – an exemplar who has, as he bitterly remarked, more than a passing resemblance to medieval heretics who were tortured and killed as witches. And certainly his self-pitying litany of personal failure and suffering is accurate.

But despite this it is evident that the followers did indeed revere him as a charismatic figure, whose "eyes were hypnotic" (Watson 1978: 68), and who was in touch with the forces of the universe, revealing magical powers to heal, read thoughts, tell the future, even to raise the dead. Manson himself admits that "sometimes I was God to some of those kids" (Manson quoted in Emmons 1988: 232). And even though he claims not to have believed in his own divinity, the worship of his followers did affect him, leaving him with the double sense of emptiness and power that Hitler also manifested, and that is typical of the charismatic:

Half way believing it, and yet knowing that I was truly a nothing, I let the girls feed me the myth until it has finally burned me so bad, I'm not sure what face I should be wearing. . . . I hear it so much, sometimes I believe it – believe it so strongly that I think the world should bow down to me and ask forgiveness. Not forgiveness for what they did to me, but forgiveness for what they do to themselves. (Manson in Emmons 1988: 222, 231)

Yet Manson also had a faith in his own apotheosis long before his heady elevation by his admiring followers. He has often mentioned his spiritual power, and even in Emmons's demystifying account, Manson recalls visions of Jesus he had as a child, and a spectacular revelation in San Francisco where a holy figure in a long white robe lifted him into the air, showed him a multitude of people and intoned "These are your loves and you are their need" (Manson in Emmons 1988: 126). In another, even more revealing account of his shaping transformation he says: "It happened one day in prison. The Infinite One just came into my cell and opened up my head. He showed me the truth, but I didn't want it. I cried and yelled at him, 'No. No. Not me.' But he showed me the truth" (Manson quoted in Atkins 1977: 106).

In this instance, Manson's vision was of himself on the cross, surrendering to death, and then suddenly, expansively merging with the world – imagery of personal death and rebirth as a transcendent being that is typical of the charismatic calling. From then on he claimed to have escaped from his suffering by being at one with the universe, beyond ambivalence or impotence. His own ego-shattering rage was warded off by his claim to operate at a higher level than ordinary human beings;[13] both completely empty in himself, and yet encompassing everything in the universe.[14]

> I'm dead since 1951.... I died in a penitentiary in solitary confinement. . . . I don't break laws. I make laws. . . . I live in the desert, I live in the mountains, man. I'm big. My mind is big, but everybody's trying to crowd me down, twist me down, and make into all these little things they need me to be, and that's not me at all, man, that's not me. (Manson quoted in Rivera 1988: 19–20)

Like Hitler, Manson protected himself from the fragmentation, abandonment and shame of his history by a grandiose vision which allowed him to fill his inner vacuity and vent his anger at the world which had rejected and injured him. He imagined himself to be a conduit, a possessed vehicle responding immediately and intuitively to the voice of an inner, transpersonal awareness. As such, he was destined to lead, since he was attuned to universal powers and therefore "only he, and he alone, was on top of his thought, in complete control, unprogrammed by anyone or anything" (Bugliosi 1974: 378). And, like Hitler's, his leadership had to be absolute. "The only way anyone can live on earth is *one world under the last person.* I am the last and bottom line: You will all do what I say or there will be *nothing*" (Manson quoted in Schreck 1988: 20).

Of course, there are many individuals, some psychotic, some simply mystically inclined, some charlatans, who make similar claims. What is interesting for us is how Manson's "sacred" quality manifested itself in an ability, such as we have seen already in Hitler, to transform himself in response to his surroundings:

> I'm a guitar, a cup of coffee, a snake, a pocketful of names and faces. I see myself in the desert as a rattlesnake, as a bird, as anything. You guys are stuck play-acting as humans. I don't need to be human. I don't want to be anybody in particular. I already am everybody three times around the clock. (Manson quoted in Schreck 1988: 18–19).

It was exactly this uncanny capacity to reveal a vast and evanescent range of roles and characters that compelled the attention and awe of the converts:

> He had the most delicate, quick motion, like magic, as if glided along by air, and a smile that went from warm daddy to twinkely [sic] devil. I couldn't tell what he was. (Fromme 1969)

One moment his movements would be slow, almost trancelike, and then the next he could be exploding with a violent energy that shook off him to set everything around him on fire. He changed his hair and beard constantly, and with each change he could be born anew – Hollywood slicker, jail tough, rock star, guru, child, tramp, angel, devil, son of God. (Watson 1978: 67).

Manson explains this capacity with characteristic candor: "I've got a thousand faces, so that makes me five hundred schizophrenics. And in my life, I've played every one of those faces. Sometimes because people push me into a role, and sometimes because it's better being someone else than me" (quoted in Emmons 1988: 229).

Like a "borderline" personality, Manson escaped from his own emptiness, rage and fear by empathetically reflecting the desires of his listeners; discovering, echoing and amplifying their inner states; imitating their actions, expressions and movements; returning them to themselves in exaggerated form as reflected through the magnifying and distorting lens of his own deep anger and shame: "I am only what lives inside each and every one of you. . . . I am only what you made me. I am only a reflection of you" (Manson quoted in Bugliosi 1974: 389). "What you think in your mind as you look at me is how you're judging yourself and the world" (Manson quoted in Schreck 1988: 22).

Coincident with his sensitivity to the inner states of others was a Wittgensteinian understanding of ordinary language, which Manson dismissed as a destructive restriction on his personal revelation. "You invented the words, and you made a dictionary and you gave me a dictionary and you said 'These are what the words mean.' Well, this is what they mean to you, but to someone else, they have got a different dictionary" (Manson quoted in Schreck 1988: 56). Words for Manson are not cognitive, they are emotionally evocative and symbolically multivocal, shifting meaning and tone as Manson himself shifted shape. And along with a fluid discourse, Manson relied as well on paralinguistic cues to create for the receptive follower intense sensations of recognition and participation – as we can see in Susan Atkin's account of her first meeting with him: "I experienced a moment unlike any other. The stranger and I, dancing, passed through one another. . . . It was beyond human reality. As we turned to one another again, we mirrored each other perfectly. He moved as I moved, I moved as he moved. We were perfectly together – one. Something of him was in me" (Atkins 1977: 5).

Manson's mirroring ability was carried through into his doctrine, as he taught that his converts should strive to empty themselves and reflect back whatever was projected toward them.[15] The Family members made intensive efforts to achieve this passive state in a literal fashion, believing they would then fuse together with the eternal force of cosmic love and permit the pure mind to shine forth. Child training, which aimed to create adults who were "unprogrammed," therefore meant repeating back to the child whatever it did; if the child cried, the caretaker cried back (Sipe 1976).

It is in this context that we can understand Manson's statement that he was not the leader of the Family, but just reflected the desires of the following; whatever they did, they were responsible, not he. He was, after all, the exemplar of the essential selflessness and abdication of responsibility the followers sought – he was the empty space in which they found unity by obliterating their separateness.

But those who emulated Manson in becoming reflective did not then begin creating their own realities, as Manson did. Instead, they took on more and more of what they intuited his character to be, since it was his volatile intensity that manifested true being. "We were tuned into God – at least Charlie was, and the rest of us through him" (Atkins 1977: 114). Following Manson, trying to become Manson, brought the disciples subjectively near what was imagined the ultimate source of power. And, indeed, the closest converts who imitated Manson most avidly – who became empty mirrors – felt themselves to be acquiring his magical abilities. Susan Atkins reports that when she was delegated to command some of the followers, she found herself able to read their thoughts and to manipulate them, just as she believed Manson did. She too began writing music and playing the guitar, and thought she was a conduit for a transpersonal power source.

The identification became so complete that the converts believed Manson had actually become a part of them; that they and their leader had fused, and that he was looking out through their eyes: "I became Charlie. Everything I once was, was Charlie. There was nothing left of me anymore. And all of the people in the Family, there's nothing left of them anymore, they're all Charlie too" (a convert, quoted in Bugliosi 1974: 461).

Manson now had a chorus to echo his lyrics as he sang: "Cease to exist / Just come and say you love me / Give up your world / . . . Submission is a gift / Go on, give it to your brother" (quoted in Schreck 1988: 73). And the following felt the pleasure of giving themselves up into this encompassing community that overcame the ambivalences and differences of ordinary life: "We lived together as one family, as a family lives together, as a mother and father and children, but we were all just one, and Charlie was the head" (a convert quoted in Bugliosi 1974: 318).

The Downward Cycle

But the community of love had a short life. Manson's own inner demons, the expectations of the followers, and the impact of a hostile society all conspired to propel it into a final cataclysm. Yet in the beginning, the destructive conclusion did not seem inevitable. "In 1967 when all my travels began, I had a heart crying for love. And there isn't much doubt about my craving some attention and wanting to be accepted. . . . Things that were originally good and meant always to be good somehow got turned around later" (Manson quoted in Emmons 1988: 110).

In fact, it seemed at first to Manson and the Family that as the group grew and took form something wonderful was happening. The perceived corruption and falsity of ordinary life was being replaced with a community in which "love, togetherness and fulfilling each other's needs bonded us as one" (Manson quoted in Emmons 1988: 143). Within the adoring circle of the Family, Manson was secure at last in a world which was nothing but an extension of himself. Meanwhile, the acolytes began to see the Family as an empowering force to revitalize the world; and to take Manson as a new Christ.

This worship had a destructive effect on Manson's already unstable personality. In his previous life as a petty criminal or convict, his paranoia and grandiose fantasies of domination had been constrained by reality. But when his dreams came true, and he was the adulated leader of the Family, the fragmentation and inner rage that lay behind his charismatic ability to play a thousand roles threatened to emerge; to maintain safety he was forced to expand his community and his influence – an effort that was augmented by the followers' fantasies which fed into and amplified his. "He shared the madness he created in us; he was finally its most ardent disciple" (Watson 1978: 27). While not the passive totem imagined by Durkheim and Bion, Manson, like Hitler, was also not simply an evil genius. He existed in a formative dialectic with those who followed him, as leader and followers manufactured their own shared reality – a reality that became ever more excessive and paranoid.

Nonetheless, for some time Manson did keep a connection with the mundane world through his music, which he hoped would make him famous and accepted.[16] When that fanciful dream was thwarted by what Manson thought was a conspiracy,[17] his deep resentment against society overcame his hopes. In compensation, he asserted himself more in the Family. Simultaneously, as the community grew larger and more unwieldy, the necessity of providing food and shelter became more difficult. Love could not feed everyone. "I was pushing to get things done and pretty heavy into being the voice of authority. It was a thing that crept up on me" (Manson in Emmons 1988: 175). In his efforts to maintain and expand the group, he soon was involved in illegal activity. But again, Manson was not a successful crook. The police were alerted, and tensions mounted, leaving Manson with a terrible fear that his laboriously constructed world was starting to fall apart: "When things stopped working out, it all seemed to fall right back in my lap. Then the head starts reeling, pressure mounts, tension increases, frustration starts and there ain't no rhyme or reason to a fucking thing" (Manson in Emmons 1988: 171).

Manson's innate response to pressure was to withdraw. He wanted to hide deep in the desert away from the society that was threatening him. But it was impossible to retreat much further and still survive as a group, and Manson's powerful identification with the community that had made him a god held him prisoner: "I often had the urge to get my things together and head for unknown places, but I was so caught up with those kids and the role I played in their lives, to leave would have been like ripping my heart out. Something inside me needed them, more than they thought they needed me" (Manson in Emmons 1988: 183).

The situation deteriorated rapidly as Manson's already polarized imagination began to envision the outer world as ever more dark and dangerous. "The cops, the niggers, the establishment – they're all after us" (Manson quoted in Atkins 1977: 117). The commune became an armed camp, and Manson was consumed by "hate for a world that denied. Contempt for people who can't see or understand" (Manson in Emmons 1988: 185).

In his anxious state, he now started to emphasize fear as a way of enhancing vitality. The Family were to become like the coyote who was "always in a state of total paranoia and total paranoia is total awareness" (Manson quoted in Sanders 1971: 129). Wearing knives became the rule, and Manson himself wore a "magic sword" which he brandished at his acolytes. The followers drove around tricky cliff roads at high speeds to increase their capacity for fear-awareness, and Manson sent his closest devotees on "creepy crawls" into people's houses, where they would secretly rearrange the furniture. While they were on these expeditions Manson told them to think about killing, and discussions of torture and violence became more prevalent in his nightly talks. He began as well to show signs of severe stress, flying into rages, beating his disciples and smashing things. For the acolytes, this violence was both another challenge to identity, and a test of their belief in Manson and the Family.

As their leader's paranoia and rage increased, the Family members were drawn into even greater intimacy and isolation. Those who had joined the Family found what they felt to be their deepest selves; they shed their personalities in order to experience the ecstasy of fusion in the group, they escaped from ambivalence and participated in a vision larger than themselves. They loved each other because they all loved Manson, and he loved them, or rather, he loved himself in them. Now, for the sake of his love and all that they had gained by it, and to ward off the demons that threatened that love, they were prepared for the final stage of the drama.

Whether suggested by Manson, or by some of the group members, it is clear that the thought of murder sprang from the matrix of the situation – the group could neither go forward nor back, and the explosive rage that built up within it, as a reflection of Manson's psychological condition, the increasing external pressures and the group dynamic, had to be released or the community would collapse. Manson's own polarized millenarian doctrine had prepared the way, since he imagined a vast cataclysm which would destroy the powers of darkness completely and usher in the new age. The murders committed by the Family were therefore legitimized, at least in part, as ways to speed the arrival of the Apocalypse.

But behind the ideology was pure virulent hate. "One by one this fucked-up society is stripping my loves from me. I'll show them! They made animals out of us – I'll unleash these animals – I'll give them so much fucking fear the people will be afraid to come out of their houses!" (Manson in Emmons 1988: 199). In the meantime, the elect would hide themselves in a secret pit in Manson's beloved desert where milk and honey would flow. On the earth's surface the bestial Negro would war with the decadent whites, leaving the Family to emerge later and usher in the millennium and Manson's final apotheosis as Saviour.[18]

And so Charles Manson sanctioned and participated in the grotesque murders that made him famous, and ended his dream of complete love and acceptance in a bloodbath. In his rational moments, he knew the murder plot would never work, he knew the group could not survive for long in the desert, he knew the killings would lead to imprisonment, but "bitterness and contempt for a world I didn't give a shit about allowed me to go along with anything. . . . So goes the feeling of power when coupled with hatred" (Manson in Emmons 1988: 200–1). Rather than being abandoned again, Manson was willing to kill – to destroy everything he had hoped for.

After the slaughter, the Family did indeed stay together, isolated in a hideout deep in the desert, bound even more tightly by their common crimes, although the love was gone, replaced by mistrust and fear, and also by a pride in the violence they had shared. But after Manson and the actual murderers were arrested and convicted, the transcendent myth that he had personified came alive once more, fueled by those left behind, who remembered their paradise lost and chose to forget the darkness or to blame it completely on a society that had not permitted them to realize their dream.

The fantasy preached by his followers and embodied by Manson appealed greatly to many members of the public. So while he has become the devil for some, he has become a god for others, and he continues to receive thousands of letters a year from those who see in him the eschatological potential for dissolving the time-bound world into the "eternal now." For these believers, however, Manson has little sympathy. After all, as he says, "Humans need gods, gods don't need humans" (Manson in Schreck 1988: 29), and Charles Manson, as a god alone in his cell, needs no-one.

> I want you to know that I've got everything in the world, and beyond, right here. My eyes are cameras. My mind is tuned to more television channels than exist in your world. And it suffers no censorship. Through it, I have a world and the universe as my own. So, save your sympathy and know that only a body is in prison. At my will, I walk your streets and am right out there among you. (Manson quoted in Emmons 1988: 227)

10

"The Only God You'll Ever See": Jim Jones and the Peoples Temple

You'll never be loved again like I love you.
Jim Jones quoted in Reston 1981

I see Jonestown as a tragedy in which I share responsibility.
Looking backward, I can see many actors playing their parts,
making decisions and acting, and all moving inexorably toward
destruction. . . . The actors were not so different from the rest of
us. The actors on the world stage are making their decisions, and
moving step by step toward a climax. The die is not yet cast. We
are among the actors. Options are still open, but the movement is
toward unimaginable tragedy. To suppose that Jonestown cannot
happen to the world is folly.
John Moore, the father of two women who died in Jonestown,
quoted in Moore 1986: 395

Jim Jones and his followers offer an instructive example of a charismatic
movement that begins from very different premises and appealed to a
different constituency than the Manson Family, but aroused in its
membership the same ecstatic communal selflessness, stimulated the
same paranoid intensity in the leader, and ended in a similar catastrophic
bloodbath – though in the Temple the members killed themselves as
well as others. It remains the most enigmatic modern cult movement,
since the mass suicides at Jonestown that shocked the world in 1978
were and remain difficult to conceptualize except by postulating insanity
or else the use of force.

The evidence, however, does not indicate either insanity or force to
be the case. The armed guards who surrounded Jonestown drank the
poison that killed their friends when they could easily have escaped,
and the only shots that were fired took the lives of Jones himself and
Anne Moore, one of his closest disciples, in an apparent double suicide.[1]
Some converts who, through happenstance, were not at Jonestown
killed themselves later, and others who remained alive expressed regret:
"I wanted to die with my friends. I wanted to do whatever they wanted
to do" (a survivor quoted in Gallagher 1979). Nor were the members

of the commune "insane" in any clinical sense. In fact, as one
commentator writes, "the frightening thing about most of Jones's
followers is that they were amazingly normal" (Richardson 1982: 21),
and even hostile witnesses testified that the Jonestown populace were
"far from the robots I first expected" (Reston 1981: 229).

The Peoples Temple

To understand the tragedy of Jonestown, we first need to look at what
it offered to those who participated. Unlike the Manson Family, the
Peoples Temple (it was always written without an apostrophe) was not
based on an antinomian belief system that repudiated the reality of the
world. Instead, the Temple combined Pentecostal faith-healing with left-
wing political activism. It opposed the divisions of modern society, and
the invidious distinctions of racism, and favored instead a new communal
ideology in which everyone would be treated equally and share in the
common good, welded together in a loving community of healing and
mutual caring under the leadership of Jim Jones.

The group itself was a much more complex and powerful organization
than any of the other communes that thrived in the California
atmosphere, involving about 5,000 followers at its largest. In attempting
to implement his political program, Jones could mobilize his supporters
in letter-writing campaigns and picket lines, giving the impression that
his support base was even wider than it really was; he therefore was
courted by a number of politicians, and was appointed to a city
commissioner's job in San Francisco. The Temple in its prime was not
a group that withdrew from the world; it was active, visible, and
powerful; operating within the system to change the system.

Much of the early success of the Peoples Temple came because of
the tremendous appeal Jones had for the black community, and this
also differentiates the Temple sharply from most countercultural
organizations, whose membership consisted of young, white, middle-
class ex-students. While Jones did draw in a middle-class base of ex-
political radicals and activists, as well as a cadre of white fundamentalist
believers from his early evangelizing in the midwest, he was most
successful at proselytizing impoverished and culturally oppressed blacks,
who were impressed by the fact that the Temple was an encompassing,
interracial community where people worked and lived together in
harmony, without fear of hunger, loneliness, prejudice, or poverty.

Of the membership in the fully formed Peoples Temple, 80 percent
were black, two-thirds of them women, many elderly, many from
extremely impoverished backgrounds, many ex-drug addicts or ex-
criminals. Even in his early days in Indianapolis, when his church was
mostly white, Jones had had a special capacity to appeal to the outsiders

and the stigmatized. As one of his followers from that era says, Jones attracted "the kind of people most folks don't want to have nothing to do with. Fat, ugly old ladies who didn't have nobody in the world. He'd pass around hugs and kisses like he really did love them, and you could see it on their faces what he meant to them" (quoted in Feinsod 1981: 17). Within the Temple the deprived, the downtrodden, the unloved found a better world, working together and united by Jim Jones's love and caring, which apparently went beyond all social boundaries. He loved them all, he would take care of them all, he would struggle tirelessly for them, he would sacrifice himself for them without any concern for material rewards. "Here's a man who says as long as I have a home, you have a home. Here's a man with only one pair of shoes and no car, one suit of clothing – I think the suit he's got on tonight was borrowed. Here's a man who works over twenty hours a day. Here's JIM JONES" (Jones's introduction at a revival meeting, quoted in Reiterman and Jacobs 1982: 307).

Indeed, this portrait was a true one as far as it went. Even though the Temple took in enormous sums of donations, and had a bankroll of about twenty million dollars in its final days, Jones, as a true charismatic in the Weberian mold, had little interest in wealth. According to one convert, "It [the money] became almost a joke with Jim. . . . We used to wonder what to do with it all. But we never spent it on much" (quoted in Kilduff and Javers 1979: 82). And Jones did devote himself completely to the church, and to his congregation, working almost around the clock to achieve his dream of an interracial socialist community.

Another appeal of the Temple, aside from its mixture of classes and races, and the loving commitment of the leader, was the fact that many whole families participated, including, in some cases, three generations. This again is very unlike other cultic groups, which generally appealed to a narrow age range of converts. In the Temple, on the other hand, one did not have to give up attachments to one's closest relatives.

Being in the Peoples Temple was therefore a far cry from membership in an isolated, powerless group living on fantasies. It was a large community with a strong socialistic ideology of sharing and activism. It had achieved real successes and had real power. Many members testified that they had faith in Jones and in his vision precisely because, as one ex-temple member recalls, it seemed that "Jim has the knowledge and ability to make this world a better place. This is the only place I've seen true integration practiced" (Mills 1979: 137). Organized as a cooperative community, with Jim Jones as the orienting element, the Peoples Temple offered an alternative to lives of desperation, isolation and humiliation; a new vision was not only talked about, it was lived. Middle-class whites, as well as impoverished blacks, found in the experience of the Temple something of absolute value. They chose to live in this community, and many of them chose to die rather than forgo it. That this was so is not a testament to the insanity of the Peoples Temple as much as it is an indictment of the ordinary world.

"Always Alone": Jim Jones

But the direction this idealistic charismatic community took toward paranoia and suicide is not only a reaction to a negative social milieu; it is also partly a consequence of the character of its leader, who gave it its shape, and whose dark fantasies were magnified by the deep desires of the followers.

Jim Jones, like many other charismatic figures, was an outsider; a small-town boy whose "Indian" complexion and aberrant family life made him unusual among his classmates. His father was an invalid, a distant and embittered man who died when Jones was a boy – the typical father for a charismatic. Jones had a close tie with his mother, a relatively well-educated woman with artistic pretensions who had married down; a non-conformist who swore, drank, smoked, and worked in a factory, leaving her young son alone all day.[2]

From an early age Jones was filled with a sense of anger and isolation that stayed with him throughout his life.[3] "I was ready to kill by the end of third grade. I mean, I was so fucking aggressive and hostile, I was ready to kill. Nobody gave me any love, any understanding. . . . I'm standing there. Alone. Always was alone" (Jim Jones quoted in Reiterman and Jacobs 1982: 16–17).

Young Jones vented his anger by cursing, for which he was paid by amused laborers. Later he would help unleash the repressions of his congregations by leading them in cursing sessions. He knew well the emotional effect of language, and of public indulgence in the forbidden. At the same time, with the encouragement of a neighbor who took him to a local Pentecostal church, the boy found solace in another type of language. Participating in the services, Jones found he could speak in tongues and preach spontaneously, gaining a reputation as a possible child evangelist. In the heated atmosphere of revival meetings, he found both the approval, and the emotional release, he sought. But the price was high. His career was cut short when he began having the frightening nightmares and insomnia which troubled him for the rest of his life. Only later, after a typical charismatic revelation, would he have the inner strength to return to preaching.

Having dropped out of the church, Jones built himself a little world of his own at home in a loft. There he arranged and directed theatrical performances, reading and orating to his friends, sometimes cruelly testing their loyalty. He liked to perform experiments on animals, and claimed to have an ability to heal. Already, Jim Jones had begun to create environments where he could be in complete control, and where he could act out fantasies of omnipotence and violence as the regulator of life and death. He would replicate this environment later, in the Peoples Temple.

At the end of junior high school Jones dressed himself in a sheet and set out to evangelize in his home town. This venture won him no converts, but later he began hitchhiking to larger towns and preaching on the street, especially to poor, black people, who were willing to listen and respond to him. After a lackluster college career at the University of Indiana, Jones married and had a number of unsuccessful jobs. He found some relief from his dissatisfaction by owning a menagerie of pets, including a monkey.

It was during this difficult period that Jones, in common with other charismatics, underwent a transforming experience. In his case, the revelation was connected to the executions of Julius and Ethel Rosenberg, who were electrocuted while the 22-year-old Jones was in a feverish and semi-conscious coma, suffering from a long and debilitating bout of a disease he diagnosed as hepatitis. "I wept when I got out of that coma, wept until the sheets were soaked. I wished I had died. Someplace along the line, I quit crying. Don't cry anymore. It's rough being a Communist" (Jim Jones quoted in Reston 1981: 50).[4] This experience left him with the sense of self-estrangement that is the mark of the charismatic. "Don't love your life. Move on like I have until you hate your life. Move on till you lose it, then you find it" (Jim Jones quoted in Reiterman and Jacobs 1982: 226).

After his revelation Jones came to terms with the nightmares that had terrified him as a child, and could begin his career as an itinerant Pentecostal preacher and healer,[5] offering his audience spiritual cures for their ills through participation in the hyperemotional service. His gift for speaking spontaneously had matured, and the rush of energy he felt and conveyed in his preaching exhilarated him and his audience. At the same time, he discovered that some people really did seem to be cured by his touch, giving him increased confidence in his own magical powers.

Building from his success, Jones decided to organize a Pentecostal church in Indiana where his dreams of a unified community with himself at the center could be realized. To solidify the church, he demanded the parishioners donate all their worldly possesions in return for a promise from Jones that every need would be met in the future by the Temple. Services were long, exhausting and highly emotional, a rollercoaster of fervent highs and lows that left the congregation both fatigued and inspired. Jones himself was vibrant, a dynamo of energy, who often called his associates in the middle of the night to discuss an idea, and who was always ready to offer condolence or advice to any parishioner.

As his congregation grew, Jones made increased claims for charismatic elevation. His exaggerated self-presentation was modeled on Father Divine, the black leader from Harlem who called himself God, and who controlled a large and active following. Jones presented himself to his black congregation as the spiritual successor to the recently deceased Father Divine,[6] imitating a number of Divine's practices, including interrogation and public confession. These helped create a strong sense of merger in the group, and served to ratify Jones's position as communal center, orchestrating emotional outbursts, collective purges, and group catharsis:

> Transgressors were encouraged to come forward and kneel before Jimmy and confess not their sins but their ill feelings toward others. Jimmy would direct the supplicants to make peace with their adversaries by verbalizing their animosities. Once stated, the ill feelings would vanish in a tearful outpouring, to be replaced by gusty emotions of unity, brotherhood, and Christian fellowship. (a convert to the Indiana Temple, quoted in Weightman 1983: 20).

Jones now argued that since God is the force of love, the most loving person therefore is God incarnate. And this person had to be Jones himself. At the same time, Jones told his inner circle, "of course I'm not God, of course I'm not Jesus. But these people are so religious that in order to bring them around to socialism I have to tell them these things" (Jim Jones quoted in Yee and Layton 1981: 158).

Yet even as he claimed to be both God and the leader of a secular socialist revolution, Jones became more and more fearful; his old nightmares returned, but in concrete form, as he saw plots against him, prophesied nuclear destruction, and claimed that extraterrestrial voices warned him to relocate the church. Threats and even shootings occurred; incidents which Jones probably fabricated himself. The manufacture of episodes of attack set a pattern that was repeated throughout Jones's life, and served to unite the congregation behind him in opposition to the unseen, but dangerous, "others." But his manufacture of enemies had another, psychological purpose, since in arranging dramatic menaces he brought his inner terrors into the world of the Temple, where the community could help him to fend off personal disintegration.

But despite community support, during this fevered period Jones had a mental breakdown that led him to retreat to Brazil for two years.[7] In Brazil he, his wife, his son, and his interracial family of adopted children lived a very marginal life. His own conventional moral values, never held very deeply, were challenged by the Brazilian atmosphere of sexual freedom and emotionally charged cultic activity.[8] In response, he continued his transformation, shedding his middle-class inhibitions and constructing a theory of self-sacrifice and millennial social change.

When he returned to Indiana, Jones claimed himself to be "the only God you'll ever see." He now was prepared to initiate the final phase of the Temple, leading it first to California, where he won many more converts with his message and style, and then to Guyana, where his grandiose vision ended in the convulsions of cyanide.

"Jim Loves You": Living in the Temple

The modes in which membership in the Temple was solidified developed over time, ending finally in the complete self-loss of the disciples in the group, and ultimately in the grave. We can see this process occurring quite clearly among the elite PC (Planning Commission),[9] which began pragmatically in Indianapolis as an administrative staff, but quickly evolved into a confrontational encounter-group where hostilities were aired and all aspects of personal and group life were debated. Jones served as arbiter and focus of the meetings, offering final words and resolution of conflicts.

After he returned from Brazil the meetings came to focus on "antisocial" aspects of behavior, in particular sexual practices. People were obliged to take turns accusing each other of selfishness, sexual misconduct, and other crimes against the community, with one's closest relatives and loved ones called upon to lead the attack. "Sessions started with verbal sniping, slipped into verbal brutality that brought people to tears, and gradually plunged into the sphere of physical violence" (Reiterman and Jacobs 1982: 161).

In these meetings, personal identity and trust of others was undermined while simultaneously Jones's centrality and the dominance of the group over the individual were reinforced. All the PC members were crowded together in a small, hot room, nearly immobilized, with little to eat or drink, for up to 20 hours, while continual confrontation and occasional violence occurred under their leader's expert orchestration. Lounging on a couch above the fray, Jones would intersperse the attacks with long passionate harangues, often telling of his sacrifices and sicknesses, which he suffered for the sake of the Temple, of his sexual prowess and his selfless willingness to satisfy PC members whose own sexuality was distorted, of his struggles to achieve an absolute community, struggles thwarted by the weaknesses of the PC members, of his undying love and his great dream.[10]

Not only the elite, but all the followers, were told again and again that the only true love was Jim Jones's love: it was a love that could never be reciprocated because it was so all-encompassing, so draining of him, so selfless, so absolute. As he told one of his disciples who had left the fold:

The love you get out there will not sustain you, honey, because it isn't love like you know love to be. You'll never be loved again like I love you. You never will. . . . My God, if I'd had someone love me as much as I love some of you, that's all I'd have needed in life. Nobody's ever loved me that much. (Jim Jones quoted in Reston 1981: 98)

The ideology was expressed in the salutations exchanged between Temple members. "This mandatory phrase of greeting, departure, and encouragement – 'Jim loves you' – instilled in members the belief that *only* Jim could love with purity and unselfishness" (Yee and Layton 1981: 137). All expressions of love had to be aimed toward Jones and derive from Jones; any other form of intense attachment was denigrated. Any involving relationships outside the group were absolutely prohibited:

It's time for you to cut your family ties. This church is your family now. Blood ties are dangerous because they prevent people from being totally dedicated to the Cause. . . . Families are part of the enemy system. They do not love you. If you were in trouble, only Jim and his church family would be there to help you. (Jim Beam quoted in Mills 1979: 241)

Meanwhile, within the community framework the family unit was reworked and diffused; childraising was shared, and members were encouraged to adopt interracial children to help break down racial barriers and encourage a collective awareness. Jones himself set an example by adopting a number of children. In this context, family disputes and punishments were mediated through the group and through Jones:

Now that we all belonged to a group, family arguments were becoming a thing of the past. There was never a question of who was right, because Jim was always right. When our large household met to discuss family problems, we didn't ask for opinions. Instead, we put the question to the children, "What would Jim do?" It took the difficulty out of life. (Mills 1979: 147)

Romantic dyads were also undercut. Jones assigned people to partner each other, being sure they were not mutually attracted. And, like other communal leaders, he discouraged any spontaneous love affairs within the community, breaking up relationships between couples who seemed to be fond of one another, since their sexuality detracted from their commitment to him and to the community. "When people try to hold onto [life] through sex . . . their romance has turned to bitter, bitter agony already" (Jim Jones quoted in Reiterman and Jacobs 1982: 226).

The husband and wife tie was also attacked. Jones assigned new partners to married couples, and demanded pledges of celibacy from his following, arguing that "the only reason sex would ever become necessary would be to produce children, and of course at this time in history, when we are concerned about an impending nuclear disaster, we don't need any babies in our group" (Jim Jones quoted in Mills 1979: 228). Only he, the leader who embodied them all, should produce children.

While he was demanding abstinence from his following, Jones was increasingly stressing his own sexual energy, claiming that, because of his inner connection with the infinite, sex with him was equivalent to the experience of transcendence. As proof, women were asked to confess that actually they hated sex with their husbands and lovers, and that they experienced orgasm only with Jones, while the men were obliged to admit their latent homosexual attraction to him. According to Jones, all the other members of the Temple were "hiding their homosexuality . . . having heterosexual relations was simply a masquerade" (Reiterman and Jacobs 1982: 173). In contrast, Jones defined himself as the only true heterosexual, a "Man of Steel, though I feel every ache and pain" (Jim Jones quoted in Reston 1981: 224). His insistence on his lack of ambivalence is a stance we have seen already in Manson and Hitler, and probably was a response to his own increasingly fragmented identity and polymorphous sexual desires, which came to light publicly when he was arrested for homosexual solicitation in a men's room at a movie theatre.[11]

Whatever the causation, Jones's doctrine served to focus sexual energies upon himself and to heighten the personal guilt and anxiety of the following. All the Temple members were required to write confessions that they had imagined Jones making love to them. "I've come to one of you! I've come to all of you! As I said, you'd all be happier to admit it" (Jim Jones quoted in Reiterman and Jacobs 1982: 150). Men too were obliged not only to admit but also to enact their sexual desire for Jones:

> Those who showed an interest in the opposite sex – and were therefore "compensating" for their homosexuality – were humiliated, or sometimes sodomized by Jones to prove their homosexuality. . . . Jones's sexual contact with men generated tremendous conflicts within some of them. He made his lessons in buggery all the more humiliating by always assuming the dominant position. As he conquered his partners, he told them again and again that it was for their own good. He derived no pleasure at all from the act, he told them, but made sure they did. (Reiterman and Jacobs 1982: 173–6)

The dominated other had to thank Jones for "helping me to know my true nature." After sexual encounters, Jones would often discuss intimate details in public, in front of the PC or even the whole congregation, humiliating his partners, denigrating their sexual identities, while drawing them deeper into the community through the physical enactment of fusion with the community's embodiment – himself.

The actual intensity of Jones's sexual appetite is hard to judge, but certainly there was a general attempt by everyone to portray his sexuality as overwhelming. As one apostate says:

> We all knew what we were supposed to say because we had seen it all before. We were supposed to say that *we* had approached *him*; that he had helped us psychologically; that he had the biggest penis we had ever seen; that he could screw longer than anybody; and that we had never had an orgasm until we had sex with him. Until that moment I had always believed that what all the others previous to me had said was true; now I knew differently. (Debbie Layton quoted in Yee and Layton 1981: 177)

This anecdote illustrates one of the most striking aspects of the Peoples Temple, namely the degree that the members, especially the elite inner cadre, colluded together to maintain the myth of Jim Jones's omnipotence, in both the figurative and literal sense. The PC were, in fact, privy to many of his weaknesses. They knew of his drug addiction,[12] his ill health, his sexual predilections. They even knew that the "miracles" he used to draw in his religiously fundamentalist black followers were fraudulent. But the PC membership consciously agreed that these failings and lies should be overlooked because of the need to bolster Jones's posture of infallibility for the good of the group. As one member of the PC said, "a leader must maintain an image in order to command the respect of his followers" (Mills 1979: 140). Therefore, Jones should be treated and portrayed *as if* he were the Messiah.

This argument was openly made by Jones himself, who, like Hitler, was very aware of the necessity of playing his part without any faults or breaks in the facade. In PC meetings, for instance, he was immune from attack during the heated encounters. "I would love to be able to accept your criticisms," he told the PC members. "Believe me, everything you say about everyone else, I do look to in myself. But brothers and sisters, we need a strong leader here, and it would not be wise" (Jim Jones quoted in Yee and Layton 1981: 150). The converts thus connived in their own subordination; they "did not obey him because he disciplined them; they accepted his discipline because they had made him their leader" (Weightman 1983: 160).

Yet, despite this self-conscious awareness in the elite members of the way in which Jones's image was built and the ways in which commitment was manufactured, the experience of the community, and of Jones's leadership, acted to estrange them from themselves, breaking down each individual's personal separateness to the extent that "like an unstable chemical radical he hunger[ed] to combine with whatever [came] within his reach" (Hoffer 1951: 83). What they combined with was Jones, whose fantasies brought them all together. As in Tarde's metaphor of the photographic plate, knowledge of the process did not prevent it from occurring. But where Tarde and the crowd psychologists thought that the cognitive ego would naturally, but futilely, resist self-loss in the group, the Temple members instead consciously sought and helped to engender group immersion.

Consequently, as in the Hitler cult, the elite cadre not only promoted, but also actually believed strongly in their leader's charisma. They had faith that Jones did have a magical power to heal, but that using this power exhausted him unduly, so that fakery was necessary to keep him alive. They believed in his Godlike qualities, and "were convinced that Jones could foresee the future, that he had information that no one else was aware of. These members also believed that the Temple was the only antidote to all the ills of the world" (Yee and Layton 1981: 165).

This process of destabilization of the individual personality and recombination into the charismatic group was accomplished incrementally through a number of methods we have already noted: constant confrontations and public confessions which revealed each person's weaknesses and sexual inadequacies, as well as the untrustworthiness of friends and family; the denial of all emotional bonds between individuals and a focusing of affect on Jones; obligatory participation in group rituals of emotional intensification; propaganda that played upon the corruption and evil of the outer world; forced, self-incriminating confessions of homosexuality, and so on.

Their shared deceptions about Jones's ability to heal, about his sexuality, about his omnipotence, which were originally engaged in for the sake of group solidarity, also increased commitment among the elite by eroding their own ability to distinguish between truth and falsehood. Lies constantly repeated have a transforming effect, redefining reality not only for the listener, but for the speaker as well, who sees that the delusions become reality, and that assertions of transcendent power are associated with the actual inner experience of transcendence.

Commitment was further solidified by the requirements Jones made of his disciples. All worldly goods had to be invested in the Temple; children had to be given up into the Temple. Jones continually demanded that his followers cut their ties with the past completely and move from place to place, first from Indiana to California, then to the even greater isolation of Guyana. There solidarity reached its maximum, stimulated by Jones's absolute control of information, by the near continuous group meetings, by the fatigue and hunger of the members, by the blaring of loudspeakers bringing Jones's message to the people at any hour of the day, and by the atmosphere of paranoia that Jones emanated and cultivated.[13]

This process of amalgamation into the group took place within a typically charismatic command structure in which rules were strict, rigid and highly elaborated, as the community reflected the leader's struggle to construct a world that would contain and channel his rage and fear. At the same time, the rules could change instantaneously, according to the leader's whim. As a result, "well-intentioned people, trying to obey the rules and regulations, often committed . . . crimes without realizing it" (Mills 1979: 288). The followers had to learn to live in a total universe where complete arbitrariness was combined paradoxically with obsessional regimentation. The anxieties aroused by this situation pressed the disciples to greater identification with Jones as the sole point of orientation and guidance.

Jones's charisma was also maintained by the distance he kept from actual policy implementation. The community was run on a daily basis by an administrative core of eight to ten young white women.[14] They stood above the PC and were Jones's closest and most loyal associates and confidants. They served to deflect any hostility felt by the rank and file for the direction of the commune. When things went wrong, they were to blame, not Jones; like Hitler, he kept his pronouncements on a transcendental plane.

The identity-challenging techniques, the community structure, and the willingness of the group to participate thus all combined to create a powerful communal experience centered around the volatile personality of Jim Jones. Those who gave themselves up to the experience found themselves within a total community that they had helped to construct. And once it was built, most of them did not wish to escape it. When Jones asked them to destroy others, and then themselves, they did so.

"Spiritual Energy": Jim Jones's Charismatic Appeal

But a stress on social context, on technique and on the willed participation of the group can ignore the intrinsic charismatic appeal of Jones himself, whose emotional intensity and powerful expressiveness in enunciating his visionary message was the original source of the group's cohesion, and continued to be the locus of the community. Like all charismatics, Jones had a great capacity for emotional displays of extreme forcefulness. For instance, just as Hitler's close associates feared his tirades, Jim Jones's inner cadre were in fear of his sudden mood swings, and particularly of his intermittent attacks of fury, which Jones attributed to insulin deficiencies. Guards needed to be near him at all times, Jones said, to protect the PC members from outbursts of his righteous indignation, since he feared he might kill someone while in a frenzy of rage.

At the same time, Jones had an uncanny capacity to draw the audience, whether an individual or a group, into felt communion with him. "He listened as no man could listen, with dark eyes mirroring understanding, empathy and love" (Reiterman and Jacobs 1982: 100). He appeared as a being "magical and strange" (Kerns and Weed 1979: 37), who, like Charles Manson, had a magnetic appeal for the animals that followed him as if he were the Pied Piper. His flamboyant dress added to his attraction, as did his dramatic jet-black hair and the dark glasses he wore because his hypnotic stare "was too powerful – he wore them to shield others from his gaze" (Weightman 1983: 115).

But also, as when he rolled up his shirtsleeves to work with the laborers in the fields of Jonestown, he knew "how to make you feel everybody, including him, was all in it together" (Ordell Rhodes quoted in Feinsod 1981: 115). Along with a capacity for empathy came tremendous vitality, an ability to work 20 hours a day, to go for a week without sleep. The sheer physical power Jones radiated was interpreted as "spiritual energy" that experientially validated Jones's ministry to his flock, since they too felt energized by his presence.

Jones's addiction to amphetamines probably had a great deal to do with his incredible stamina and fervor, but we can, from our theoretical position, postulate that his compelling intensity and expressiveness is fundamentally linked to Jones's seminal struggle with psychic fragmentation, which ended in his merger with what he felt to be transcendent powers; a merger achieved only at the cost of a sensation of inner deadness and detachment.

As with other charismatics, this reconfiguration of personality gave Jim Jones a fantastic quality; he was the man able to walk the tightrope above nothingness, to play with the deepest human fears of death and dissolution, to express the most vivid feelings, to intuit and meet the inner desires of others, to shift and change at will, while still maintaining his control. Jim Jones became a man who could make others feel as they had never felt before, an empathic mirror for their sufferings and desires, so that even those who later left the Temple testify that Jones seemed to have paranormal abilities to intuit their thoughts and feelings.

It was from this matrix that Jones convinced his followers of his ability to heal, to forestall death, to foretell the future, to read people's thoughts, to merge into their minds: "Twice while I was at work, I had actually felt as if Jim Jones were in my head and I was looking out at the world through his eyes" (Mills 1979: 126).

The major way Jones revealed his spiritual power was in his sermons; they were carefully constructed to heighten his immediate emotional appeal by a dramatic setting and choreography. Jones, the evangelical showman, knew how important theatricality was for creating the proper

mood for achieving charismatic transference. In his earlier performances
he stressed his ordinariness and his similarity to the audience in order
to gain their trust, but as the congregation increased in size, as his
reputation grew, and as his personal magic no longer could be applied
in one-on-one confrontations, he relied more and more on trappings
and effects that set him conspicuously apart from the community. The
congregation encouraged him in this. They now knew him as God, and
they wanted their God to be elevated.

So, in his Californian church, infectious gospel music, often proclaiming Jim Jones as the Messiah, preceded his arrival on stage and provided
an atmosphere of excitement and anticipation. He dressed in a
scintillating red satin robe and sunglasses; surrounding him were
his multiracial, red-shirted, black-tied aides, who merged into an
indistinguishable enthusiastic chorus that echoed his sermon. Jones sat
in a high chair above them all, in a setting that combined spiritual and
national symbols: an American flag on one side, a framed Declaration
of Independence on the other, a magnificent stained-glass window in
the background.

In his sermons, Jones united preaching and an overt sexual appeal.
"He gave earthy commentaries that made the audience howl. With a
clever sense of humor, he tossed off all pretensions of piety, adopting
the language, intonations and vocabulary of his inner city people. . . .
Jones spoke with candor, giving off the sexual magnetism of a crooner"
(Weightman 1983: 30).[15] Having drawn the audience into collusion,
he then denigrated the corrupt outer world, comparing it with the
brotherhood and equality of the Peoples Temple where people were
empowered by their unity:

> I'm here to show you as a sample and example that you can bring
> yourself up with your own bootstraps. And you can become your
> own God! Not in condescension but in resurrection and upliftment
> from whatever economic condition, injustice or racism or servitude
> which you have had to endure. Within *you* rest the keys of deliverance.
> (Jim Jones quoted in Reiterman and Jacobs 1982: 147)

Aside from his specific message, like other charismatics Jones had the
capacity to react immediately to his audience in a way that worked his
listeners to a fevered pitch of emotional intensity. He and the crowd
shouted together in call and response rhythms to develop a state of
"joyous frenzy," drawing each other to greater expressive heights, and
eventually meeting in an ecstatic shiver of communion.

Using his skills to generate fervor in the audience and in himself,
drawing them into a felt identification with him and the potency of the
group, Jones was able to convincingly affirm his deification, which he
associated with the apotheosis of his believers, who transcended

themselves through their participation in the Temple congregation and their worship of him as the embodiment of the community.

> We ask for no condescending saviors that has been pawned off on every breast. And I, God that came from earth of earth, this dust of this toils and fields, hardships of labor, from the lowest of economic positions, from the misery of poverty near the railroad tracks, I came to show you that the only God you need is within you. . . .
>
> If you don't need a God, fine. But if you need a God, I'm going to nose out that God, He's a false god. I'll put the right concept in your life. . . .
>
> I want you to realize that *you* must be the scripture, that any other scripture other than you and the word that I am now imparting is idolatry.
>
> I know where I am going. I know what I believe. And I know what I'm doing. And I've got a principle that will carry me on if the world passes away.
>
> When your world has failed you, I'll be standing. Because I am freedom. I am peace. I am justice. . . . *I AM GOD!!!!* (Jim Jones quoted in Reiterman and Jacobs 1982: 147–9)

The socialist worker God, Jim Jones, then called on all the followers to find the God within them, to discover themselves in the merger of the group under his direction and bearing his stamp. As we have seen, he used many techniques typical of charismatic organizations to further that discovery, and to ensure that the true self the followers found would be the image of Jim Jones. But his fundamental appeal consisted of enacting his emotional journey through death to self-deification in the pulpit before the crowd, redeeming his own inner vacuum by filling the world with his voice, calling on the audience to participate with him in the ecstatic moment in which boundaries between self and surround were dissolved and man becomes God – at least for the moment.

Revolutionary Suicide

His techniques, coupled with the intensity of his charismatic personality and the desires of the followers for community, did indeed increase members' ties to the Temple. It was, as we have seen, a highly successful enterprise, both economically and politically. But there was a time bomb within it, since the communal dynamic demanded continued expansion; yet as the group grew, it reached its outer limits. Jones could no longer interact with everyone and fuel them with his fire; the necessities of bureaucratic planning and group maintenance meant that work was harder and less rewarding; the expansion of the group became more difficult. But most threatening were defections. In fact, withdrawal from the group paradoxically reflected the Temple's very success at giving its members improved senses of self-worth and empowerment. Some of them now felt they could deal with the world on their own terms.

But Jones and the Temple could not accept anyone growing beyond them. For Jones and the committed members, the community was everything; it provided the structure that kept them from falling into the void. Jones had spent his entire life creating relations of dependency, warding off emptiness by placing himself in the center of the worlds of others, absorbing them into his expansive fantasy. He, who had not had love, would give love completely; he, who never trusted, would command absolute trust; he, who was torn by ambivalence, would be a rock; he, who had a damaged family, would manufacture the perfect family – but it was a family no one could ever leave; it had to be eternal, and it had to engulf the world.

The community was caught in a downward spiral as Jones's paranoia and desire to maintain control created tensions that led some members to reconsider their ties to the Temple. The last straw for Jones was the effort by one apostate couple to gain custody of their child, whom Jones claimed as his heir.[16] In response, Jones sent many of his followers to Guyana to build a refuge in the jungle which would form a nexus for a new, millennial society, and provide as well a safe place where his enemies could no longer threaten him. Of course, the demons could not be warded off; they were too deep in Jones's soul.

Furthermore, the truly heroic struggle by the emigrants to build Jonestown undercut community solidarity. Productive work in common gave many who participated an increased belief in themselves, a feeling that they were active and creative individuals. As Eric Hoffer writes, "the taste of continuous successful action is fatal to the spirit of the collectivity" (1951: 120). Jones could not countenance this challenge to the group and to his dominance. Therefore, when he arrived in Jonestown he immediately acted to erode the achievements of the pioneers who had preceded him and who had almost unbelievably managed to construct a viable enterprise in the middle of the jungle. He began to implement increasingly irrational procedures and focused on ideological indoctrination instead of farm production. And he soon talked of abandoning the commune in favor of migration to the Soviet Union. This led to resentment, to further defections, and more paranoia, in a fateful movement toward the eventual mass suicide.

The thrust toward death had long been part of Jones's character and the ideology of the Temple. Like Hitler, his fascination with death was revealed as he frightened and coerced his associates by saying he might soon give up the life he hated. He was, he said, already dead at heart, and it was only his compassion for others who depended on him that kept him alive:

Ever since as a child I saw a dog die, I wanted to commit suicide. It was the first time I felt guilt. But I still had some little dogs and cats alive, and I had to keep care of them, so I stayed alive for some thirty-nine-odd years more. . . . Then a little later, my mom needed me, and then some poor soul down the road, poor and minority. Then always blacks wanted me for their champion. It's always been that way. (Jim Jones quoted in Reston 1981: 263)

This stance had a function. By his display of a lack of interest in life and his continual litany of self-sacrifice, Jones made it clear that while his disciples needed him, he did not need them; he could touch them, but they could never touch him. In expressing his inner state of estrangement and isolation Jones increased his power over the following, since "someone who is indifferent arouses our desire to be recognized. . . . Afraid of his indifference, not understanding what it is which keeps him aloof, we come to be emotionally dependent" (Sennett 1981: 86). The followers could never hope to do enough to compensate Jones for the emptiness and alienation he suffered, supposedly on their behalf. They were thus prepared to sacrifice themselves for him as an act of gratitude and love.

But his portrayal of himself was not constructed for the purpose of increasing the loyalty of the group. It obviously came from his own inner core, and correlates with the sense of fragmentation and rage he had felt from childhood. To Jim Jones, life meant difference, change, uncertainty, betrayal; all of which dissolved the monolithic structure of dependency and omnipotence he had built up – but death would halt transformation in the refuge of the tomb. Jones was therefore glad to die, and, looking at his life, in which he was drugged, sick, in constant pain, hopeless, paranoid, laden with unreachable delusions of grandeur, burdened by his acceptance of absolute responsibility for those around him, tormented by projections of rage, hatred and fear of abandonment, one can understand his desire to destroy himself and those who were merged with him in the community.

We can note as well an ideological slant that pressed the commune toward suicide (see J. Hall 1982). Because he was "god socialist," Jones could not offer an eschatology of suffering and redemption after death in the same way a more mystically oriented leader could. Heaven was obviously not located in Jonestown, nor was it likely that the socialist millennium was actually near. And the Soviet Union, which he now pictured as the final refuge, showed no interest in permitting him or his commune to emigrate, leaving him without any place in the real world to play out his fantasies. All that was left was the immortality to be gained by entering the historical record.[17]

When Congressman William Ryan's investigating team arrived in Jonestown from the United States to see if members were being held against their wills, Jones felt his paranoid vision was coming true. At first, he managed to keep himself under control, and even provided hospitality and entertainment for his guests. The breaking point came when a few Temple members asked to leave Jonestown with the congressional party. This meant that even in Guyana, betrayal and disintegration were possible. The social world of the Temple no longer was solid; it was being torn apart by the blandishments of Satan.

For some weeks Jones had been preparing for this moment, claiming that CIA troops were already in the jungle, and manufacturing fake attacks on the compound – just as he had manufactured attacks on his early church in Indiana. This time, however, there was no place to run. Jones burned his bridges by having the congressional party attacked. He thus took revenge on America and on those who had betrayed him. Then he told his followers that instead of succumbing to the inexorable power of the state, the Peoples Temple would destroy itself in an act of defiance.

Suicide was proclaimed a revolutionary victory, an escape from inevitable corruption, an entrance into history, and a claim for the power of the love of Jim Jones, a love that would carry the followers to their ultimate merger with him in the unity of death, which Jones typically sexualized as "the orgasm of the grave" (Jim Jones quoted in Reston 1981: 265). Jones could see this as a triumph because it matched his grandiose vision and permitted him the positive expression of his self-hatred. The fates of his individual followers were of no concern to Jones; they were nothing more than extensions of himself, poor weak beings whom he could not leave behind on his journey to death: "I did not bring you to this point to leave you without a future, without someone who loves you, who will plan and care for you" (Jim Jones quoted in Reiterman and Jacobs 1982: 451).

The only thing that could save him would be if he could have faith in something outside himself: "If I had a leader – oh, how I would love to have a leader. . . . If I had a God – and oh how I wish I had a God like you . . . because I'm the only one there is as far as I could see. And I have searched all over heaven and earth and I certainly looked through the belly of hell" (Jim Jones quoted in Reiterman and Jacobs 1982: 226).

But Jim Jones found no escape, no matter where he looked, neither in the world, where he saw himself rejected and persecuted, nor in his heart, where the love of the Temple could no longer ward off rage and fear. Meanwhile, the community had been practicing for mass suicide for some time. The notion of death had lost its terror for them. Like their leader, they believed themselves besieged by a hostile world; the defections of their fellows solidified them all the more, and they were ready to share the ultimate emptiness with the man who had brought them together for eternity. It was not Jim Jones, but the world, that was driving them to self-destruction:

> Jim was the most honest, loving, caring concerned person whom I ever met and knew. . . . He knew how mean the world was and he took any and every stray animal and took care of each one. His love for humans was insurmountable. . . . Jim Jones showed us all this – that we could live together with our differences, that we are all the same human beings. . . . We died because you would not let us live in peace. (Anne Moore's last testament quoted in Moore 1986: 285–6)

Because Jim Jones had brought them together, because they had lost themselves and been reborn in the Temple, because they could not imagine any alternative to their unity, because they believed themselves to be under attack, the members were ready and willing to give up their lives rather than lose their community or the leader who crystallized it. As one of them said, "any life outside of this collective is shit. . . . All I want is to die a revolutionary death" (quoted in Reston 1981: 265–6). And so they killed themselves just as they killed Congressman Ryan and his party; quite willingly, and without compunction. Far from being inhuman, the suicide was a quintessentially human act; one derived from the power of the group, and the dream of transcendence.

11

"Technicians of the Sacred": Shamans and Society

Man is born broken. He lives by mending.

Eugene O'Neill

I am he who puts together.

A Mazatec Indian shaman, quoted in Munn 1973

We have now seen three modern manifestations of charisma at different social levels: one movement that engulfed an entire nation, another that emulated a family, a third that gathered together an interracial congregation of thousands. All ended in tragedy, despite the promises made – and kept – that participation would absorb the membership in an encompassing community, energized by the intensity of a charismatic leader. The most frightening aspect is that many participants apparently welcomed the deluge, and colluded with the leader and the group to undermine the very defenses that might have shielded them from submersion; that is, their personal identities and values.

The paradigm of charisma illustrated in these movements is like the images given us by crowd psychologists and their Freudian followers, and far from the cosy model of resocialization and comforting community offered by modern sociology. The dark charismatic advents of our age have also made Durkheim's approval of collective effervescence seem terribly naive, while Weber's yearning for a charismatic prophet is now sometimes unfairly interpreted as evidence that his thought was a precursor to Nazism. But we need to remember that these two men imagined charismatic involvement not as the horror we have witnessed in the modern age; instead they pictured it in the simplest of societies, revealed positively in spontaneous expressions of group unity and heroic action.

Crowd psychologists reversed this evaluation of the primitive; for them, simple social formations were equivalent to the regressed, the infantile, the somnambulist. Spontaneity and group immersion meant yielding to exactly the primitive destructive urges which civilization had to repress in order to sustain itself. More than other crowd psychologists,

Freud recognized the cost of this repression in terms of neurosis and enervation, but felt its necessity nonetheless. Events seem to have proved him and his colleagues correct: unleashing "savage" charismatic power appears to be unremittingly destructive.

But how much does this negative paradigm actually apply to the premodern societies that Durkheim and Weber used as their models? Ethnographic research can provide us with a portrait of societies where the charismatic experience is an expected and even ordinary event. In the next few pages, I want to consider charisma within these premodern contexts. We can then decide whether charisma actually is the eternally destructive force it has been portrayed as by crowd psychologists – or whether Durkheim and Weber were closer to the truth.

But before discussing the ethnographic material, let me reiterate briefly the Durkheimian and Weberian understanding of charisma in primitive society. For Durkheim, charisma was an unpremeditated collective event that occurred whenever men and women gathered together. A totem was worshipped as the locus of the charismatic power of the community, revealed in the vitalizing rites of intensification where individuals lost their separate identities and fused with one another in a state of entranced ecstasy.

Although he admitted that the totem could be a human being, Durkheim's interest was solely in the group's power to transform participants by taking them beyond their petty personal interests within the morally uplifting communal ritual. But in his anxiety to deny individuals any role in sociology, Durkheim ignored the fact that actually totemism requires a practitioner, one who knows the secrets of the totem, and can reveal its power in his person. Such a spiritual individual is a kind of shaman, a "technician of the sacred," in Mircea Eliade's famous phrase, who has "a special, mysteriously derived, dangerous, supernatural power" (Fried 1965: 618). And it is not totemism (which is actually quite rare), but shamanism – the revelation and worship of an embodied divinity – that is the paradigmatic archaic religion.[1]

Max Weber begins this theory of charisma precisely with the sacred performer Durkheim leaves out. Weber understands the shaman to be a virtuoso of trance whose "ecstasy is linked to constitutional epilepsy, the possession and testing of which represents a charismatic qualification" (Weber 1946: 246).[2] But even though Weber focuses on the individual, he intersects with Durkheim when he notes that the shaman's extraordinary capacity for frenzied self-loss acts to draw the audience into similar states of entrancement. In this induced state of ecstatic communion, the devout escape from the ordinary miseries of isolation, pain, and the fear of death in "the objectless acosmism of love" evoked by the shaman's paroxysms (M. Weber 1949: 330). The shaman, then, is the deified human agent whose emotional effusions precipitate the collective effervescence of the group.

The Shaman and the Modern Charismatic

Of course, neither man knew much about shamanism or the collective rituals they precipitated, though Durkheim had done extensive research to corroborate his incorrect theory that totemism is the religion. However, original ethnographic work has since shown that their initial understandings of charismatic primitive religion as an ecstatic event were essentially correct; and we know as well that the shaman who is the center of the rite is "a specialist of trance, generating in himself that state, and the related state of the entrancement of the others, which they are prepared both by themselves and through his intermediation to receive" (Krader 1978: 184).[3]

In fact, the Weberian and Durkheimian emphasis on the ecstatic aspect of religious performance in simple societies resonates with the meaning of the term "shaman" itself, as it is understood by the Siberian Tungus speakers from whom it was first appropriated by Western explorers. As a noun the Tungus "saman," from which the word "shaman" is derived, signifies "one who is excited, moved, raised." As a verb it means "to know in an ecstatic manner." The shaman is thus indeed the charismatic figure par excellence – one who actually displays the presence of the sacred while in a state of ecstatic trance. As Weston LaBarre writes, "the real difference between shaman and priest is who and where the god is, inside or out" (1970: 108).

A cursory reading of ethnographic texts relating to these extraordinary figures and their congregations shows remarkable resemblances to modern charismatic revelations – so much so that Robert Ellwood has written that "the cult phenomena could almost be called a modern resurgence of shamanism" (1973: 12). For example, those who become shamans do not usually choose this arduous occupation willingly. Like modern charismatics, they are "called" by spirits who lead the initiate into realms of intense, and often terrifying, sensations of personal suffering, powerful emotion, and the disintegration of identity. The ferocity of the initiatory phase varies individually and cross-culturally, but very often the spirits are said to rend the initiate, tearing the flesh from his bones, dipping him in boiling oil, eviscerating him and breaking him into bits – all vivid symbolic representations of the decomposing process we have seen as typical of the altered state of entranced consciousness, and as a precursor to charismatic immersion. An account from Nepal gives the flavor of one shaman's initiatory visions:

> I did not know what was happening. I began to shake violently and was unable to sit still even for a minute. . . . I ran off into the forest, naked, for three days. My grandfather and the other spirits . . . fed me earthworms and I had to eat them or die. . . . I saw many evil

spirits, some with long crooked fangs, others with no heads and with eyes in the middle of their chests, still others carrying decaying corpses. They attacked me and, before I knew it, they were all over me devouring my body. (quoted in Peters 1982: 23)

During this initiatory stage, under the influence of visions of disintegration, initiates typically manifest familiar symptomatic behavior such as withdrawal, extreme depression, hallucinations, hysterical seizures, depersonalization and so on, to the extent that they often appear to be "insane," or at least seriously mentally disturbed.[4] Nonetheless, in every culture where shamanism occurs, the people themselves clearly distinguish between the authentic shaman's mental state and the truly insane, whom the Siberian Tungus say are afflicted with a "shadowed heart." This distinction is made even though the actions of both may be similar, and in spite of the fact that "insanity" (often culturally defined as spirit possession) is the sign of the shamanic gift in an initiate. But the differences between a shaman and someone who is driven insane by spirit possession are crucial. Those unfortunates who have been possessed by a spirit and who, in their frenzy, speak forbidden words, run naked into the forest, and exhibit great strength and stamina in their convulsions, are simply acting out the whims of the deities who inhabit them. On the other hand, the shaman, even though he begins his career as a possessed lunatic, and may show the same symptoms of insanity, gains control over the possessing demons, and can therefore enter a dissociated state when desired and leave it more or less at will (Noll 1983). In acquiring this ability, the shaman tames the possessing spirits and is cured of being under their thrall. Thus entering the role of shaman, like becoming a modern charismatic, is a movement from an initiatory phase of identity disintegration through painful self-reconstruction, and on to rebirth as a transformed practitioner able to control and reveal the potent spirits that fragment other, weaker, souls.

As the Akawiao Indians say, "a man must die before he becomes a shaman" (Lewis, 1971: 70), and the imagery of death and rebirth is universal in shamanic lore. It is exactly the shaman's conquest of death and psychic fragmentation that is at the center of his charismatic status. "His ultimate triumph [is] over the chaotic experience of raw power which threatened to drag him under. Out of the agony of affliction and the dark night of the soul comes literally the ecstasy of spiritual victory" (Lewis 1971: 188).

This epic battle forms the basis for the shamanic seance, which follows a general dramatic sequence that recapitulates the shaman's original initiatory experience of disintegration and reintegration. Archetypically, the performance begins with slow chants and repetitive music and dances and accelerates to an increased pitch of emotional power, climaxed by the shaman's entrance into trance. There he displays "an intensification of affect [and] . . . contextually appropriate expressions of this affect for public display" (Noll 1983: 454), including "violent distortions of the face, changes in the voice, cramp and other signs of obsession" (Hultkrantz 1978: 45). The shaman also shows himself to be a volatile shapechanger who "sheds his ordinary identity to pass through a succession of impersonations. He becomes the spirits to whom he calls for supernatural aid, the patient who seeks healing, the drum that is fragmented and reassembled, and the entranced seer of appropriate techniques for healing" (Grim 1983: 52). These sometimes furious metamorphoses are clear in this account of an eighteenth-century Ojibway curer: "At intervals the surgeon dances, chants, makes hideous grimaces, rolls his eyes and casts them down, turns up his nose, thrusts forward his jaws and dislocates the lower jaw; his neck now stretches and now shortens; his lungs expand and his stomach swells; his fingers, hands and arms are extended and withdrawn" (Cadillac quoted in Grim 1983: 141–2). The performer then may fall into a state of "stupor and catalepsy" from which he finally, triumphantly returns with magical healing powers, having made his mythic journey to the world of spirits and demonstrated his own powers of transfiguration and transcendence of death (Hultkranz 1978: 42).

Evidently, as in modern charisma, a shaman's power is revealed primarily in his emotional intensity, and by his uncanny capacity for transformation. Claude Lévi-Strauss has therefore argued that the shamanic performance of energetic transcendence of the self can be best conceptualized by the psychoanalytic concept of abreaction; that is, "the decisive moment in the treatment when the patient intensively relives the initial situation from which his disturbance stems, before he ultimately overcomes it." The shaman is thus "a professional abreactor" (Lévi-Strauss 1963: 181).

But, as Lévi-Strauss observes, the re-enactment of the shaman's call, in all its compelling emotional potency, is the reverse of the psychoanalytic situation, where the patient tries to reach a state of mundane equilibrium by reliving a psychic trauma under the watchful but coolly uninvolved eye of the analyst. In contrast, the shaman cures others by repeatedly re-experiencing his own trauma in public, exciting a sympathetic outpouring of emotion among the onlookers, who are molded into a unified ecstatic group as they share in the shaman's expressive revelation. It is obvious that this is parallel to the modern charismatic relationship as we have seen it in our ethnographic accounts.

The powers the shaman acquires through his struggle with chaos are also similar to the powers attributed by believers to charismatic figures everywhere, namely an ability to read minds, an ability to see at a distance, the power of X-ray vision, as well as magical capacities to heal (and cause) illness, to predict the future, and to travel out of the body, often becoming one with a spirit familiar in the animal world.[5] All of these qualities symbolize a belief in the charismatic's transcendence of the limits of the body and ability to empathetically merge with others.

Another striking similarity is that even while in ecstatic trance the shaman, like the modern charismatic, maintains a degree of detachment, so that he "is able to stand back, so to speak, and manipulate his visionary contents" (Peters 1982: 35). Experienced shamans are distinguished from initiates precisely because "among the candidates extasy [*sic*] usually turns into a half delirious hysterical condition; among the shamans it remains on the very dividing line between the two: normal stable state and abnormal unstable state" (Shirokogoroff 1935: 274). In a way that is familiar to us, the shaman is therefore a curiously divided figure, who, as an Alaskan practitioner says, "go[es] out of his mind, but not crazy" (quoted in Murphy 1964: 58). He is both caught up in, and yet outside of, the trance; a self-conscious actor,[6] as well as the enraptured participant.

So far I have focused primarily on the character of the shaman, but as with the modern charismatic, shamanizing is never a solitary occupation; the shaman exists only in a collective arena, where a responsive audience both witnesses and participates. This participation takes place within a highly dramatic and well-organized setting that cleverly uses staging to help the audience to experience what the performer experiences, feel what he feels.[7] The theatrical methods that achieve this end are familiar; the seance is usually enacted late at night in a darkened, close room, and involves a number of trance-inducing techniques such as rhythmic chanting, repetition, and drumming which infect not only the shaman but the onlookers as well. The Tungus seance described by Sergei Shirokogoroff is typical:

> The rhythmic music and singing and later the "dancing" of the shaman gradually involve every participant more and more in a collective action. When the audience begins to repeat refrains together with the assistants, only those who are defective fail to join the chorus. The tempo of the action increases, the shaman with a spirit is no more an ordinary man or relative, but is a "placing" for the spirit; the spirit acts together with the audience, and this is felt by every one of the audience. The state of many participants is now near to that of the shaman himself, and only a strong belief that in the presence of the shaman the spirit may enter only into the shaman detains the participants from being "possessed" in mass by the spirit . . . In shamanizing the audience consists at the same time of actors and participants. (Shirokogoroff 1935: 33).

From the ethnographic evidence it seems clear that there are considerable parallels between shamans and modern charismatic leaders. Both reveal emotional intensity, exhibit facility in role playing, and show a fluidity of identity and a capacity for empathy combined with inner detachment. We have seen as well that the charismatic shaman generally achieves his status as a result of suffering an existential crisis of identity, a crisis that is re-enacted in his abreactive seance; this appears to be much like the shattering of the self and the rebuilding of a charismatic persona postulated by psychoanalytic researchers to be at the heart of the modern charismatic's performance. It is significant in this context that the shamanic practitioner is literally regarded as a borderline figure – one who crosses the boundary between human and cosmic – who embodies in his person the ambiguity of a liminal state in which nothing is fixed, nothing is as it seems, and dream can become reality.

Furthermore, both shamans and modern charismatic figures enact a polarized vision of the universe that fits the Freudian hypothesis of the charismatic as a locus for the denial of ambivalence. The shaman always heals by repudiating the evil principle that has infected his patient, and always gains power by wrestling with demons. And finally in shamanism as in modern charisma the leader stimulates ecstatic participatory states of communion in the audience, offering them the lived vitality of immersion in the abreactive performance.

The !Kung

But, even though the shaman clearly is a charismatic figure, he is not a radical opponent of the system. Instead, shamanism serves as the accepted revelation of the holy, and the practitioner is integrated into society. To illustrate this more concretely, let me use an example from a social formation which resembles the sort of group envisioned by Durkheim and Weber when they developed their theories.

The !Kung San Bushmen of Africa's Kalahari Desert are highly mobile hunters and gatherers with a very simple technology.[8] Their flexible, individualistic and egalitarian society has long been thought to recapitulate the social pattern characteristic of the earliest human cultures. Whether this is true or not is a moot point, but it is certain that the manifestation of charisma among these people does provide us with a type case against which to test our negative image of charisma in modern times.

Among the !Kung, there is only one specialized role; this is the role of shamanic curer. The curer is the man, or sometimes the woman, who has learned to master the inner vital energy the !Kung San call n/um. The healer uses this energy for curing the people of the community during an ecstatic state called !kia, brought on by all-night parties of dancing and singing.

But even though the healer is a specialist, he or she is hardly an unusual person. Fully half the men and ten percent of the women become healers, and all of the !Kung take part in the healing ceremonies, which occur as often as once a week, and even more – whenever, in fact, a large animal is killed, or someone is ill, or there is a big gathering, or a visitor arrives, or simply when people feel they would like to !kia, since experiencing !kia is considered to be an absolute good in itself.

The dance that stimulates the rising of the vital energy of n/um begins when the women gather around a fire that has been lit in the central area of the camp in the late afternoon.[9] "They sit side by side in intimate physical contact, legs intertwined, shoulder to shoulder, forming a tight circle around the fire" (Katz 1982: 40). Such close physical contact is a central characteristic of shamanic performance in general; the more people, and the more dense the crowd, the greater the energy that is thought to be generated – verifying Durkheim's notion of collective excitement.

Once the women are gathered, the dancers then begin to circle them. The women sing and clap rhythmically and, as the evening wears on, the singing, clapping, and dancing intensify, pressing the dancers to greater exertions. Special songs are used, and "when they are sung strongly – that is, enthusiastically, with feeling, and especially by many singers – they help heat up the dancer's n/um" (Katz 1982: 122–3).

As the songs and clapping become more abandoned, the mood is heightened, and the dancers pound the ground and are bathed in sweat. Some now begin to go into trance; a process that can occur gradually, marked by trembling, staggering and eventual collapse; or suddenly, as the performer shrieks and somersaults out of the dancer's circle. Whether gradual or rapid, the sensation of entering !kia is painful:

> In your backbone you feel a pointed something and it works its way up. The base of your spine is tingling, tingling, tingling, tingling, tingling. Then n/um makes your thoughts nothing in your head. . . . Your heart stops. You're dead. Your thoughts are nothing. You breathe with difficulty. You see things, n/um things; you see spirits killing people. You smell burning, rotten flesh. Then you heal, you pull sickness out. You heal, heal, heal. Then you live. Your eyeballs clear and you see people clearly. (quoted in Katz 1982: 42, 45).

Like people in other shamanic cultures, the !Kung do not regard the sequence of death and rebirth they experience in trance as a metaphor. Instead, they say that "It is the death that kills us all. . . . [but] healers may come alive again" (Katz 1982: 116). As is true elsewhere, learning to enter the death of trance is not easy, and those initiates who dare to cross the boundary of the self show signs of derangement. They become hysterically violent, falling into an epileptoid fit, rolling in fire, hitting people, throwing coals, running wildly into the bush, and acting in antisocial ways that are prohibited in ordinary life by the !Kung ideal for non-violence.[10]

The unrestrained, chaotic behavior of the novice shows that he is in touch with vital powers, but the paroxysm is dangerous; it undermines the social world, and must be brought under control, just as the "insane" behavior of apprentice shamans everywhere must yield to a more measured and stereotyped ecstasy. Among the !Kung, this is achieved as the teachers of the initiate and others also entranced press to the novice, shake in rhythm with him, rub him with sweat or perhaps cool him with water, teaching him to restrain and channel his n/um.

This immediate expression of the physical and psychic unity of the collective draws the initiate back into its folds, and with time he learns to overcome disorientation and violence, to control the !kia, and to use it for healing. The burning energies of n/um, having purified the initiate, now allow him to restore well-being to the society, just as he himself was returned to a state of harmony by the loving attention of the group. Accepting the death of !kia thus not only leads to personal rebirth, but also revitalizes the community. It is for this reason that n/um is especially associated with fertility and generative power.[11]

Learning to become entranced may take many years. The result, however, as we have seen elsewhere, is a capacity to re-enact in public the initiate's own psychic death and rebirth. Once a person has become an expert at achieving this liminal state, he or she can then go quite quickly into trance, sharing n/um with the collective by rubbing them with healing sweat, pulling disease from them by laying on hands which are vibrating as if palsied. In this performance, the personal identity of the shaman is lost as energy overflows the boundaries of the entranced individual, cementing the group into an invigorated collective unit.

Those who become experts at !kia acquire personalities that are different from the personalities of other !Kung. In ordinary life experienced healers are "more emotionally labile. They are said to be more *xga ku tsiu*; that is, their 'heart rises' more, they are more 'expressive' or 'passionate' " (Katz 1982: 235). Undoubtedly these changes are due to the fact that while channeling the vital force of n/um the !Kung performer, like the charismatic everywhere, is in a state of "hyperactivity, increased excitement, and vigorous, often violent, expenditure of energy" (Lee 1968: 49), in which "emotions are aroused to an extraordinary level, whether they be fear or exhilaration or seriousness" (Katz 1982: 42).

Psychological tests also show the healer has a much richer fantasy life than other !Kung, and a far more permeable body image, indicating "the central importance of fluid psychological processes and transitions that break out of the body's ordinary anatomical boundaries" (Katz 1982: 235). These findings fit with the scientific studies of the consequences of long-term experiences of Altered States of Consciousness for personality structure, and with the psychoanalytic picture of the charismatic "borderline" personality.

There is a definite, though sometimes disputed, hierarchy of healers: some can slip easily into !kia and are more efficacious at curing than others, and a very few elderly healers are designated "ama ama," great ones, who are regarded by the !Kung with awe and a considerable degree of ambivalence. Formerly, the !Kung say, these great healers could turn into lions and eat men, though none are so powerful in the present era.

But these distinctions are meaningless in ordinary life, and even the greatest experts have no influence outside the realm of the dance. Even though they can embody and express the sacred better than others of the tribe, their expertise is regarded simply as an innate personal capacity – like good eyesight – that can be used to benefit the community. They are not thought sacred themselves, and must work and live just like everyone else. As Durkheim thought, in this community the individual is subsumed into the group. However, the dominance of the commune is by no means absolute.

In fact, when the Bushmen come under the sway of the neighboring and more hierarchical and complex Bantu peoples we begin to see a transformation occurring almost immediately, as the collective consciousness changes in response to conditions of subordination. Under these circumstances, some expert !kia dancers become full-time specialists in evoking n/um. These men are paid professionals with their own travelling troupes of musicians, going from place to place, dancing and embodying the sacred power of the Bushmen before wildly excited and adulatory audiences. They are few in number, wealthy, prestigious and "widely idolized" by boys and young men, who imitate their idiosyncrasies and their songs (Guenther 1975: 164). Both the Bushmen and the Bantu also fear these ecstatic dancers, believing them to have a potent power to kill, as well as to cure.

Here, among Bushmen deprived and impoverished by the Bantu, the great !kia dancer is no longer "first among equals," participating alongside his less gifted fellows in collective ritual, and then returning to daily life. Instead, he has achieved a new, permanent status as the living symbol of beleaguered Bushman pride and as the center for resistance to the Bantu. In other words, he has been "assigned the potential role of the charismatic political leader with far-ranging authority" (Guenther 1975: 165). A Weberian charismatic authority figure thus lies very near the surface of even the determinedly egalitarian Bushman collectivity; when external pressures and historical conditions permit, he is likely to arise and proclaim himself – and be proclaimed – as a deified leader.[12]

Pathology and Structure

What are we to make of this premodern revelation of charisma? For psychoanalytically inclined theorists influenced by crowd psychology, the characteristics shamans share with modern charismatics may be interpreted to indicate that the shaman too must be struggling with a fragmented identity. And it does seem to be true that in these shamanistic societies the experts who are better at immersion in trance are recognized by the people and by themselves as possessing unusual mental capacities, including a blurring of the distinction between self and surround, a rich fantasy life, and heightened emotional expressiveness combined with a marked capacity for inner detachment – all conditions typical of borderline pathology. A psychoanalytic argument would be that this character type must be a result of problematic familial relationships – according to the theoretical stance of the analyst, either an Oedipal question of sexuality and authority, or a disintegrative early infancy that has led to a fragmented identity.

There are, however, grave difficulties in this model. It assumes, for instance, that a behavior indicates that a prior pathology must exist. More important is the fact that the psychological model is strongly value loaded. It assumes that the desire for self-loss *must* be a result of antisocial and regressive id drives as opposed to the positive states of ego integrity and "adult" individualism; this assumption requires an automatic negative value judgement against societies such as the !Kung where the ecstatic shaman is an accepted and honored individual. The "primitive" is thus rendered equivalent to the infantile, and shamanic pathology is taken for granted.

But the ethnographic material makes it clear that, in simple societies with shamanic religions, the "borderline" personal manifestations of fluid identity and disengagement from the body that are regarded in Western culture as indicative of incipient psychosis are instead favored as pathways to spiritual power, used for invigorating the community at large. Because these abreactive psychic states are favored, special individuals who, for whatever cause, may have a psychic predisposition to charismatic seizure are given community support and appropriate role models to imitate, as well as a forum for acting out their disintegrative states within the public sphere; bolsters which the modern charismatic does not have. In this context, the trance is not a chaotic, boundless frenzy, nor is it an assertion of antisocial power by a Nietzschean superman, nor is it a manifestation of regressive violence and rage that tends to spiral into psychosis. Instead, as we have seen, shamanism is expressed within a relatively formal, ritualized, dramatic structure that directs the performer's overflowing emotional superabundance for the benefit of the audience.

Furthermore, learning is central in attaining shamanic status, as initiates are taught to act *as if* entranced as a road to actually *becoming* entranced. The role of learning in charisma gains even more credence when we recall that the study of trance states shows that repeated engagement in trance seems to change the capacity of the brain, allowing the individual easier access to primary process thought, and a more vivid expression of emotions. The fact that the shamanic condition is a desired status that can be, at least to a degree, learned, undercuts the psychoanalytic attribution of pathology to the charismatic figure in these environments, and leads us to wonder how much the modern charismatic is also socialized into his position.

Moving from the shaman to the audience, it is evident that, even if we diagnose the charismatic seizure itself as a manifestation of the practitioner's pathology, we cannot characterize attraction to the charismatic's performance as deviant. Clearly, among the !Kung and other societies where trance is highly favored, *many* persons can participate in the shamanic performance, exhibiting the ecstatic behavior that is associated with the charismatic experience in more complex social formations, while even those who are lacking the capacity for trance find the gatherings positive and revitalizing.

Indeed, the evidence from less complex societies seems to indicate that a positive vision of charismatic involvement is rather more the rule than the exception in human communities, and that such involvement acquires a negative value only as society becomes highly centralized, impersonal and rationalized. From this point of view, one can argue that the automatic imputation of insanity to charismatic followers and leaders can be correlated, in large measure, to a social configuration which has a deep ambivalence toward immersion in immediate, communal, transcendent experiences, and therefore presents such experiences in an unrelentingly negative and threatening light – in contrast to the social world in which the shaman lives, where charismatic participation is conceptualized in far more auspicious and less absolute terms.

The interplay between social form and charismatic advent is not just a hypothesis, but is borne out in ethnographic material; for example, the enhanced power, permanently exalted status, and ambiguity gained by the !Kung expert shaman when his people are dominated by the Bantu. Under similar conditions of hierarchization, colonialization and the centralization of power structures, indigenous shamans everywhere gain similar special powers, and may be denounced by the dominant authorities as energumens – defined as witches, cannibals, or communists, according to the local demonology. At the same time, participation in the ecstatic trance may be denigrated by the hegemonic powers as demeaning, polluting and destructive (see Douglas 1970, Krader 1978, Lan 1985, Lanteneri 1963, Lewis 1971, 1986 for elaborations and examples).

On the other hand, for the downtrodden, the witch-shaman now offers not only a cure of ills, but a way of asserting power outside the accepted hierarchy through the immediate experience of ecstatic trance. The personal attraction of the charismatic stands against the institutionalized authority of the ruling order, since he (or she, as many such cults are made up of women protesting their inferiority and marginalization in a patriarchal society) has the potential to tame and embody the spirits feared by the establishment, to reject the world as it is, and to bring immediate communion to the disaffected. Charismatic revelation thus becomes, in Victor Turner's apt phrases, a manifestation of the "power of the weak," a moment of "antistructure" and warming "*communitas*" in social formations that have become too rigid and oppressively cold, and that have ignored and oppressed the dominated or peripheralized groups (1982).

Ordinarily, these manifestations serve primarily as safety valves and "rituals of reversal," reinforcing the status quo by redirecting challenges to it into the realm of the theatrical and the spiritual. But the ruling elite are well aware of the shaman's dangerous potential. The British, for instance, were quick to incarcerate the charismatic prophets who arose spontaneously out of the shamanic clans of the Nilotic African Dinka and Nuer tribes in response to colonial encroachment. Even within an existing state structure, history shows us that the assertion of the shaman-witch's attractive ecstatic experience can become a serious threat, and is especially insistent and compelling when the society itself is regarded as unstable and illegitimate.

I have already discussed perhaps the greatest example of a charismatic uprising in my chapter on Hitler, but the process of disenchantment and charismatic revelation is evident in many other places as well. For instance, Norman Cohn shows that charismatic millennial cults flourished in medieval Europe "amongst the poor and oppressed whose traditional way of life [had] broken down and who [had] lost faith in their traditional values." Such cults were especially prevalent "where there existed an unorganized, atomized, population, rural or urban or both ... who were not simply poor but who could find no assured and recognized place in society at all" (Cohn 1970: 52, 282).

Of course, throughout history, there have been social uprisings for purely practical causes – lowering of rent, fairer wages, better conditions for workers, and so on. But sometimes, among truly disaffiliated, disappointed or hopeless people, the demand may be for something far more radical: an "age of bliss in which the faithful would preside over societies without injustice, illness or conflict" (Adas, 1979: 287). To meet these demands a leader cannot be a pragmatist, but is instead an ecstatic, shamanic individual whose inspiration of the group can "shade into true prophetic movements, where the possessed mediums and shamans not only answer recurring problems within their own cultural tradition, but in response to new stimuli and pressures announce messianic revelations" (Lewis 1986: 45). In other words, when people are alienated and oppressed, the shaman does not remain a "technician of the sacred," but instead comes into his own as the saviour, who by virtue of his ecstatic inner revelation may "decree for his followers a communal mission of vast dimensions and world-shaking importance. . . . a mission which [is] intended to culminate in a total transformation of society" (Cohn 1970: 60; see Wallace 1956 for a classic statement of this process).

And, as this process occurs, charisma can also change its character, moving from a simple affirmation of the felt brotherhood of all participants in healing communion toward an increasing apotheosis of and identification with the leader and a demonization of opponents. As Cohn writes of the cults surrounding the Prophetae of the People's Crusade:

> They were his [the leader's] good children and as a reward they shared in his supernatural power. It was not only that the leader deployed his power for their benefit – they themselves, so long as they clung to him, partook in that power and thereby became more than human, Saints who could neither fail or fall. They were the bright armies, "clothed in white linen, white and clean." Their final triumph was decreed from all eternity; and meanwhile their every deed, though it were robbery or rape or massacre, not only was guiltless but was a holy act. (1970: 85)

Ruthless hatred and absolute self-righteousness against the corrupt world therefore became a part of the charismatic message – as a medieval rhyme put it, "the children of God, that we are, poisonous worms, that you are" (Cohn 1970: 87).[13]

This is the world-rejecting form of charisma that we have seen most powerfully displayed in our examples and in history, and that remains potent in the third world, where revolutionary social movements unite millennial dreams with political action, stimulating the selfless commitment of a following in revolts of the weak against the strong; revolts which rational consideration would preclude as too risky. Leaders such as Gandhi, Sukarno, Trotsky, Castro, Mao and Khomeini all are charismatics in this millennial mode, combining powerful dramatic personalities, transcendent messages of transformation and the destruction of corrupt oppressors with absolute religio-political authority, in a way that commanded the complete loyalty and unreflective worship of the believers.[14]

But such millenaristic charismatic movements become less and less possible as the general evolution toward centralized bureaucratic structures increasingly restricts the potential for success, as Weber correctly informed us. This is because of the power of the center, which prohibits revolt, and also because of rationalization itself, which demystifies and disenchants the world, making belief in a charismatic revelation more difficult. Furthermore, the conditions of oppression and peripheralization that are a precursor to millenaristic charisma are less obvious and salient, due to the tremendous technical success of bureaucratic instrumental rationality.

Yet, as we have seen, crowd psychologists and other theorists of modern life have argued that rationalized contemporary society, while not overtly oppressive, does severely restrict exactly the feeling that charismatic immersion offers: the expansive vitality that accompanies participation in a movement that transcends the limits of the self. Instead, people are enmeshed in systems that have no communal warmth but that permit and encourage expression of individual separateness and antagonism as a route to success. For these theorists, it is axiomatic that the desire for communion, when repressed, will nonetheless remain beneath the surface, increasing in intensity, distorted in aim, to erupt whenever and wherever the structure permits an outlet. The form taken by charisma in any society will therefore indicate the type and the degree of repression that must be overcome for it to appear within the social structure.

Evidently in modern society the extraordinary forms we have witnessed charisma take indicate great pressures and great passions, as the charismatic relationship is warped and exaggerated. The social attribution of insanity and evil to the ecstatic practitioner is countered by the community's own claim for its leader's absolute deification. This dichotomy is lived out within the soul of the leader himself, and within the group, who affirm ever more extravagant claims to offset doubts and opprobrium, and who often repudiate completely the larger society that has treated them with such contempt. Furthermore, as in medieval millenaristic movements, charismatic involvement is defiantly affirmed as a whole way of being for the devotees, absolutely opposed in its negation of the self to the selfishness of the ordinary world.

The demand within this milieu is for lived, immediate community which is not momentary, but eternal. The charismatic whose energetic revelation embodies the revitalizing force then ceases to be an expert incarnating the god occasionally; for the followers he becomes the god now and forever, ever-present and all-powerful; a transcendent identity the followers jealously guard and defend, both against the leader's own, too human, weaknesses and against all external influences.[15]

As we have seen, the end result can be a group loyal to an individual who certainly appears outside of any conceivable form of rationality. But it is evident that the cycle of paranoia, isolation and fear we have witnessed in modern cults, and in millennial cults throughout history, is not located solely within the psyche of the charismatic. Unlike his shamanic predecessors who had the support of the community at large, the charismatic leader who dares the ostracism of contemporary society has no model to imitate, no accepted way of coping with his own internal fragmentation. And if the postulate of the charismatic's volatile, borderline-like personality is correct, then such a man is particularly susceptible to psychotic collapse when not given needed social support.

There is then an evident correlation between labeling of deviant groups and their leaders as mentally deranged and the actual spiral into insanity, as the label is lived out in practice within the heated and highly pressured atmosphere of the commune. In this situation, the underlying tendencies toward mental disintegration and psychotic fantasy within the leader are exaggerated by the followers' incessant demands for a permanent and totalizing experience of transfiguration – a demand that places even greater pressure on the leader, as well as permitting him greater excursions into fantasy.

The ethnography of shamanism and the transmutations of shamanic revelation over history make it evident that social structures and their accompanying values, as Weber long ago pointed out, are central for the way in which charismatic ecstasy will be experienced, understood and evaluated. But where Weber thought rationalization would make charisma disappear, instead it has rendered charismatic revelations increasingly distorted and fanatical. The excesses of charisma today reflect the inability of the social system to meet fundamental human needs for communion. The transformation of love into hate, peace into violence, ecstasy into paranoia, that is so depressing a constant in charismatic movements, is more a consequence of social structural factors than of charisma per se; a shadow that by its darkness indicates the outline of our own dilemma.

Part IV

Conclusion

12

Charisma Today

I have argued in this book that there is a deep human desire to escape from the limits of the self; a desire taking on various guises according to social circumstances. We have seen that one way people can achieve this extraordinary state of selflessness is in a group brought together by the inspiring figure of a volatile charismatic leader. In shamanistic societies, such experiences of charismatic participation are integrated into the round of life, and reinforce the world as it is. In more complex social systems, where people are downtrodden and oppressed by a system they consider illegitimate, or enervated in a society that appears meaningless, they may look to a charismatic saviour who not only offers participation in an ecstatic communion, but also promises to lead a transformative crusade against the corrupt world. This is the situation, common in the Third World, in which radical millenaristic movements are most likely to arise, as I noted in the last chapter.

Yet neither of these conditions fits the modern Western world very well. Certainly we do not have the simple face-to-face society that favors shamanism. On the other hand, most people do not feel oppressed, nor do they consider the dominant power structure to be illegitimate or meaningless. Nonetheless, according to the sociological portrait of modernity there are many aspects of our world, including personal isolation and rapid mobility, competitiveness, and an absence of values beyond those of emotivism, that should press toward some form of compensatory charismatic revelation at weak points in the social framework. Our cases – Nazi Germany, the Manson family, and the Peoples Temple – are reminders of the intensity of this pressure toward communion and revitalization through charisma.

However, these specific cases are exceptional; it is evident that charismatic movements have not yet toppled the rationalized social order, nor does such an overthrow seem possible in the foreseeable future. Nazism, which came closest, was a response to extreme conditions of malaise and disruption in a context of resentment and racism that hopefully will not be repeated. The other movements I have documented, even though extraordinarily powerful for their members, have remained as fascinating and disturbing newspaper items for most of us; to be remembered only when we read of new cults in the tabloids. Nor is this relegation of charisma to the periphery of our consciousnesses unexpected, since the dominant rational mode of thought must seek to deny strength and authority to movements that pose a challenge to the taken-for-granted world.

Yet it is obviously not simply a hegemonic, rationalized system repressing its opposite that is at work here. In truth, despite social conditions that would seem to promote charismatic reactions, charismatic movements are not as widespread nor as overwhelming as we might expect. In this chapter, I want to argue that this is because people in the modern Western world do in fact have experiences of self-loss that are analogous to, but usually weaker than, those given by charismatic involvement. Unlike charisma, these sensations have been channeled, shaped or diffused so that they do not offer a threat to the social structure, and in fact support the status quo, as charismatic involvement itself did in shamanistic society. But I will also point out that this support is often fragile, and sometimes these states may become more involving, expansive, potent and perilous.

Public Secular Alternatives to Charisma

There are a number of alternatives operating in the most mundane areas of the modern world that give a mild and tamed taste of the fervor offered by charisma. For instance, in America the ethic of consumption has an important communal function, since it demonstrates for the public that the goals set by the ethic of free enterprise are realistically reachable, and that everyone can participate and succeed, given perseverance and a little luck. The potential for indulging one's preferences, and therefore demonstrating one's value, through conspicuous consumption provides a feeling of sharing despite the competitive framework. All the antagonists take heart from their belief that the world does what they expect it to do, and gives the rewards they are taught to desire. Furthermore, the immense productivity of the system means that middle-class malaise is offset by the very real and abundant material pleasures offered by the culture. Man may not live by bread alone, but a plenitude of bread can compensate for loneliness and thereby generate considerable loyalty.

In this context, the act of buying is an exercise in community, as the shopping mall becomes an arena in which to congregate with others and to enjoy a pleasurable disjuncture of ordinary awareness within a group (see Jacobs 1984). The fact that depressed people often go on a buying spree says less about the lure of goods than it does about the appeal of this weak form of communion.

But it is not the gathering of people en masse that conveys a muted sense of power and participation. People are, after all, packed every day in subway cars without generating anything more than irritation and fatigue. There still needs to be a focus of the gathering, a catalyst that stimulates the crowd and gives it its special character. In the case of the shopping mall, the catalysts are the personalized images that have been connected to the products – images of sexual power and glamor, and also images of national pride. These symbols serve to convince the shoppers that while purchasing goods they are simultaneously participating together in a shared experience of a more vital and sensual world. Those who fail in the race for success tend to blame themselves, rather than society, and to deal with their frustration and futility through personal introspection, or by self-medication with the drugs and entertainment the expanding market makes available. If disturbance becomes too great, the individual may have recourse to ameliorative psychotherapy (itself an alternative "safe" form of charisma, as I shall argue below), or religious conversion, but rarely to any movement challenging the premises of society itself, which, because it delivers what it has promised, appears dauntingly solid.

As long as the marketplace continues to succeed on its own terms, material satiation and a general sense of participation forestall involvement in any more compelling, and risky, charismatic movements. Of course, should the economy falter, people may lose confidence and search for a new way to recover collective strength, possibly through charismatic immersion.

Another alternative to membership in charismatic movements is found in the strong attachment fostered between individuals and the nation as a whole. The heightened affective relationship of people to the nation is directly connected to the disintegration of family and neighborhood ties, with the result that the nation then becomes the major source of a sense of participatory community. The identification of the self with the nation-state is particularly evident in the US, where the country is portrayed not as an abstract concept, nor as a set of political institutions and bureaucracies, but as a living entity – a gigantic individual. Citizens are taught, through intensive propaganda and sophisticated advertising, that America has a distinct personality equivalent to the ideal personalities of Americans as individuals; that is, benevolent, neighborly, competitive, rich, egalitarian and strong. This imagery allows isolated citizens to transcend or ignore their own faults and failures via identification with the potent, encompassing nation.

At the center of this nationalist imagery is the president, whose personal life is felt to be merged with the essential character of the country and its citizens. As long as the personalized nation and the president who embodies it remain successful at giving a positive impression of power and control, the public gains a feeling of activity, pride, and community that is a watered-down and distanced form of charismatic commitment.

Once again, however, the linking of the person with the larger system works only as long as the system itself is perceived to work. Events which challenge the national image therefore engender social unrest far beyond what would be expected from objective conditions. Such challenges are subjectively felt by the public as challenges not so much to pragmatic interests, but to the individual's own transcendent identity gained through membership in the nation. This crisis of identity can lead to the advent of charismatic politicians who strongly exemplify the idealized character traits that have been undermined by attacks. An example is the upheaval in America caused by Iran's nose-thumbing at American power during the hostage crisis. The imagery of impotence that was attached to the Carter administration, and hence to Americans themselves, made Ronald Reagan's charismatic style especially appealing. In more serious crises, far less avuncular charismatic figures may arise to embody the threatened, sacred nation.

Other mundane forms of participation that siphon energy away from charismatic movements include the idolization of sports heroes and entertainment figures that so marks modern Western culture. Athletes, movie stars, singers, famous artists, certain politicians, and other icons, all are popularly held to be charismatic figures. This attribution is correct insofar as all do indeed provide centers for the gathering of crowds and for an expression of charismatic unity among the fans. In these circumstances, charisma has become, as Bryan Wilson has claimed, "merely for fun" (1975: 125), providing the masses with a momentary redemption from boredom, a reminder of an unregulated life, and a fleeting opportunity for titillation, primitive sensation, personalized relations, and imagined physicality – at a price.

As permanent liminal figures who enjoy the patronage of the system, these entertainers and artists have a protected place not permitted to more radical charismatics.[1] In these enclaves, a degree of experimentation is permitted, and alternative worldviews are envisioned and acted out in the glare of publicity, which emphasizes the larger-than-life and extrarational characteristics of the "stars." These alternatives ordinarily provide only occasional amusement for the public at large, who can vicariously identify with lives lived at a high emotional pitch while not daring any risk themselves. But the influence of these exemplary persons is actually fleeting and remains on the surface, even if their message is quite radical, since continual shifts in style mean that few idols have very long in the limelight. This is charisma as a "safety valve," diffusing repressed popular energies into ritual and fantasy, while simultaneously fueling capitalist consumption.

But in times of social crisis, theatrical individuals can serve as centers for charismatic gatherings, and their life styles can gain an appeal beyond the artistic enclave. We should remember as well the close association between failed artists and charismatic leaders. When the artistic community – the place in modern society where deviance and volatile emotionality are fostered – becomes so professionalized and rigid that it cannot accommodate marginalized visionaries, then these visionaries are likely to find their audience in cultic circumstances, and may attempt to apply their aesthetics to politics.

Charisma in Religion

So far, I have only considered secular substitutes for charisma, but charisma has also been institutionalized and tamed within the context of modern religions. The great charismatic enthusiasm that marked the beginnings of Methodism, for instance, is now forgotten, while Mormonism, which Weber cited as an American charismatic faith, has become staid and respectable. And the Unification Church of Reverend Moon, the modern "type case" for a religious charismatic movement, has evolved a well-formulated doctrine and a complex bureaucratic infrastructure. But the quandary for all these faiths is that as rationalization increases, church membership decreases, and those who are members are often unenthusiastic, reporting their beliefs to be founded primarily on habit.

Simultaneously, in the United States, and increasingly in Europe, the orthodox religious community has been disturbed by an upsurge not only of radical, world-rejecting cults, which are less radical versions of those we have already documented, but by apparently far less threatening – and far more widespread – "new age" religions such as spiritualism, alchemy, magical "Aquarian" practices, as well as Scientology, est and their many successful offshoots that have entered the corporate mainstream.

At first, it would seem these "world-affirming" beliefs, with their highly pragmatic messages, do not come under the rubric of religion at all, much less of charismatic religion (see Wallis 1984 on this terminology). They begin by preaching accommodation with the world as it is, with a special emphasis on success, which is valorized as "the *result* of a transpersonal perfection that can be experienced here and now" (Tipton 1982: 211). With their strong materialistic ethic and advertisement of a "technique for happiness" that can be purchased for a fee, these groups do not appeal to radical outsiders, oppressed minorities, or drugged hippies; instead they attract middle-class workers interested in finding a quick way to upgrade their careers and enrich their lives.

These practical followers who are looking for helpful knowledge could be regarded primarily as apprentices; a far less intense relationship than the devotee or disciple committed to a world-transforming cult

(Bird 1979). And, indeed, the rank-and-file membership of these world-affirming movements tends not to be strongly attached to any particular message or leader. Like anyone else in a marketplace, the consumers shop around for the best product, the most arousing message, the quickest form of gaining the success they seek; and they switch brands from power crystals to pentagrams with no great pangs of remorse.[2]

But despite the apparent pragmatic utilitarianism of the membership, these groups too tend to spiral, at least among an inner circle of initiates, in the direction of charismatic cultism. In Scientology, for example, the large but fluid outer circle of part-time adherents was led by a small, highly disciplined and fully committed secretive central organization, the Sea Org, marked by their special uniforms and complex regulations, who formed an inner elite circle of virtuosi living in a closed community surrounding the charismatic leader L. Ron Hubbard, proclaiming their devotion by signing "billion year contracts" of service to him. A similar pattern is seen elsewhere, as networks of adepts solidify and mark themselves out against the outer world as the possessors of esoteric knowledge. Often this solidification entails the worship of a charismatic leader, whose revelation is the foundation for the group's existence.

A combination of elements accounts for the seemingly strange appearance of a fanatical world-rejecting inner cadre at the core of pragmatic secular world-affirming movements such as est, Scientology, and other "new age" groups. For instance, in terms of ideology all preach a devaluation of social mores and ties and accept the premise of an internally motivated, emotionally validated, free choice as the sole grounds for commitment. They also use various training techniques that undercut personal identity, stimulate intense abreactive emotions, and draw converts into a tight network of other highly committed believers. As we have seen, these ideologies and techniques are typical of incipient charismatic organizations.[3]

As a result, individuals who join a world-affirming group may find that "intimacy, community and intra-movement elite status have gained a higher priority than worldly achievement or self-realization as originally envisaged." In consequence, there follows a general shift from a practical apprenticeship toward total absorption in a millennial charismatic cult, as within the atmosphere of the collective circle of converts "the self and personal identity . . . become subordinated to the will and personality of the leader," who is envisioned as the embodiment of the group (Wallis 1984: 122–4).[4]

But if "new age" movements tend toward charismatic revelations despite their seeming pragmatism and secular character, so too is there a parallel trend within orthodox religion. Pentecostalism is a burgeoning religious movement in America, and it rests precisely upon the capacity of the charismatic preacher to excite in the congregation a felt ecstatic moment that validates their shared religious faith. The power of this movement is most obviously demonstrated in America by the immense popularity of entrepreneurial television evangelists. The priority of person over doctrine in these "televangelical" ministries is witnessed when many devotees remain loyal even though the leader has been shown to have feet that are very muddy indeed. But even aside from these mass media figures, every American town has local Pentecostal preachers who acquire a fervent following through their charismatic expressiveness. The relative detachment of these individuals from any strong bureaucratic structure permits them tremendous leeway in their preaching, and always includes a danger of developing along the lines of the Peoples Temple.

But charisma also has appeared in a more Durkheimian manner within the most highly formal church systems, and even within the strict hierarchy of the Catholic church. The eruption of charismatic "antistructure" is exemplified in the so-called "charismatic renewal" movement, in which Catholics gather outside of the confines of the official church to participate in practices of immediate inspiration, such as speaking in tongues.

Any degree of charismatic inspiration within such a hierarchized structure seriously threatens the precarious accommodation with the mother church, since these experiences stand as an alternative, and more immediate, conduit to transcendence. Nonetheless, out of the desire for enthusiasm and communion, charismatic figures and anti-establishment movements continue to evolve within the orthodoxy to provide a spiritual base for revitalization of moribund faith – as they have in the past, and will undoubtedly continue to do in the future. And when this occurs, radical consequences can result, as we presently see in the revolutionary Catholicism of Latin America.

Intimate Relationships

Within the European-American context, however, the major alternative forms of charisma are found not in public, secular realms of capitalist consumption, nor in the worship of the nation, nor in entertainment, nor in religion, either orthodox or magical. Instead, people experience merger and self-loss in more intimate circumstances. For instance, as "haven in a heartless world" (Lasch 1977), the home in middle-class America ideally provides an atmosphere of intimacy and warmth where feelings of unconditional participation in the group are supposedly not only allowed, but favored. It is thus the locus for private community that stands opposed to the struggle and antagonism of the public world.

But the hoped-for unity of the family is undercut by social reality. Although the family exists as the source of and model for intense relationships of unalloyed caring, emotional expressiveness and sympathy, yet it must train its members in independence and distancing, and in the skills of negotiation and entrepreneurship. As a result, instead of a fusion in a loving unit, children and parents become independent bargaining agents, seeking "to accrue claims for future privileges justifiable on the basis of one's past concessions" (Erikson 1985: 317).

Furthermore, the ever greater intrusion of experts helps to create a degree of self-consciousness and emotional distancing in the family. Meanwhile, a number of social factors, including the economic necessity of two incomes, the greater number of single-parent households, and the low status of work in the home means that children are increasingly placed within institutional frameworks, and experience isolation and a lack of emotional bonding (Kohut 1977).

Additionally, ambivalence within the household is heightened because the modern family is not an ongoing extended unit; instead it exists only to disintegrate, since the children are expected to leave home and live out the autonomous existence for which they have been trained. Due to all these factors, the protection the family offers is fleeting, the warmth contingent. Yet the quest for a haven becomes more and more compelling as the frigidity of the public world is more and more numbing, and the demands made of the family to provide a refuge of warmth and vitality become greater just as those demands are harder and harder to meet.

Because so much is now required of the family in terms of personal fulfillment, many have been disappointed in what is actually delivered. It is for this reason that many countercultural communes, such as Manson's group, called themselves "families" and attempted to live out in the commune a fantasy of what they believed families ought to be. It is also noteworthy that student activists in the late sixties ranked nurturance highest in psychological need hierarchies (Geller and Howard 1972), and that attitude tests of countercultural "revolutionaries" of the period showed them to be motivated not by egalitarian ideology or concern for the underdog, but by a desire "to recapture the warm, effortless security that was theirs during the formative years" (Lesse 1969: 589).

A second form of imagined intimate community is that of friendship, which, like the family, is idealized in the public mind, but which also has serious difficulties in delivering what is promised; that is, an emotionally rewarding, caring, timeless, egalitarian relationship that stands outside the competitive marketplace. The fact that Americans move homes so often clearly undercuts the desired intimacy and shared companionship of friends. Also, the segmentation of social life and a greater emphasis on work means that very many people now find almost all their friends within the workplace, where competitiveness and rivalry must taint the relationship. Or, if friends are found outside work in the special-interest enclaves that are increasingly the gathering points for people, the extent of the interaction is limited by the range of the shared interest, so that the friendship is likely to remain one that has little depth or intensity.

Disappointment in family and friends often leads to therapeutic relationships that, like "new age" movements, ostensibly aim to teach people how to escape from their neuroses and to realize their individual potentials. Whether this quest is successful or not is irrelevant for my argument; what is important is that therapy provides clients with interaction in an accepting, empathetic environment where strong feelings of solidarity (and antagonism) can be expressed in an extremely supportive setting. The therapeutic setting is, quite literally, thought of as an alternative family, where adoration of and "falling in love" with the therapist are expected and encouraged as the necessary road to working out emotional problems generated by early childhood traumas. Patients also often have an opportunity to establish collective community with others in the therapy groups organized around the central figure of the therapist.

But, since therapy is a charismatic relationship that is stimulated precisely in order to eradicate itself, the therapist retains a professional and therefore anticharismatic stance, and does not allow the relationship to get beyond the bounds of the session. Even empathetic, identity-oriented therapy, while favoring greater emotional interaction with the patient, stops short of advocating a relationship that oversteps the professional contract between advisor and client.[5] Given the studied unresponsiveness of the therapist, the transference that does occur in psychotherapy is therefore a striking vindication of the Durkheimian argument that the charismatic figure is created in order to form a node for the experience of self-loss and abreactive emotional intensity.

The Romantic Dyad

There is one final form of relationship which, more than any other, has the characteristics of charisma. This is romantic love – recognized in popular culture as the most important, most moving, and most common form of idealized attachment in the modern era, serving as the counterweight in personal life to the deadening effects of the institutional framework, compensating for expulsion from the natal family, providing a permanent friend and an intimate dyadic relationship in which transcendence can be immediately experienced.[6]

The parallels between romantic love and charisma are multiple. For instance, in Western ideology, romantic love, like charisma, is believed to completely implicate the parties involved, making claims to timelessness, and is marked by the mutuality, emotional intensity, and expressiveness expected (but rarely found) in the family, or among friends. And where all other social ties are obligatory, like kinship; or chosen, like friendship; romantic love, like charisma, "just happens" when the subject is overwhelmed by the magnetic charm of the desired other, who appears as "the unambivalent object, in which duty and pleasure coincide, in which all alienation is extinguished" (Alberoni 1983: 23).

When they reach their goal, lovers, like followers, feel themselves immolated in merger with the beloved other. As Georges Simenon says: "Love is being two in one. It is being so close that when one opens his mouth to speak, the other says exactly what you meant to say. Love is a . . . fusion" (1984). From a Freudian object-relations viewpoint this merged state is sought by both lovers and charismatic followers as an attempt "to undo their separateness and find a way back to the state of bliss they had known before individuation" (Bergmann 1980: 75). And in love, as in charisma, the loss of the self in the other is experienced not as diminution, but as "exaltation, ecstasy, and exaggeration of the ego" (Chasseguet-Smirgel 1976: 356).

While in this expansive condition, great self-sacrifice is possible, since the follower/lover is so enmeshed in the beloved other that personal safety becomes irrelevant. Sacrifice then becomes not only painless, but a pleasure, if it gives pleasure to or protects the beloved one. Indeed, the attraction to the other takes precedence over all other relations and values, so that life without the beloved is felt not to be worth living, while simply being close to the desired one is an ultimate value in itself.

In romantic love also, as in charisma, the relation between the lovers is thought to oppose social constraints, so that lovers, like communal groups, are believed capable of obliterating boundaries of age, class and race in their quest for unity.[7] And, again as in charismatic relations, the great sins against love are the intrusion of planning or rational calculation or the assertion of selfish egoism. The relation, in principle, stands outside of any measure, and transcends the boundaries of self.

Furthermore, romantic love, like charisma, is aroused in situations where personal identity has been devalued and challenged by feelings of loss and isolation, and persons prepared to fall in love or join a movement are first plagued by "a sense of incompleteness and nostalgia, a desire to belong" (Reik 1972: 43). Otto Kernberg's statement that "loneliness . . . is a precondition for transcendence" thus fits both love and charisma (Kernberg 1977: 96).

According to theory, romance therefore gains currency through precisely the conditions conducive to charismatic movements; that is, as a response to social alienation, competitiveness, and fluidity in a world where old duties and connections have crumbled and the self has become contingent, problematic or threatened. Under these identity-challenging conditions there is "an inability to find something that has value in everyday life" (Alberoni 1983: 69) and a deep impulse to transform the self and revitalize the subjective world. Love, like charisma, provides a transcendent experiential truth that makes existence worthwhile:[8]

> What love does ... is to satisfy man's most urgent psychological needs, those produced by social isolation, by lack of any conceptual hold on the world in which he lives, and by lack of work satisfaction. ... Reduced through technological progress to a negligible nut in an incomprehensible machine, confused by tumbling and contradictory moral values, he can regain the feeling of self-importance only in love. (Beigel 1951: 333).

Finally, the parallel between charisma and romantic love is of course most evident in the apotheosis of the leader/beloved. In both cases we see "the same kind of elevation, idealization and incorporation that endows the leader-lover with special status and powers" (Miller 1980: 205). By identification the follower shares in the leader's power, just as the lover finds self-fulfillment in pleasing the beloved. Both follower and lover recognize the beloved other as vividly extraordinary, full of intense emotion, and the embodiment of all that is good and desirable; in other words, as "charismatic." Because of these imputed qualities, the lover, like the follower, wants to obey the adored beloved, and tries to intuit and immediately meet the desires of the other. Devotion to the beloved one in both charisma and romance is felt as ennobling and ecstatic, so that selflessness is a gain, not a loss. Due to these extensive parallels, falling in love is therefore, as Francesco Alberoni says, "the simplest form of a collective movement," replicating in small scale the ecstatic sensations and transformative patterns of great revolutions (1983).[9]

Love versus Charisma

There are, however, considerable differences between the experiences. In contrast to the hostility and opprobrium that tend to mark relations between charismatic groups and society at large, romance, despite the lovers' own subjective sensation of rebellion against structure and norms, can and does exist within and support the modern Western social system, and is considered to be a normal, if disruptive, relationship. This is because love, unlike charismatic involvement, is culturally recognized as a necessary stage in the developmental process, providing the emotional glue needed to cement together a couple in the absence of other binding mechanisms.

Love has another function too. It gives an accepted image of rapture and communion; an escape from the world of competitive individualism. All the world loves the lovers because the lovers' regard for one another is a reaffirmation for everyone that transcendence over human hostility and alienation is possible. The lovers also are a pleasurable reminder to each onlooker of his or her own experience of or hope for falling in love and escaping from the antagonisms and irritations of daily life. The tremendous quantity of love songs, stories, movies, poems testify to the function of love imagery in soothing and pacifying the public, and reducing the tension of existence in the modern world.

Romantic love, because it is so powerful and so involving, and yet so harmless, is the best and most efficient safety valve for the intense emotions that might otherwise be channeled into dangerous charismatic social movements. Instead of being turned against the world, in love the potent desire for transcendence is confined to the mutuality of the dyad, where the lovers create their own intimate world as they withdraw from the social environment – a withdrawal symbolized and legitimated by the institution of the honeymoon (Slater 1977). This symbolic withdrawal is socially approved, but only on the condition that the couple then return again to undertake their primary job of serving as the reproductive base for the society at large.[10]

Clearly, charismatic groups and lovers' dyads "constitute alternative and competing strategies for solving many . . . psychological dilemmas individuals encounter" (Miller 1980: 208). These strategies compete and are antagonistic because of the excessive, irrational commitment demanded by each; that is, a complete identification of self and other in intensive and emotionally evocative relationships which permit no simultaneous affective relationship of equal force. A person therefore cannot submit to merger within a charismatic group and still be in love.

The antagonism between charismatic group and personal romantic relationships is evident in theory and practice. For instance, Otto Kernberg writes that "submission to the leader" is always accompanied by "an intolerance for the formation of couples" (1980: 39). And indeed, within charismatic communities we find a consistent effort to devalue and break any intense dyadic bonds while focusing sexual desires upon the leader who arouses powerful sensations of merger with the group (Zablocki 1980: 131). The promiscuity demanded by Charles Manson was simply one form of this process.[11]

The opposite pattern also holds true; as Freud noted, "lovers are sufficient to themselves" and are hostile to the demands made by the group (1961: 55). Ex-cult members regularly attest that their decision to leave the group was a direct consequence of establishing or managing to retain a romantic dyad in spite of group pressure. The words of an ex-member of the Unification Church could apply to all of these cases: "Love, when it is allowed to flourish between two thinking beings, brings a heightened perception of value. . . . To us, it represented a gradual return to sanity" (Wood and Vitek 1979: 169).

If charisma and romance are structurally opposed but subjectively equivalent expressions of a deep desire for an ecstatic transcendence of the self in merger with the beloved other, and if romance is the dominant way this desire is expressed in the modern world, then we have to ask what will happen if the ideal of romantic love is devalued. According to many social theorists this is exactly what is occurring in modern Western society, particularly as the ideal of self-actualization replaces that of romantic attachment. This ideology is one we can recognize from our earlier discussions of modern emotivism, and from the rhetoric of the counterculture.

The priority of self-actualization based on realization of an inner core of sensation over dyadic relations of interdependence means that "the partners in a relationship remain autonomous and separate, each concerned about what he will have gained, what he will take away when the relationship is over" (Swidler 1980: 137). The quality of a dyadic relationship is measured by pragmatic calculation of the degree the individuals involved feel their inner selves are helped to grow and evolve through their ties with one another – an attitude that opposes the selfless essence of romance, and that denies any pain in favor of felt gratification.

The calculation of benefit coincides with a pervasive fear that the true, autonomous self may be lost in the responsibilities and interdependency that follow upon entering into a love relationship. Therefore, "the ability to retain control, if only . . . the fail-safe ability to disengage entirely – quickly, effectively, efficiently – is cultivated, refined and treasured" (Pope 1980: 22). An absence of commitment also makes it possible to rapidly substitute other, more gratifying relationships for those which have proven to be too demanding and not pleasurable enough. As a result "the search for *open* relationships, which is not simply restricted to the sexual realm, slides into the search for *interchangeable* relationships" (Zablocki 1980: 171).

This transformation is coincident with and probably correlated to a continuing decrease in the salience of the family unit in modern society, due to the increasing importance of work outside the home for both parents, and the subsequent appearance of more rational alternatives to the nuclear family such as day care, play groups, camps, and so forth. As the family becomes less necessary, the social usefulness of the romantic couple as the precursor to the institution of the family is steadily undercut in favor of a more self-oriented ideology. People are less willing to give up pleasures and preferences for the sake of unwanted and unnecessary chains of obligation to a partner. This shift is favored by the dominant institutions, since it frees the work force from private loyalties and dissolves the one remaining bulwark against full integration into a rationalized world.

But the model of emotional structure I have proposed indicates that the crumbling of the romantic ideology will result in a heightened pressure toward self-loss and identificatory merger in some other, alternative form of transpersonal relationship. This pressure will intensify as experiences of communion are increasingly lacking in the world at large because of the greater competitiveness, diversification and fluidity of the work environment implicit in the process of modernization. Many may numb their feelings of emptiness with tranquillizers and television, but for others self-transcendence, no longer found in intimate personal relationships and long absent in the central institutions of the society, will be sought elsewhere.

We have looked already at some of the alternatives available within the mainstream of social life which provide a diffuse form of charismatic attachment. We can expect that these expressive public arenas of sport, religion, art, entertainment, and consumption will be more and more important in people's lives if the potential for dyadic identification fades. And we can expect greater fusion between the individual and the personalized nation as well. However, such abstract and distant symbolic forms are only pale substitutes for the immediacy of the actual, physical presence of the other. They cannot fill the gap left by the death of romantic idealization.

It seems likely that a lack of commitment in love, within the modern context in which alternative forms of idealized attachment are weak or absent, may lead in compensation to participation in charismatic group relations which offer equivalent feelings of vitality and self-loss.[12] Most of these charismatic manifestations will not be as negative or extreme as those I have outlined but will be accommodated and even fostered by dominant institutions; instead of "world-rejecting" cults we will see more "world-affirmative" communities offering camaraderie, participation, and identification along with an ethic of worldly success that supports the status quo. In the workplace these groups will be marketed as giving members strong feelings of excitement, commitment and loyalty to the company and to the executive officer who embodies it. This pattern is already clear in some organizations where enthusiasm is a necessary prerequisite for the job.[13]

But this picture of numerous middle-level communal groups offering an institutionalized, less intense, more easily controlled, but nonetheless satisfying sense of commitment and emotional gratification through inner transformation rests on continued social stability, which permits the pluralistic and multiplex society to tolerate and even promote charismatic communities as a socially acceptable and organizationally functional escape from alienation. If there is a crisis, on the other hand, we can expect more radical charismatic messages and activities, and a less tolerant attitude by the society at large.

Furthermore, as we have seen, charisma in the modern context is not so easily controlled, even in its mild world-affirming guise. These groups too tend to develop world-rejecting inner cores and grandiose leaders.

Thus, despite a "normalization" of charismatic activity, the pressure of the overarching social formation and the dynamic between the demands of the group and the psyche of the leader mean that these groups may still make millennial claims, stirring up the enthusiastic fervor of the acolytes, whose intensity of commitment will often be in marked contrast to the apparent triviality or pragmatism of the avowed purposes of the group. Membership in the community will tend to gain priority over its ostensible goals and loyalty to the leader will preclude critique. We are likely then to see increasing polarization, the prevalence of mythical thought, and an unwillingness to compromise. Along with this, we will witness too the adulation of theatrical and emotionally febrile leaders who retain power by publicly mirroring and intensifying the ardor of their constituencies. Under pressure, such charismatic groups and their symbolic leaders may spiral into psychotic fantasies and collapse.

But if we continue to have relative stability, increased charismatic involvement in the modern age is not necessarily destructive. We know that charisma offers the strength and the imagination for achieving change. Yet it also can be, contrary to Weber, a factor in maintaining order. In the fragmented and isolating conditions of modernity, threats to personal identity can be warded off by membership in collectives gathered around a charismatic figure. Such a collective provides a revitalizing emotional common ground for the drifting individual in a world that seems hostile and heartless. The experience of vivid fusion with the charismatic other within the group permits a continuance of life and felt significance when the daily world has lost its enchantment. Such participation can offer a resting point and moment of transition, giving strength and support for construction of a new identity.

The problem of the modern era is not the charismatic experience per se: "charisma," after all, means a gift of grace. In essence it has no substantive content beyond being an immediate ecstatic experience, providing a visceral, transcendent moment that is outside of and opposed to the alienation and isolation of the mundane world – a memory upon which ordinary life can be constructed. The paradigm established by Weber and Durkheim, and restated by psychological theory, claims, in fact, that society is based upon a deeply evocative communion of self and other, a communion that offers not reason, but lived vitality. Without this electrifying blurring of boundaries, life no longer has its savor, action is no longer potent, the world becomes colorless and drab.

The question then is not whether such moments of selflessness and communion will continue to exist. They are a part of our human condition. The question is what form these moments will take.

Notes

1 Introduction

1 For a thorough categorization of political charisma, see Schweitzer (1984).

2 "Human Beings As They Really Are": Social Theories of the Passions

1 Of course, the content of the list of passions has not been static. Dante, for instance, listed the primary passions as pride, envy and greed, while Kant mentions ambition, lust for power and – the standby – greed. The passions have also been ranked according to their perceived mildness, malleability and social usefulness in a hierarchy that is by no means fixed, but has changed over time. As I will discuss later in this chapter, in the present era greed, once reviled as the basest of desires, is now considered to be socially valuable and even laudable (see Hirschman 1981).

2 Diderot also deserves credit for making a similar argument in his *Rameau's Nephew* (1964), where the extraordinary habits of his imaginary Polynesians compel him to admit that human morals are a function of rival and incommensurate orders of desire.

3 From my point of view, this is exactly the problem that confronts Jurgen Habermas's ambitious effort to construct a theory of communicative competence (1979). Habermas, like Kant, assumes that individuals, if given proper circumstances, will come to a rational understanding. This is, I think, a utopian view of human nature that is perfectly suited to philosophers, but not to ordinary people or ordinary interaction.

4 In making this argument, Smith was not the reductionist one might think. Smith claims that the pursuit of wealth is not for the sake of the goods themselves, but to better one's condition and gain the respect of others; the drive for economic advantage becomes the vehicle for the desire for consideration and honor, and it "became possible for Smith to concentrate on economic behavior in a manner that was perfectly consistent with his earlier interest in other important dimensions of the human personality" (Hirschman 1977: 110).

5 This is the position taken by Ernest Gellner, who writes that, as old belief systems are desacralized and the range of instrumental reason is extended, rational calculation becomes not easier but more difficult and unsatisfying, since "the more general or fundamental features of the world, though now demoted to the status of mere hypotheses, often elude rational assessment because they are unique or *sui generis* or very fundamental" (1985: 82).

6 There was a self-serving aspect to Mill's portrait, since he sought, by his argument, to "make the ordinary many see that the few unusual souls, whose natural inclinations were supremely disciplined, and who could lead society to better things, must be exempted from the rules properly binding on the majority" (Letwin 1965: 306). Mill thus hoped to justify his own unconventional union with Harriet Taylor – the relationship that had made his life worth living.

3 The Sociology of the Irrational: Max Weber and Emile Durkheim

1 Weber affirms unqualifiedly the validity of alternative ways of apprehending the world. None of these modes of apprehension, he says, are of intrinsically greater value or of any greater truth than any other. He even claims no privilege for his own thought, since "concept-construction depends on the setting of the problem, and the latter varies with the content of culture itself" (Weber 1949: 105). Weber's refusal to make judgements and his affirmation of absolute difference, along with his famous assertion of the necessity for making a choice of values ("here I stand, I can do no other") make him appear to be an existentialist, but from my point of view, he has simply accepted, on a cultural level, the emotivist premises of Utilitarianism.

2 Weber defines rationality in two ways: as increasing, systematic mastery of reality by abstract concepts, or as the instrumental, methodical and calculated efforts to reach a given practical end. According to Weber, the first form (*Wertrationalitat* or value-rationality) is associated with status positions, life styles, concepts of honor and propriety. Maximizing utility can then have to do with living up to certain standards and behaving in certain ways, since the ends of the action are defined expressively in terms of values inherent in the action itself, or in terms of following a specific code of conduct.

The second form (*Zweckrationalitat* or instrumental rationality) is inextricably connected with instrumental economic action and technical-legal-bureaucratic structures. Here maximizing utility is simply acting methodically to achieve the specific goal. Any action which facilitates efficient pursuit of that goal is permitted, so that means and ends, in this form of rationality, are severed, and social action is no longer constrained by the restrictions of values and norms. In Weber's view of history, the second form, because it is technically more functional, must slowly undermine the first, until, in the modern West, it has become the dominant mode for the orientation of action.

As Gellner (1985) notes, however, the differences between these forms are actually not so great. Both depend on the efficient use of information in order to gain a specific aim. Both also assume rule observance and consistency of behavior. In other words, both are essentially aimed toward the efficient pursuit of personal ends, and are thus grounded in Utilitarian theory.

3 However, there is some faint opening for change in Weber's conceptualization of traditional authority. This rests in the actions of the ruler himself who, insofar as he can stand outside of the constraints of custom, has the potential for independent action. Weber's example is the sheikh of a Bedouin tenting group who cannot command directly, who lacks all formal authority and all means to enforce his desires, and who can be abandoned at any time by his following. He has no power beyond his ability to set an example for others to follow, hoping that the sheer force of his personal prestige will motivate imitation. If he fails, he is no longer the leader.

It is precisely in the ability of the traditional leader to attract and motivate his following that the traditional forms of authority overlap with the second form of irrational action: charisma. Whenever the traditional leader gains and holds his following on the grounds of the magnetism of his personal character, and not from his position, he comes close to achieving charismatic status.

4 Charisma as a term, of course, did not originate with Weber. It had a long history in Christian theological discourse, and signified the gift of grace, resembling in some senses the Greek idea of the "divine man," or the Roman concept of *facilitas*, the hero's innate ability to lead a project to success due to his connection with the divine. For Christians it meant the intuitive recognition by laypeople that a saint has intimate contact with God.

5 This type of charisma, ratifying and sacralizing the world as it is, is the mainstay of tradition and could even, perhaps, be subsumed into tradition. It is often taken by Weber's followers to be the essential form. Shils, for instance, writes that "charisma is related to the need for order. The attribution of charismatic qualities occurs in the presence of order-creating, order-disclosing, order-discovering power as such" (1965: 204). Charisma in this sense is inextricably linked with the status quo.

6 This is why the teacher is not a charismatic, despite the depth of the teaching offered. The teacher has faith, and a systematic message, but lacks the passion necessary to attract a following (M. Weber 1978: 514). On the other hand, the shaman frothing in an epileptic fit or the berserk warrior in a killing frenzy most definitely are charismatic, despite the absence of meaning in their acts and words.

7 According to Weber, the development of religion is a gradual muting of these techniques for inducing a state of intoxication among the

onlookers as new, more reserved and disciplined forms of communion evolve, such as the contemplation of the exemplary prophet, or the detached action in the world demanded by ethical ascetics. Religion, like the rest of life, is progressively bureaucratically rationalized, and the original passion is lost. As the shaman becomes the priest, the hereditary king emulates in ritual the culture hero, and the judiciary repeat and elaborate the inspired words that underlie their legal code.

8 Many see Durkheim primarily as a systems theorist because he argued so forcefully that human thought is "not simply isolating and grouping together the common characteristics of a certain number of objects; it is relating the variable to the permanent, the individual to the social" (1965: 487); a relationship achieved by developing ever more inclusive classification systems. But it is worth recalling that Durkheim's symbolic structures had an affective base, grounded in the first place in the collective's experience of solidarity. And, in fact, all of his contributions began from the same basic premise.

9 It was for this reason especially that Durkheim repudiated individual self-interest and utilitarian economic action as a possible basis for community life since, he argued, it is the "sole form of social activity that has not yet been expressly attached to religion" (1965: 466) – and therefore not attached to the affective well-springs of community.

10 Recent writers, such as Lynn Hunt (1984), François Furet (1981), and Mona Ozouf (1988) have accepted Michelet's assertion of the importance of understanding the Revolution from within the Revolutionary moment itself. Their reinterpretations have emphasized the rituals and symbols generated by the Revolution in a way that Durkheim would have surely approved. These new interpretations tend, however, to over-intellectualize the act of participation, and to downplay the passion for selflessness that is so central to Michelet's, and Durkheim's, portrait of the Revolutionary moment.

11 Many commentators have made fun of this aspect of Durkheim's thought, arguing that the image of conceptless elders engaging in rituals which then impose concepts upon them is absurd. I would argue in return that it is certainly no more absurd than supposing, as contract theorists continue to do, that society is a result of intelligent and self-interested but somehow non-social individuals reaching an agreement on how to behave. Furthermore, as Gellner has commented, Durkheim's vision is at least logically defensible, since it uses a deeper level of the mechanics of collective participation to explain the social world (Gellner 1985: 155).

12 For both Durkheim and Weber the orgy, which symbolized for them the most powerful and intense form of the disintegration of personal distinctiveness and the unconstrained release of erotic energy, is the archetypical charismatic moment.

    Both Weber and Durkheim then agree that although the charismatic experience empowers the society, and gives vitality to individuals through the intense emotions generated, it also depletes the individual's personal vitality, just as drunkenness or sexual excess deplete.

13 Durkheim felt it would be socially healthy to maximize opportunities to experience the rejuvenating collective experience. This is why, like de Tocqueville (1969), he advocated smaller intermediate groups between the individual and the state. But where de Tocqueville thought men would learn democratic action and autonomy in such groups, Durkheim believed they would offer an arena for the necessary loss of the self that would permit wider loyalties.

4 Hypnotism and Crowd Psychology: Mesmer, Le Bon, Tarde

1 As we shall see in chapter 11, Mesmer's techniques recapitulate some very ancient forms of spiritual healing. But the specific precursor of mesmerism is probably found in the paroxysms of the Parisian Jansenists who had astonished Paris fifty years previously by their antics at the tomb of Saint Medard. There one could find "men falling like epileptics, others swallowing pebbles, glass, and even live coals, women walking feet in air. ... You heard nothing but groaning, singing, shrieking, whistling, declaiming, prophesying, caterwauling" (quote of an eyewitness in Knox 1950: 377). Many of these ecstatics also cured ailments through their spiritual power. The government, fearful of a possible uprising, banned the demonstrations in 1732; the convulsionists were dispersed to become private practitioners of trance, meeting in the homes of the well-to-do, where they provided healing and a connection with "higher" forces.

2 The equalizing aspect of mesmerism helped give it a political tone, since it proclaimed in its practice the unity of all in a deeply empathetic entranced communion, which Brisson likened to the "state of a nursing mother" (quoted in Darnton 1968: 96). Mesmer himself remarked that "I am not astonished that the pride of persons of high birth should be wounded by the mixture of social conditions at my house; but I think nothing of it. My humanity encompasses all ranks of society" (quoted in Darnton 1968: 73).

3 This form of mesmerism became dominant in the days prior to the fall of the *ancien régime*. Seances, manipulation of spirits, and large-scale meetings became more and more popular, and the treatment of disease less important. The miraculous abilities of the entranced subjects are typical of the supernatural powers claimed in other analogous situations cross-culturally, as we shall see.

4 This imagery much resembles Swanson's portrayal of the social world as one of people more or less in a state of trance (Swanson 1978). It also is close to Weber's picture of traditional society, in which unconscious repetition is the normal mode of being.

5 Because of this premise, Tarde envisioned no Weberian movement to rationalization. Nor did he agree with the notion of progressive historical

cycles, or even with the Durkheimian premise of increasing organic organization of society. For him, as for the cyclic thinkers of the Eastern tradition who so inspired Nietzsche, humanity was doomed to endless repetition of invention and collapse.

6 It is within this theoretical framework that Willner has done her excellent comparative research, showing the variation in the revelation of charisma across cultures (1984). Gandhi's sexual abstinence fitted with the Indian notion of accumulation of power, while Sukarno's sexual appetites enhanced his charisma in the Indonesian context; Hitler's anger would have been inappropriate in the United States, while Roosevelt's folksiness would have been ineffective in Germany.

7 This image of the leader is thus distinguished from that drawn by Machiavelli, whose famous dictum was that "it is much safer to be feared than loved" (Machiavelli 1988: 59). Love, Machiavelli wrote, is an obligation broken for expediency, but fear binds a following. Furthermore, "whether men bear affection depends on themselves, but whether they are afraid will depend on what the ruler does" (Machiavelli 1988: 60–1).

But, as we shall see, the love of the follower in crowd psychology has within it a strong taint of terror, while Machiavelli was not so one-sided as is usually supposed, and also wrote that for the prince "the best fortress is found in the love of the people" (1988: 108).

8 The underlying sexual imagery of leadership has been acted out often enough in group relations, both symbolically and in fact. Napoleon, for instance, characterized France as his mistress. "I have slept with her!" he declared. Napoleon spoke figuratively, but other leaders have been much more literal in their sexualization of the relationship with their disciples, as we shall see.

5 Oedipus and Narcissus: Freud's Crowd Psychology

1 This dynamic perspective has retained its appeal although many later analysts reject the highly abstruse cosmic interpretation Freud gave these speculations, and his rather dated biological assumptions. There remain as well great differences in the technical and theoretical understandings of this dynamic. For instance, Melanie Klein and her followers insist that the child is tortured by an inner, pre-existing opposition of love and hate (Klein 1975), while the object-relations school argues the child is fundamentally whole, and is only divided by interaction with the mother and the environment (for example, Winnicott 1965, Fairbairn 1954). Recently, some theorists who have studied the behavior of very young children claim that the infant actually has a great deal more autonomy and active will than is generally admitted by either of these schools (see Demos 1988).

Nonetheless, a survey of the literature shows that most theorists still accept, sometimes covertly, Freud's fundamental hypothesis of an inherent conflict between human desires for merger and the necessities of reality and growth which require differentiation and separation. This dialectical movement may be considered as metaphysical and innate, or as derivative from extended nurturance and the intense mother–child tie, or both; but whatever the causation, humanity continues to be defined in this literature by this model.

2 There were other similarities between Freud and the crowd psychologists as well. The Freudian portrait of the construction of a personality structure by imitation and internalization of the characteristics of significant and admired others obviously resembles very much Tarde's image of the "piling up of slumbers" in the growth of the individual, and in fact one critic has remarked that "in many regards Freud's ideas appeared to be those of Tarde transposed in psychoanalytic concepts" (Ellenberger 1970: 528; see also Moscovici 1985 for an interesting discussion of the relationship between Freud, Le Bon and Tarde).

3 Over time, this idealization expands beyond the parents to admired peers, authority figures, and even to abstract cultural objects. Like Durkheim, Freud thus saw morality, as enforced by the superego, to be an irrational force emanating from the pressures of the group dynamic, but the mechanism is quite different. For Durkheim, morality derives from the powerful pleasure of immersion in the collective, while for Freud morality is a product of the rechanneling of thwarted aggression into the punitive superego.

4 Freud found evidence for the ambiguity of devotion to authority in the rites of primitive kingship, and the prohibitions that surround god-kings. As he writes: "The ceremonial taboo of kings is *ostensibly* the highest honor and protection for them, while *actually* it is punishment for their exaltation" (1950: 51).

5 Freud does note in passing that working together for a cause and sharing interests and characteristics can bring about a sense of empathetic group identification even when a leader is absent. But according to Freud these mundane factors do not provide enough passion to keep the group from disintegrating into sexual dyads riven by jealousy and desire.

6 Modern psychoanalytic thought generally agrees with Freud's picture of the inner life of these fragmented selves. Researchers have elaborated the category of "paraphrenic" disorders to go beyond the full-blown psychoses in which all distinctions between self and object disintegrate and ordinary reality testing is completely lost. The category now includes less excessive "borderline" syndromes and narcissistic personality disorders, where the patient can function in the world, but only at the cost of a deep sense of inner emptiness, an inability to tolerate ambiguity, and an incessant desire to find an identity in fusion with others. Many analysts claim the majority of their patients now belong in these categories.

7 Freud distinguishes between identification and idealization. Idealization, according to Freud, can only occur after differentiation of self and other, and is characteristic of the Oedipal stage and development of the superego. The father is idealized as a superior being by the son who surrenders to

him. Idealization has, however, a core of identification, of not simply looking up to the other, but of *becoming* the other. The process of identification is defined by Freud as "the earliest expression of an emotional tie with another person" (1959: 37); the type case and original form is the infant's symbiotic bond with the mother.

The distinction between ego-ideal and superego, as developed by theorists such as Chasseguet-Smirgel (1976), runs parallel with the distinction between identification and idealization. In this model, narcissistic primal unity is expressed in the ego-ideal, which is a manifestation of infantile merger with the mother. The ego-ideal is loved as the undifferentiated self was loved in infancy, whereas the superego is a punitive emanation of the father, fueled by guilty aggression. Fusion with the ego-ideal is thus equivalent to identification, and corresponds with a charismatic relationship.

8 The distinction between neurotic and narcissistic group dynamics underlies Kohut's distinction between idealized, morally superior messianic leaders – who resemble Freud's punitive, patriarchal superego figures – and grandiose charismatic leaders – who express more regressed narcissistic drives as they offer the followers identification and rapturous experiences of merger and power (Kohut 1985: chapter 7; see also Lindholm 1988a).

9 Freud's shift in perspective is clear when he writes that "the state of being in love, which is psychologically so remarkable, *is the normal prototype of the psychoses*" (Freud 1950: 89 – my emphasis). I remind readers that in Freudian terminology psychosis is another term for paraphrenia, and, unlike neurosis, is connected to pre-Oedipal questions of identity formation, and that the terminology, despite its value loading, essentially denotes two different psychic structures.

6 Charisma as Mental Illness or as Resocialization

1 A well-known variant on this thesis was proposed by the political scientist, Harold Lasswell, who claimed that all public figures are seeking power as compensation for low self-esteem (1960). The job of the researcher then is to find evidence of factors that would cause low self-esteem in the childhood of the leader.

2 Note that the familial constellation of the Oedipal model for charismatic leaders and the model offered by theorists of identity and object-relations is similar. The first, however, stresses the child's problem with trying to be like the distant father; the second stresses the child's problem in trying to become separate from the mother – a problem exacerbated by the father's absence.

3 From this point of view, it is perfectly possible to have a female charismatic figure, whereas the orthodox Freudian position, with its emphasis on masculine rivalry, would imply that only men could fill the role of charismatic leader. I shall, however, continue to use the masculine

pronoun, since the number of female charismatics has been relatively few. Why this should be so is a question for further research, but I suspect it has to do with cultural images of authority.

4 Bion based his conclusions about crowds and leaders on his work with small therapy groups in which he took a non-interventionist stance and then watched the dynamic develop. This experience convinced him that groups spontaneously take on a psychotic character that overwhelms the more rational motives of the individual members. In this condition, the person who is selected leader is usually the most pathological member of the entire group. The situation that Bion initiated by refusing to give the group any formal leadership or any rules or norms resembles a society in chaos, when old values and leadership are delegitimized. I would argue that his experiments are most useful for understanding this sort of extraordinary circumstance – not for understanding mundane group interaction.

5 The propensity of individuals with a damaged and negative identity to join cults is well exemplified in the recruitment of ex-heroin users into inclusive charismatic organizations such as Synanon, which were ostensibly organized to provide a cure for addiction, but instead ended as authoritarian communities (cf. Rebhan 1983). Another well-known study attempts to demonstrate that converts to the Unification Church had considerable psychological problems before joining (Galanter et al. 1979), while yet another claims that converts to cults tend to have weak egos and difficulties in establishing relationships (Spero 1983). The psychoanalytic perspective that posits mental derangement among followers is particularly plausible when applied to many of the groups in the sixties and seventies which drew in psychedelic casualties and other fragmented individuals, and is often extended as well to charismatic movements which are religions of the weak and oppressed, who, it can be argued, have had childhood experiences of deprivation that might reasonably lead them to seek relations of dependency and self-loss.

6 Others have argued from a different point of view that immersion in charismatic groups is a positive adaption to modern institutional non-rationality, serving to "teach healthy individuals to cope with crazy systems" (Westley 1982: 153). This perspective is especially applicable to world-affirming cults such as est, which teach adaptability and deny the possibility of any given order, while at the same time favoring acceptance of authority. This perspective too has a degree of validity, as studies of members of world-affirming cults do show that the devotees believe they have gained a greater ability to cope with their work environment due to their cult training.

7   Synthetic Theories

1 The obvious example in the modern era is the worship of Stalin in the Soviet Union.

2 One noteworthy attempt is Bourguignon's coding of the manifestations
  of special forms of consciousness for the purpose of constructing
  typologies and distribution patterns cross-culturally (1968).

3 A more meaning-centered approach, also inspired by crowd psychology,
  is taken by Swanson (1978) for whom "trance" experiences are
  charismatic, since they involve encounters with superordinate forces that
  are external to the self, but that shape the action orientation of the self.
  In fact, all of society is envisioned by Swanson as immersed in a
  somnambulistic trance, an image that repeats Tarde. There is, however,
  no personal, transformative or ecstatic component in this image of
  charisma.

4 The ASC experience, and the experience of charismatic involvement, have
  strong analogies with neurological disorders such as temporal lobe
  epilepsy, Tourette's syndrome and other forms of what Sacks (1985) has
  called mental superabundances, or disorders of excess, in which the inner
  dynamic of growth and energy shades into morbidity, and illness presents
  itself as euphoria. Weber, who characterized the first charismatic as an
  epileptoid, was thus close to the mark. The allure of these morbid states
  is evident when Dostoyevsky writes, "You all, healthy people, can't
  imagine the happiness which we epileptics feel during the second before
  our fit . . . I don't know if this felicity lasts for seconds, hours or months,
  but believe me, *I would not exchange it for all the joys that life may
  bring*" (quoted in Sacks 1985: 137).

5 Maya Deren, who experienced possession trance in her research on
  Haitian voodoo, describes this condition when she discusses the importance
  of drumming and dancing in inducing dissociative states of identity
  diffusion: "At such moments one does not move *to* the sound, one *is*
  the movement of the sound, created and bound by it" (1953: 257). We
  will find similar imagery of self-loss to be a pervasive theme in reports
  from other charismatic movements.

6 This image of an anxious and faltering modern consciousness, struggling
  to maintain identity by manipulating even inner emotional states to
  conform with social expectations, finds some verification in objective
  studies. Fiske, for instance, concludes from her large-scale longitudinal
  study of the attitudes of lower- and middle-class Americans that "there
  is an increasing need to be told how to think, feel and behave" (1980:
  239).

7 It is impossible to say whether this reporting is an artifact of what the
  therapist expects, or reflects a real change in the style of mental disfunction
  in the modern era. Theoretically, the latter argument makes good sense,
  but in any case it is clear that people are more concerned with such
  disorders than they were in the past, indicating a general social focus on
  questions of identity that is significant in itself.

8 The "Possessed Servant": Adolf Hitler and the Nazi Party

1 I rely in this chapter on standard historical accounts of the origins and workings of National Socialism, including Stern (1961, 1972), Mosse (1964, 1981), Childs (1971), Taylor (1988), Holborn (1970), Craig (1978), and Neumann (1942). Other references are cited in the text.

2 A number of historians of ideas have connected the relative fragmentation of German identity and the weakness of the nation with Hegel's apotheosis of state power, with Nietzsche's quest for a superman, and with the ideology of "authenticity" that marks German phenomenologist philosophy. Heidegger's early support of Hitler is not surprising in this context, since he at first saw Hitler as the exemplar of vitalizing action in a world where all philosophies seemed impotent.

The appeal to *volki*sh traditions of the hero, so important in Nazi ideology, is the popular equivalent of this quest for authenticity and authority, and also springs from the same desire to assert some deep-seated and emotionally grounded community crystallized by the great, active, mystical force of the leader.

3 German storm-troopers were given special training to be ruthless and extremely flexible. They regarded themselves as an elite and were allowed a degree of informality and relaxed discipline denied the regular line troops.

4 In this context, it is striking how often and openly homosexuality was practiced in the Free Corps and later in the SA.

5 Kracauer writes that "instead of proving immune to Nazi indoctrination the bulk of the Germans adjusted themselves to totalitarian rule with a readiness that could not be merely the outcome of propaganda and terror. ... Since the Germans opposed Hitler on the political plane, their strange preparedness for the Nazi creed must have originated in psychological dispositions stronger than any ideological scruples" (1974: 204).

Hitler himself was proud of his vast base of support, and continued to hold plebiscitary elections throughout his reign, where he routinely gained 98 percent of the vote. As he said himself, "I am not a dictator and never will be a dictator. As a dictator, any clown can govern" (quoted in Fest 1974: 418).

6 Hitler's appeal was weakest among Catholics, committed Communists and labor unionists. Aside from ideological issues, it is clear that strong community institutions among the resistant elements protected them from the alienation, isolation, and sense of anomie that made much of Germany susceptible to Hitler's attraction.

7 Eric Hoffer notes that the radical contrast between the pomp and color of mass meetings and the drabness of ordinary existence served to

further devalue individual lives and heighten idealization of and immersion in the group (1951).

8 A number of psychoanalytic theorists have occupied themselves with trying to discover the source of Hitler's hatred of Jews. For instance, Binion (1976) cites as a contributing factor Hitler's rage at the Jewish doctor who treated his mother in her final illness. And, of course, others have cited Hitler's supposed belief that he had a Jewish ancestry. It is certain that Hitler strongly wished to repudiate his past. "People must not be allowed to find out who I am" (Hitler quoted in Fest 1974: 14).

Whatever the specific causation, clearly Hitler's image of Jews is linked to his deep fear of pollution and reflects his excruciating anxiety over inner splitting and disintegration. Exterminating the Jews was undoubtedly Hitler's way of exteriorizing and objectifying psychic conflicts that would otherwise have led to utter collapse.

9 In this context, it is worth citing Rauschning's insight that "the parallel with the Roman Emperors is entirely misleading. It is the Shaman's drum that beats round Hitler" (1940: 259).

10 The imagery of contagion, ignition and conflagration that we shall see in shamanistic rituals was also characteristic of Nazism, where torchlit parades and gigantic bonfires symbolized in dramatic form the charismatic involvement of the crowd. Hitler himself was fascinated by fire. He wished to have a fireplace in every room of his estate, and loved to throw logs on the flames. See Canetti (1978) for more on the symbolism of crowd excitement.

11 Some critics (cf. Bensman and Givant 1975) have argued that Hitler's charisma is actually "pseudocharisma" because he relied on sophisticated propaganda and dramatic techniques. But if, as Weber says, charisma is an attribution by the audience, then this critique is mistaken. Furthermore, as I have noted, it is evident that the very people who were instrumentally "manufacturing" Hitler's image were themselves true believers, not manipulative cynics pursuing rational interests. And it is also clear that Hitler sincerely believed in his own divine inspiration.

12 See Binion (1976) for a controversial, literal interpretation of this metaphor. According to Binion, the doctor who treated Hitler for hysterical blindness hypnotized him and planted the suggestion that henceforth he could conquer all obstacles by sheer force of will. Binion believes that this suggestion, in combination with Hitler's background and the German situation, was crucial in developing his charismatic appeal.

13 There is a feedback loop operating as well, since the very control that the charismatic achieves over the spontaneous revelation of feeling helps him to dampen the ambivalence and hesitation that usually adulterate unselfconscious emotional disclosures. In other words, the powerful expression of emotional intensity is not opposed by self-aware simulation, as we, with our ideology of authenticity and spontaneity, tend to believe, but instead the convincing expression of strong feeling actually *coincides* with theatricality and detachment (Goffman 1959).

14 See, for instance, Smith (1967), Binion (1976), Erikson (1985), Wolfenstein (1967), Kohut (1985), Langer (1972), Waite (1971, 1977) for a representative sampling. These theories focus on Hitler's family dynamic – a distant, authoritarian father who was much older than his overprotective mother. The father died when Hitler was quite young, and his mother died painfully when Hitler was in his young manhood.
   Waite (1977) also cites some circumstantial evidence to show that Hitler's lack of a testicle had an effect on his psychological state.

15 Hermann Rauschning reports that one of Hitler's aides was called into his bedroom where he found the Führer "looking wildly around. 'He! He! He's been here!' he gasped. His lips were blue. Sweat streamed down his face. Suddenly he began to reel off figures, and odd words and broken phrases, entirely devoid of sense. ... Then he suddenly broke out – 'There, there! In the corner! Who's that?' " (1940: 256). The accuracy of Rauschning's reporting has been questioned, but this apparition is not an unlikely occurrence, given what we know of other aspects of Hitler's character.

16 The proclivity of would-be or failed artists to charismatic revelation has been noted by Hoffer (1951), who argues that failed creativity is at the heart of the charismatic's rage against the world. But we should note that in the romantic tradition the artist, like the charismatic, believes himself or herself (and is believed by the public) to be a conduit for higher powers, to have a transcendent message, and, most of all, to have the capacity to remake the world by pure will and creative action. It is perhaps worth remarking here too that Lommel (1967) has made a claim that the shaman, the prototypical charismatic, is also the first artist.

17 This is, of course, a story that Hitler tells to validate his own truth, and we will see similar legends told by other charismatics. These stories always claim that there has indeed been a break in personal identity, and a transformation has occurred. They may be a reinterpretation of what was actually a very gradual process, but the similarity between Hitler's report, the reports of other modern charismatics, and what we know of the advent of shamanism seems to show that such stories are not merely self-justificatory lies, but do have a deep significance for the charismatic leader, and for his ability to imagine and present himself as a transcendent force.

18 In fact, even the final collapse of the charismatic does not always eliminate the believer's deeply ingrained faith; a faith that has become central to his identity. For instance, von Ribbentrop burst into tears when he saw a film of Hitler during the Nuremberg trials. "Can't you see how he swept people off their feet?" he exclaimed. "Do you know, even with all I know, if Hitler should come to me in this cell now and say 'Do this!' – I would still do it" (quoted in Gilbert 1950: 195–6).

19 Hitler was always careful to say that National Socialism was a movement, and not a party, thus emphasizing the element of change and process.

20 In this context, it is worth noting that the SA troopers, purged by Hitler and killed, died with a "Heil Hitler" on their lips. They could not believe that the Führer had betrayed them.

21 This pattern of charismatic rule resembles very much Weber's picture of sultanism, where the ruler's personal fiat is law, where institutions purposely overlap and oppose one another, and where the courtiers vie for the ruler's favor. The difference is that the sultan as a type is constrained by tradition and aims only at retaining power, whereas Hitler believed himself to be creating a new world, and power was a means to this end. The techniques used, however, are remarkably similar, verifying the intersection between Weber's models of traditional and charismatic leadership.

22 An analogous pattern in a quite different cultural configuration was the Cultural Revolution in China, which Mao Tse Tung quite consciously promoted to break down the evolving lines of bureaucratic authority and thereby retain the primacy of "revolutionary ideology." Parallel patterns occur as well in smaller charismatic groups, as we shall see.

23 Once again, parallels are obvious in other charismatic state systems, such as Khomeini's Iran, where the ruler sought to retain absolute power by focusing hostility outwards and portraying the world as an immanent threat to his eschatological vision.

9 "Love is My Judge": Charles Manson and the Family

1 In popular parlance, the term "cult" has acquired a pejorative meaning, evoking images of hypnotic and satanic leaders enslaving a robotic following. But it originally simply signified the devout actions of true believers, with an emphasis upon the expression of the adoration felt by the devotee for the personified deity, as in the cult of Mary.

The sociologically standard definition of "cult" also stresses personal devotion and expressive action, but reserves the term to refer to a proto-religion in its fragile and usually short-lived formative phase, when the prophet is still alive and doctrine has not yet been rationalized and solidified (Yinger 1957; Nelson 1960). Others differentiate cults from sects, with the latter considered as protest reform movements within an orthodoxy, while the former are synthetic, stressing personal ecstasy and novelty (Shupe 1981). More complex typologies of cults include: a distinction between secret-knowledge cults, liberation-of-inner-power cults, and cults of a saved community (Wilson 1976); a distinction between devotees, disciples, and apprentices (Bird 1978); a differentiation between traditional-dualistic and relativistic-monistic cults (Robbins and Anthony 1978); a trichotomy of world-rejecting, world-affirming and world-accommodating cults (Wallis 1984).

But for the purposes of this book, these divisions are less important than the charismatic revelation and communal ecstatic experience that are typical of cultic formations (Ellwood 1973). This definition allows us to consider as cults political action groups such as the Symbionese Liberation Army, or the Internationalists of Toronto (O'Toole 1975) which have overtly antireligious ideologies, but which are characterized by charismatic leadership and the intensified group experience typical of charismatic immersion.

2 This is not to discount groups which brought in disadvantaged individuals, particularly groups associated with black power, where charismatic individuals often held sway. Martin Luther King is an especially salient case. We shall see as well that the bulk of Jim Jones's following came from the disenfranchised black community.

3 In contrast, as Lipset notes, "in Europe, one sees the continued, even though declining, strength of deferential norms, enjoining conformity to class standards of behavior" (Lipset 1963: 123). But even these remnants of class distinction are fast dissolving, as Europe comes to be more "Americanized" in ways that are far deeper than commercial penetration.

4 Elsewhere, the reaction to the erosion of traditional ties and the pressures of modernity can, and often do, take nonreligious directions – for example, in the communist East where the state, under the authority of the great leader, has been apotheosized as the redeemer of the masses. Even in rationalistic England, recent eruptions of violent mass behavior have occurred among the disenfranchised classes, while some middle-class people have turned to more sedate escapes from modern pressures such as spiritualism, magic, and arcane ritual, and the young have discovered their idols in the world of music. In all these instances the pattern of charismatic involvement remains discernible. The American cases, however, are particularly illustrative because of their clarity and excessiveness.

5 We should recall as well that young people in Western society, regardless of wealth and status, are always susceptible to the enticement of a collective, due to their transitional structural position. They have left or are trying to leave the family; they have not formed permanent romantic dyads; they are relatively unconnected to the overarching values and artifacts of the culture at large that give adults a sense of participation and continuity with the world around them. As people seeking new lives and new alliances, the youth have less to lose and more to gain by joining charismatic cults and groups, and their recruitment into these groups is really no surprise, though the excesses of the groups are surprising.

6 Of course, not all members of cults were ex-drug-users, though very many were. And different groups attracted different clienteles. The Divine Light Mission of Guru Maharaj Ji, for example, had a very high proportion of ex-drug-users in its ranks, while the Unification Church of Reverend Moon had a relatively low proportion.

7 A similar solipsism is expressed in the therapeutic jargon of "finding yourself" and "self-actualization."

8 Later, Manson told his followers that women were the source of the

dreaded "ego programming" and should not be allowed to influence their children. In one of his songs, the chorus was "I am a mechanical boy, I am my mother's toy" (quoted in Schreck 1988: 75).

9 Manson has repudiated this biography, as he has repudiated everything written about him. It is clear that the language of the book is undoubtedly considerably sanitized and reorganized. But Emmons did interview Manson extensively, and the stories told in the book coincide in their basic outlines with those told by other participants, even if the emphasis is different. Furthermore, the biography in general has a ring of truth and a coherence with what we know of charismatic figures that makes it worth using in the same cautious way as we use the biographical material about Hitler.

10 The Process members deny this allegation (Bainbridge 1978).

11 One of Manson's prison friends said the conversations were "about Main Old Ladies – a pimp's number one girl who controlled all the others; stables – more than one girl working for you; and we talked mostly about how to turn chicks out" (quoted in Sanders 1971: 23).

12 The Family's isolation on the Spahn Ranch was considerable, but Manson tried to move the Family even further into the desert, to the abandoned Barker Ranch. This move was resisted by many of the members, who feared the loneliness and harsh environment.

13 Manson's anger was revealed not only in the killings he initiated, but also in some of his taboos. Like Hitler, Manson practiced strict vegetarianism and was extremely squeamish about taking the lives of animals, or even insects. He would be enraged if a follower killed a fly, and actually permitted flies to swarm on his lips. From a psychoanalytic point of view, these excesses may indicate an overcompensation for violent urges which Manson feared would come to the surface and shatter his personality. This is not to claim that all vegetarians are hiding violence, but in Manson's case the contradiction between the ideal of peace and harmony and the actuality of murder is obvious.

14 Manson, under the influence of literature on magic which he devoured avidly, also identified himself with mystical power figures, particularly with Abraxes, the shape-changing cabbalistic entity who supposedly frees men from the tyranny of time and allows participation in what Manson always called "the eternal now."

15 Manson also used mirrors in his seductions to reflect, multiply and distance the sexual act, expanding sexuality out of immediate bodily sensations and into the realm of observation, breaking down the intimate and inner privacy, the personal mystery, of sexuality. Eroticism, which is, as Riesman (1961) notes, the last refuge of felt inner truth for the outer-directed person, thus loses its private essence and becomes an experience of otherness. This helps denude the individual of the last vestiges of autonomy, and prepares the way for later fusion in the group orgy.

16 The reader will recall that Hitler too was a failed artist who took into politics and personal relations the artist's vision of a reality that can be

molded by the action of creative will.

17 There was some justification for Manson's belief. He had befriended one of the members of a famous singing group and also knew their manager. He had hoped to sell them some of his songs, and a slightly altered lyric of Manson's was actually used in one of their albums ("cease to exist" became "cease to resist"), but Manson was not given credit.

18 There was another, more mundane reason for the killings, which was to distract attention from the murder of a local man by some Family members who were extorting money from him. The idea was that the police would blame black militants for the murder. It is unclear how specific a plan of action Manson actually had in mind when he began his killing spree. It is likely that, as Atkins writes, he was responding to his increasing paranoia by attacking, hoping to instigate action to which he could then instinctively react, trusting to his connection with higher powers to guide him correctly (Atkins 1978). Certainly he himself believed in the existence of the magical pit, and led his followers out into the desert to find it after the murders had been committed.

10 "The Only God You'll Ever See": Jim Jones and the Peoples Temple

1 Although tape recordings make most of the sequence of the mass suicide clear, the final act remains equivocal. Jones sent some of his closest followers out of Jonestown with large sums of money before the carnage, leading some to think he may have intended to decamp, but was killed before he could escape. However, his own words seem to indicate a man very tired of living.

2 Jones always kept a close tie with his mother, and she died in Jonestown shortly before the mass suicide.

3 Jones refashioned his early life in a taped autobiography found in Jonestown, making himself out as a political radical and rebel from an early age. We need not accept this attempt to create a heroic self-image at face value, but we should take seriously Jones's psychological self-portrait – especially when it is relatively unflattering, and when that portrait fits with what we know of charismatic personality types.

4 Again, what is important here is not so much the specific content of the revelation, nor even its actual occurrence, but the imagery of transformation and inner detachment.

5 The dramatic performance of faith-healing is a theatrical genre rather reminiscent of carnival magic shows; it follows a set sequence demonstrating the magical power of the traveling evangelical tent preacher. First the performer "discovers" facts about the audience, demonstrating his mystical ability of telepathy. Then, having gained their confidence, he preaches, calling on God to enter him and to cure

the sick who line up before him. The bolt of healing power channeled through the preacher often knocks down the seekers, who rise cured from their afflictions. Jones had a knack for the tricks of the trade, and even originated his own variation, a "cancer" of rotted chicken innards that he miraculously extracted from awestruck members of the audience.

Later, he used the young women of the elite cadre of the Peoples Temple to prowl through garbage cans and enter houses in order to find information that Jones could later magically discern during his sermons. These women even developed an elaborate filing system of "secrets" which could be revealed to convince the gullible of Jones's authority.

6 Jones made an attempt to take over Father Divine's wealthy church and actually converted some members into his congregation by pretending to raise the dead and to perform other miracles. Father Divine's wife, who had succeeded to the leadership of the church after her husband's death, was not impressed by Jones, and ordered him off her property.

7 It is noteworthy that during this self-imposed exile Jones retained control of the mother church by the same methods Hitler used while he was imprisoned, i.e. by adroitly appointing different leaders and keeping any rivals split. Noteworthy as well is the pattern of withdrawal and return, which is a common motif for charismatic figures.

8 Jones later claimed to have made money for his family while in Brazil by becoming a gigolo.

9 The PC was the upper echelon of believers, made up mostly of the better-educated white followers, and it more closely resembled the "cult" as it is ordinarily thought of, while the rank and file of believers were more like a millenarian religious sect.

10 During these sessions, Jones graphically exemplified his exalted position by eating fruit and steak while the PC members went hungry, and reclining while his feet were massaged by a specially privileged member of the community. It must be stressed that the PC members felt this was completely appropriate. Jones did not ask to have himself exalted – they did it for him, reasoning that they could never do enough to repay Jones for his suffering on their behalf.

11 According to Reiterman and Jacobs (1982), Jones solicited an undercover police officer in the men's room of a cinema showing *Dirty Harry*.

12 Jones became drug addicted in the late fifties, when he first began evidencing paranoia and showing the pattern of collapse in times of stress that he would repeat throughout his life. At the time, he claimed the injections he took were B12. Later he clearly became drug dependent, even though he maintained in the group a strict taboo on the use of drugs, as well as other stimulants such as alcohol and tobacco. When he died, an autopsy showed high concentrations of phenobarbital in his system.

13 In fact, Judith Weightman (1983) has estimated that of the 26 different possible commitment mechanisms outlined by Rosabeth Kanter (1972), Jonestown used 24. It is worth mentioning here that Jones, like Hitler

and many other charismatic actors, had actually studied crowd psychology and the sociology of groups, and used information in this literature to initiate new indoctrination procedures.

14 All of these women were rivals for his attention, and he was well aware how jealousy could be used to maintain their loyalty. "I tell them all I love them most," Jones said. "Actually, I love only the Cause" (Jim Jones quoted in Mills 1979: 256).

15 Jones made great use of the breaking of taboos in his sermons, abusing the Bible, and getting his congregation (who mostly came from quite conservative religious backgrounds) to join him in chanted curses. The emotional energy released by this technique was explosive.

16 Jones had managed to get Timothy Stoen, the father of the child, to sign a confession that he had asked Jones to impregnate his wife. After leaving the Temple Stoen repudiated this statement. For Jones, Stoen became the embodiment of the forces arrayed against him, probably because he threatened Jones's claimed omnipotence by initiating a law suit against him. In his last speech, Jones justified mass suicide by saying "We win when we go down. Tim Stoen has nobody else to hate. Then he'll destroy himself" (quoted in Reiterman and Jacobs 1982: 558).

17 "His obsession with his place in history was maniacal. When pondering the loss of what he considered his rightful place in history, he would grow despondent and say that all was lost" (Kilduff and Javers 1979: 118).

11 "Technicians of the Sacred": Shamans and Society

1 Although widespread, shamanism is not found in every simple society. However, I would argue that the function of the shaman, i.e. the embodiment and transmission of vital force, will be served in some fashion everywhere, though the mode may be different.

In Melanesia, for instance, the power of life is conveyed by complex, large-scale exchanges and shared production of surplus, which affirm fertility in ritual performance located around an entrepreneurial big man. But even these societies, under stress, have produced charismatic figures as symbolic heads of millenaristic cargo cults (Worsley 1968).

2 I use the masculine pronoun here, but note that shamans are sometimes women. When a society becomes larger and shamanism is marginalized, female shamans become more prevalent (Ohnuki-Tierney 1980). This is an instance of the "powers of the weak" I shall discuss later in this chapter.

3 There are, however, enormous controversies in the literature about the exact way to categorize shamans. I refer the reader to Eliade (1964), Hultkrantz (1978), and Shirokogoroff (1935) for representative statements. Considerable discourse continues to be devoted to the question of whether shamanistic ecstasy is distinguishable from possession

by a spirit, as occurs in Voodoo rituals, or whether a shaman must be aware of what occurs in the trance, or whether the entranced performer is unconscious. Does a shaman have to have a tutelary spirit, or is the relationship between ecstatic vision and a guardian spirit "dialectically fortuitous," as Benedict argued (1923: 20)? And so on. Nonetheless, the assumption of an altered state of subjective, ecstatic trance remains at the heart of shamanism, whatever other definitions are offered. And in all cases, the shaman is a public performer, whose ability to go into trance and induce trance in others is believed to be beneficial to the collective.

4 The question of the shaman's sanity has been a subject of debate, since shamans often not only look strange, they also act strangely, and a nervous and excitable temperament is cited by Bogoras as a prerequisite for the vocation (1904: 426–8; see also Jochelson 1926: 187, Kroeber 1952, Eliade 1964: 306, Devereux 1961: 1,089). On the other hand, Boyer claims that Apache shamans are actually saner than others in the group, with a greater capacity to "regress in the ego's service" (Boyer et al. 1964: 173; see also Shweder 1972, Handelman 1968). As I shall outline it, from a structural perspective, the relative "sanity" of the shaman is probably inversely related both to the degree of social complexity and the marginalization of the shaman in the culture.

However, in very simple societies, the shaman may be obliged to appear and act odd as a way of proclaiming a distinctive role as mediator in a social formation where there are no other status markers. This "oddness" is actually highly stereotyped, and often involves transvestism, which graphically symbolizes the practitioner's "border-line" status. Like the "strange" look, cross-dressing too is essentially a part of the uniform of the shaman, and does not necessarily imply homosexuality, any more than a habitually abstracted expression implies insanity (Czaplicka 1914: 243–55).

5 This is, of course, instrumental, since control of animals is crucial for hunting and herding societies. But identification with the animal world is symbolically stressed too, so that the shaman typically feels himself to be "as one with" his animal familiars (Lame Deer and Erdoes 1972: 156).

However, the blurring between the shaman's self and nature also illustrates the ambivalence of shamanism, since the shaman may acquire not only the helping power but also the violent and even man-eating habits of his animal opposites. We recall in this context the special relationship Hitler, Manson, and Jones all had with the animal world. All of them seemed to have a marked and apparently uncanny attraction for animals; Hitler even liked to call himself a wolf, while Manson portrayed himself as a coyote, and Jim Jones surrounded himself with pets throughout his life.

6 The image of the shaman as a self-aware performer means that the sincerity of the performer becomes a matter of dispute. Certainly, most shamans do use feats of legerdemain and other tricks of the trade to

increase the awe and reverence of the audience, and for some performers these tricks may be the whole content of their profession.

In actuality, however, it seems that there is usually more to the shaman than trickery. We find a fair degree of consensus among observers, both native and foreign, that the "best" shamans do indeed enter an altered state of consciousness while shamanizing. And shamans themselves also assert the validity of their trance states. Nordland reports, for instance, that American Indian shamans who have become Christians, and who strongly repudiate their old religious practices, continue to insist on the reality of their shamanistic experiences (1962).

Furthermore, a charlatan may come to actually believe in the magical powers attributed him by the audience, and to take his powers seriously, as Franz Boas has documented in the case of the cynical Kwakiutl shaman Quesalid discussed in Lévi-Strauss (1963). We see a similar process in the case of Jim Jones, who used chicanery, but who still believed in his miraculous powers to cure. It is also interesting that even total frauds are themselves often the clients of other mystical healers (Bainbridge and Stark 1980). Apparently confidence tricksters are rarely cynics, and are usually easily deceived themselves.

7 The symbiotic relationship between performer and audience is evidenced by the fact that the belief and cooperation of the audience is absolutely necessary if the performance is to succeed. For instance, Shirokogoroff notes that the Tungus shaman cannot perform before an unsympathetic audience, and Hultkrantz says that the spirit lodge shamans, like many modern spiritualists, would refuse to perform if an unbeliever were in their midst.

8 The !Kung speak a language in which tongue clicks are phonemes. (!) is a click with the tip of the tongue against the roof of the mouth, (/) is a click with the middle of the tongue.

9 Among the !Kung, fire is the archetypical n/um, and awakens the n/um within the dancers' bodies, so it will emerge during the dance in vivifying sweat. Similarly, the Nilotic Dinka imagine the charismatic generative power they call Flesh to be like a flickering fire or flaring lamp (Lienhardt 1961), and elsewhere shamans often show their power by walking on fire, or playing with fire. Elias Canetti has noted how often fire is taken as the natural symbol of the contagion of charisma in a group, spreading from a central spark to inflame the surrounding crowd (1978). We have seen already how powerfully the symbol of fire was used by Hitler.

10 It has been argued that the rampage of the new shaman is probably at least partly a reaction to the docility demanded by the !Kung in daily life; the expressions of rage and hostility show that the onset of !kia is a kind of ritual of rebellion, not against an elite, but against a social structure that denies all acts of aggression. The onlookers also get a degree of satisfaction from their secondary participation in this forbidden behavior. The apprentice shamans' actions symbolize as well entrance into a new status; they have ceased to be ordinary human beings, but are not yet masters of !kia, and their in-between nature is marked by

wildness and manifestations of loss of identity and self-restraint.

These explanations are undoubtedly correct, but one must not forget as well the existential truth of the novice's condition, as his personal identity is lost in the "death" of the trance, and the energies released are as yet unintegrated into the community at large.

11 This relationship between n/um and fertility is expressed in the variety of places n/um appears. It occurs not only in fire, but also in boiling water, in ripening plants, and in the onset of menses. In the same manner, the Dinka envision the deity Flesh which possesses them as manifested in the spurting blood and trembling body of a newly slaughtered sacrificial beast. Other shamanic symbolism shows the same association between vitality and trance.

In societies at this level, women often do not participate much in these rituals of revitalization. Their rituals are more personal. This distinction is structurally related to the fact that women are actually the centers of vital power in these cultures that are focused on reproduction. Male peripherality is compensated for in these rituals where men take the central role. As we shall see, as society becomes more complex and women's roles are marginalized, they then become more involved in compensatory shamanic charismatic cults.

12 Conversely, even in highly routinized and complex archaic social formations, the charismatic component of leadership often remained important. For instance, in Preclassical Mayan society elaborate public rituals focused on the shaman-king's manifestation of "personal charismatic power" (Freidel and Schele 1988: 550). Similarly, in ancient China the ruler was the "head shaman" who had a special capacity to incarnate the sacred (Chang 1983: 45).

13 The liberation struggles of many nations have been marked by similar charismatic eruptions. The "Shining Path" that has so disrupted Peru is a modern version of such a millennial "antistructural" movement, as was the advent of Ayatollah Khomeini.

14 Certainly many followed these leaders because of the leader's values, or for other less idealistic reasons, and in these cases the relationship was not primarily charismatic. But there is no doubt that even for those motivated in the first instance by values or by pragmatic gain, a component of powerful emotional attraction for the leader who embodied the revolutionary cause entered in, inspiring followers to risk their lives in seemingly hopeless struggles. Naturally, the personal style of each leader will differ along cultural lines, since he embodies an inspiring, ideal man, and ideals vary cross-culturally. As Willner has shown, in such situations, "the leader who becomes charismatic is the one who can inadvertently or deliberately tap the reservoir of relevant myths in his culture" (1984: 62), expressing in his person both a deep continuity with the threatened past, and a willingness to heroically remake the future. These differences, however, do not keep us from seeing these individuals as charismatics, and Willner, in fact, demonstrates that the following in all of these instances evidences the typical

characteristics of a charismatic group; i.e. an irrational willingness to accept the leader's word simply because he said it, a belief that the leader is superhuman, an abdication of personal choice and judgement in favor of absolute compliance, and an ecstatic worship of and emotional commitment to the leader.

15 Another related factor also presses toward an increase in the durability and awesome character of the charismatic in contemporary cults. Given the modern context, a successful group must marshal bureaucratic organization and technique, "the very agencies against which its basic thrust should be directed" (Wilson 1975: 113), to insure the movement's expansion and support the leader's authority. We have then the apparently contradictory spectacle of highly sophisticated fund-raising organizations and media campaigns coincident with a charismatic annunciation of the end of all rationality.

As we saw in our case studies, charismatic leaders may struggle against the rigidification and constraint these techniques and structures imply (see Wallis 1984 for examples). Nonetheless, the more the manifestations of the charismatic aura are known to be manufactured, the more strongly the believers, to escape cognitive dissonance, assert that beneath the technique is an unquestionable essence of true charismatic power. It is partially for this reason that the inner core of members, who know the secrets of manipulation, do not become cynics, but are usually stronger believers in the divinity of the leader than the outer circle.

12 Charisma Today

1 The reader will recall that shamans are not only the prototypical religious figures, but also the paradigmatic artists and entertainers.

2 There is naturally a strong effort by each group to draw people out of this peripheral status and into more and more intense commitment. This is done by promising "gains" in awareness and higher status through increased participation in cult programs and indoctrination. Recruiting new members is also enjoined as a demonstration of enlightenment, thus obliging the new convert to proselytize others and thereby solidify his or her own beliefs by making public statements of commitment. Group activities are promoted as well as ways to make progress, and work to increase solidarity.

3 Wallis has argued that the increased centralization and cultic atmosphere of secular world-affirming movements is also in part a consequence of the founder's effort to retain marketing control over the teaching he has propounded. This leads him to turn a secular knowledge system into a religion focused on himself as a charismatic messenger. If this transformation works, it provides the client loyalty that will maintain the business, prevent others from marketing similar knowledge systems,

and stabilize his authority. Wallis calls this "transcendentalising one's product" (1984: 101). But he leaves aside the question of why any member should accept the leader's grandiose claims to charismatic ascendance, though he does show why such claims make good marketing sense.

4 The world-affirming movements are evidently well-suited forms of charisma in the modern world, disguising their radical content beneath an entrepreneurial and individualistic ideology. But they are not new. Similar movements are found in European history from the time of the Greeks, as gnostic cultists sought "to surpass the condition of humanity and to become God" through shamanistic processes of self-abnegation, fragmentation of identity, and transformation under the tutelage of a deified master (Cohn 1970: 174). As in modern new age movements, the appeal of this doctrine was not to the impoverished and oppressed, but to the bored and frustrated who felt that their lives had lost zest and meaning. And, again as in modern affirmative cults, this mystical form of charismatic revelation permitted worldly pleasure and success, as well as withdrawal and asceticism, and therefore did not have the overt revolutionary content of charismatic uprisings of the poor and marginal. Nor was it centralized, and generally consisted instead, as in the new age environment, of a "cultic milieu" of seekers following various wandering adepts who travelled through the countryside. Nonetheless, even these earlier advents of mystical anarchism had the potential to become centralized and millenaristic given the right leader and the right circumstances, as Norman Cohn brilliantly documents (1970).

5 Therapeutic groups have themselves occasionally escalated into cults when a therapist of charismatic personality decided to expand his power beyond the office and to dominate the patients' lives (Kriegman and Solomon 1985b). Therapeutic techniques are also widely used by new age religions and other cultic groups as indoctrination methods – especially the reliving of traumas in public as a way of stimulating an abreactive catharsis which is then attributed to the philosophy of the cult's leader.

6 Romantic love must have the potential for mutuality, and so cannot be for a thing, or a cause, but only for a person. Unlike the love of the medieval courtier, which always emphasized the inferiority of the lover to the beloved, romantic love in the modern world is equalizing. It therefore cannot include the love of a mother for a child, or the love of God. This does not distinguish it from charisma, however, since in the charismatic relation the tie between leader and follower is conceived of and felt as mutual and as elevating for the follower, who identifies with the grandiose leader.

7 This belief is strong despite the fact that most romantic attachment is located within strict boundaries of age, race, class and even neighborhood. Nonetheless, "love conquers all" – even if the conquest is really not very difficult. What is symbolized in this imagery is the fundamental

214   *Notes*

capacity of love to break the boundaries of the self and to produce a
fusion between separate individuals. Given the strong individualism of
Western society, the self-loss of love is then rhetorically extended to
erode all of the less compelling boundaries denoted by the categories
of class and race.

8 A number of historians (for example, Stone 1978 and Shorter 1975)
   envisioned the romantic love complex in the West as a functional
   response to the breakup of kin networks at the beginnings of the
   industrial age (see Segalen 1986 for an opposing perspective). Some
   anthropologists have made similar efforts to show the function of love
   and have correlated residence patterns and relative degree of economic
   independence of spouses (Coppinger and Rosenblatt 1968, Rosenblatt
   1978, Mukhopadhyay 1979). The results of all of this historical and
   ethnographic research have been contradictory and inconclusive.
     My own material indicates that romantic love complexes are especially
   likely among people inhabiting an extremely competitive, fluid and
   unreliable environment, who have a dominant ethos of individual action
   for personal self-interest, who lack any secure identity markers to offer
   refuge from antagonism, and who also lack alternative possibilities for
   identification. An example is the American Indian Ojibway (Landes
   1969; see Lindholm n.d. and Solomon 1981 for more on the structural
   contexts favoring the development of romantic love).

9 Another similarity is that social science has generally denied the salience
   and social relevance of both experiences. Love, like charisma, is often
   conceptualized as a mask for more venal and pragmatic motives, or else
   as a kind of disease. If taken seriously, it is seen in Weberian terms as
   an irrational and non-analyzable charismatic precursor to the rational
   institution of marriage. Nonetheless, just as charismatic followers
   continue to deify leaders, attitudinal tests by social psychologists show
   that Americans continue to believe in and live out the stereotypes of
   romantic involvement (see Huston and Burgess 1979, Rubin 1973,
   Levinger 1977, Driscoll et al. 1972 for examples; for a more elaborate
   comparison of the structural similarities and differences between love
   and charisma, see Lindholm 1988a).

10 See Kornhauser (1959) for a discussion of the relationship between
   dyads and the state. Cohen (1968) makes a similar point, arguing that
   the formation of romantic dyads is actually favored by state systems as
   a way of breaking up larger, potentially dangerous social formations
   such as lineages.

11 Similar patterns are found in many charismatic communes, such as the
   sanctions against "special love" in John Humphrey Noyes's Oneida
   community (Kephart 1987). In the Nazi movement, romantic idealization
   was negated by German attitudes toward sexual relations (Schaffner
   1948). These attitudes were exaggerated by Hitler's eugenic approach
   to childbearing, which brought sexuality under state auspices. Other
   strategies for breaking the dyad may be found in the enforced celibacy

of the Shakers, or, most radically, in the castration enjoined by the Russian sect of the Skopzi.

12 In some senses, what I am predicting is a resurgence of shamanistic practice, though of course in a different guise. It may seem unlikely that the highly complex modern social system would be conducive to such "primitive" cultural traits, but the fact is that our society and some of those that are characterized by shamanism are not so far apart in many essential ways – particularly in the importance of the individual, the highly pressured social environment, the intensive struggle for survival that makes people rivals, and the feeling of being controlled by external forces. I have discussed some of these similarities, and their consequences for the revelation of emotion, in a recent work (Lindholm 1988b), and intend to write a more complex account in the future.

13 As an early est convert writes, "we weren't people selling soap. We were perfect beings on the path of enlightenment" (quoted in Tipton 1982: 210).

Bibliography

Abel, Theodore 1938: *Why Hitler Came into Power: An Answer Based on the Original Life Stories of Six Hundred of his Followers.* New York: Prentice Hall.

Adas, Michael 1979: *Prophets of Rebellion: Millenarian Protest Movements against European Colonial Order.* Chapel Hill, NC: University of North Carolina Press.

Adler, Gerald 1979: The Myth of Alliance with Borderline Patients. *American Journal of Psychiatry,* 136, 642–5.

Adorno, Theodor et al. 1950: *The Authoritarian Personality.* New York: Harpers.

Alberoni, Francesco 1983: *Falling in Love.* New York: Random House.

Allen, William 1984: *The Nazi Seizure of Power.* New York: Franklin Watts.

Appel, Willa 1983: *Cults in America: Programmed for Paradise.* New York: Holt, Rinehart and Winston.

Arendt, Hanna 1973: *Totalitarianism.* New York: Harcourt Brace Jovanovich.

Atkins, Susan with Slosser, Bob 1977: *Child of Satan, Child of God.* Plainfield, NJ: Logos.

Bainbridge, William 1978: *Satan's Power: A Deviant Psychotherapy Cult.* Berkeley, CA: University of California Press.

Bainbridge, William and Stark, Rodney 1980: Scientology: To Be Perfectly Clear. *Sociological Analysis,* 41, 128–36.

Becker, Ernest 1973: *The Denial of Death.* New York: Free Press.

Becker, Howard 1946: *German Youth: Bond or Free.* New York: Oxford University Press.

Beigel, H. 1951: Romantic Love. *American Sociological Review,* 16, 326–34.

Bellah, Robert 1973: Introduction. In Robert Bellah (ed.), *Emile Durkheim on Morality and Society.* Chicago: University of Chicago Press.

——, Madsen, Richard, Sullivan, William, Swidler, Ann and Tipton, Steven 1985: *Habits of the Heart: Individualism and Commitment in American Life.* New York: Harper and Row.

Benedict, Ruth 1923: The Concept of the Guardian Spirit in North America. *Memoirs of the American Anthropological Association,* vol. 29.

Bensman, Joseph and Givant, Michael 1975: Charisma and Modernity: The Use and Abuse of a Concept. *Social Research*, 42, 570–614.

Bergmann, M. 1980: On the Intrapsychic Function of Falling in Love. *Psychoanalytic Quarterly*, 49, 56–77.

Berne, Eric 1978: *Transactional Analysis in Psychotherapy*, New York: Grove Press.

Bettelheim, Bruno 1943: Individual and Mass Behavior in Extreme Situations. *Journal of Abnormal and Social Psychology*, 38, 417–52.

Binion, Rudolph 1976: *Hitler Among the Germans*. New York: Elsevier.

Bion, Wilfred 1961: *Experiences in Groups*. New York: Basic Books.

Bird, F. 1979. The Pursuit of Innocence: New Religious Movements and Moral Accountability. *Sociological Analysis*, 40, 335–46.

Bogoras, Waldemar 1909: *The Chukchee. Memoirs of the Jesup North Pacific Expedition*, vol. 11. New York: American Museum of Natural History.

Bourguignon, Erika 1968: World Distribution and Patterns of Possession States. In Raymond Prince (ed.), *Trance and Possession States*, Montreal: R.M. Burket Memorial Society.

Boyer, L. Bruce et al. 1964: Comparison of Shamans and Pseudoshamans of the Apaches of the Mescalero Indian Reservation: A Rorschach Study. *Journal of Projective Techniques*, 28, 173–80.

Bromley, David and Shupe, Anson 1981: *Strange Gods: The Great American Cult Scare*. Boston: Beacon Press.

Bugliosi, Vincent with Gentry, Curt 1974: *Helter Skelter: The True Story of the Manson Murders*. New York: Norton.

Bullock, Alan 1962: *Hitler: A Study in Tyranny*. New York: Harper and Row.

Canetti, Elias 1978: *Crowds and Power*. New York: Seabury.

Chang, K.C. 1983: *Art, Myth, and Ritual: The Path to Political Authority in Ancient China*. Cambridge, MA: Harvard University Press.

Chasseguet-Smirgel, Jeannine 1976: Some Thoughts on the Ego Ideal. *Psychoanalytic Quarterly*, 45, 345–73.

Chessick, Robert 1979: A Practical Approach to the Psychotherapy of the Borderline Patient. *American Journal of Psychotherapy*, 33, 531–46.

Childs, David 1971: *Germany Since 1918*. New York: Harper and Row.

Cohen, Yehudi 1968: Ends and Means in Political Control. *American Anthropologist*, 71, 658–87.

Cohn, Norman 1970: *The Pursuit of the Millennium: Revolutionary Millenarians and Mystical Anarchists of the Middle Ages*. (Revised edition). New York: Oxford University Press.

Coppinger, R. and Rosenblatt, P. 1968: Romantic Love and Subsistence Dependency. *Southwestern Journal of Anthropology*, 24, 310–19.

Craig, Gordon 1978: *Germany 1866–1945*. New York: Oxford University Press.

Czaplicka, M. 1914: *Aboriginal Siberia*. Oxford: Clarendon Press.

Dahrendorf, Ralf 1979: *Society and Democracy in Germany*. New York: Norton.

Darnton, Robert 1968: *Mesmerism and the End of the Enlightenment in France.* New York: Schocken.

Deikman, Arthur 1972: Deautomatization and the Mystic Experience. In Charles Tart (ed.), *Altered States of Consciousness,* New York: Doubleday.

Demos, Virginia 1988: Affect and the Development of the Self: A New Frontier. In Arnold Goldberg (ed.), *Frontiers in Self Psychology,* vol. 3, Hillsdale, NJ: The Analytic Press.

Deren, Maya 1953: *Divine Horsemen.* London: Thames and Hudson.

Descartes, René 1972: *Discourse on Method and Meditations.* Harmondsworth: Penguin.

Deutsch, Alexander 1980: Tenacity of Affiliation to a Cult Leader – A Psychiatric Perspective. *American Journal of Psychiatry,* 137, 1,569–73.

——1983: Psychiatric Perspectives on an Eastern-style Cult. In David Halperin (ed.), *Psychodynamic Perspectives on Religion, Sect and Cult,* Boston: John Wright.

Devereux, Georges 1955: Charismatic Leadership and Crisis. In W. Muensterberger and S. Axelrod (eds), *Psychoanalysis and the Social Sciences,* New York: International Universities Press.

——1961: Shamans as Neurotics. *American Anthropologist,* 63, 1,088–90.

Dicks, H.V. 1972: *Licensed Mass Murder: A Social Psychological Study of some SS Killers.* London: Sussex University Press.

Diderot, Denis 1964: *Rameau's Nephew.* New York: Bobbs-Merrill.

Douglas, Mary 1970: *Natural Symbols.* Harmondsworth: Penguin.

Downtown, James V. 1979: *Sacred Journeys: The Conversion of Young Americans to Divine Light Mission.* New York: Columbia University Press.

Driscoll, D., Davis, K. and Lipetz, M. 1972: Parental Interference and Romantic Love: The Romeo and Juliet Effect. *Journal of Personality and Social Psychology,* 24, 1–10.

Durkheim, Emile 1965: *The Elementary Forms of the Religious Life.* New York: Free Press.

——1966: *Suicide.* New York: Free Press.

——1973: The Dualism of Human Nature and its Social Conditions. In Robert Bellah (ed.), *Emile Durkheim on Morality and Society,* Chicago: University of Chicago Press.

——1982: *The Rules of Sociological Method.* New York: Macmillan.

——1984: *The Division of Labor in Society.* New York: Free Press.

Eagle, Morris 1984: *Recent Developments in Psychoanalysis.* Cambridge, MA: Harvard University Press.

Eliade, Mircea 1964: *Shamanism: Archaic Techniques of Ecstasy.* Princeton, NJ: Princeton University Press.

Elias, Norbert 1983: *Court Society.* New York: Basil Blackwell.

Ellenberger, Henri 1970: *The Discovery of the Unconscious.* New York: Basic Books.

Ellwood, Robert Jr 1973: *Religious and Spiritual Groups in Modern America.* Englewood Cliffs, NJ: Prentice-Hall.

Emmons, Nuel 1988: *Manson in His Own Words*. New York: Grove Press.
Erikson, Erik 1970: On the Nature of Psycho-historical Evidence: In Search of Gandhi. In D. Rustow (ed.), *Philosophers and Kings*, New York, Braziller.
——1985: *Childhood and Society*, New York: Norton.
Fairbairn, W. 1954: *The Object-Relations Theory of the Personality*. New York: Basic Books.
Feinsod, Ethan 1981: *Awake in a Nightmare*. New York: Norton.
Fest, Joachim 1974: *Hitler*. New York: Harcourt Brace Jovanovich.
Festinger, Leon, Riecken, Henry and Schacter, Stanley 1956: *When Prophecy Fails*. Minneapolis: University of Minnesota Press.
Fiske, M. 1980: Changing Hierarchies of Commitment in Adulthood. In N. Smelser and E. Erikson (eds), *Themes of Love and Work in Adulthood*. Cambridge, MA: Harvard University Press.
Fitzgerald, Frances 1986: Rajneeshpuram – Part I. *New Yorker*, 22 Sept., 46–96.
Freud, Sigmund 1950: *Totem and Taboo*. New York: Norton.
——1957: On Narcissism: An Introduction. In *The Complete Psychological Works of Sigmund Freud*, London: Hogarth, vol. 14.
——1959: *Group Psychology and the Analysis of the Ego*. New York: Norton.
——1962: *Civilization and its Discontents*. New York: Norton.
——1977: *Introductory Lectures on Psychoanalysis*. New York: Norton.
Fried, Morton 1965: *Readings in Anthropology*, vol. 2. New York: Thomas Y. Crowell.
Friedel, David and Schele, Luda 1988: Kingship in the Late Preclassic Maya Lowlands: The Instruments and Places of Ritual Power. *American Anthropologist*, 90, 547–67.
Fromm, Erich 1941: *Escape from Freedom*. New York: Holt, Rinehart and Winston.
Fromme, Lynette 1975: Memoirs of Squeaky Fromme. *Time*, 15 September, 12–14.
Furet, François 1981: *Interpreting the French Revolution*. London: Cambridge University Press.
Galanter, M. et al. 1979: The Moonies: A Psychological Study of Conversion and Membership in a Contemporary Religious Sect. *American Journal of Psychiatry*, 136, 165–70.
Gallagher, Nora 1979: Jonestown: The Survivors Story. *New York Times Magazine*, 18 November, 124–36.
Gay, Peter 1985: *Freud for Historians*. New York: Oxford University Press.
Geller, J. and Howard, G. 1972: Some Sociopsychological Characteristics of Student Political Activists. *Journal of Applied Social Psychology*, 22, 114–37.
Gellner, Ernest 1985: *Relativism and the Social Sciences*. Cambridge: Cambridge University Press.
Gilbert, G.M. 1950: *The Psychology of Dictatorship*. New York: Ronald Press.

Glassman, Ronald 1975: Legitimacy and Manufactured Charisma. *Social Research*, 42, 615–36.

Goffman, Erving 1959: *The Presentation of Self in Everyday Life*. New York: Doubleday Anchor.

——1968: *Asylums*. Harmondsworth, Penguin.

Green, Martin 1974: *The Von Richthofen Sisters: The Triumphant and the Tragic Modes of Love*. New York: Basic Books.

Greenfield, Liah 1985: Reflections on the Two Charismas. *British Journal of Sociology*, 36, 117–32.

Grim, John 1983: *The Shaman: Patterns of Siberian and Ojibway Healing*. Norman, OK: University of Oklahoma Press.

Guenther, Mathias 1975: The Trance Dance as an Agent of Social Change among the Farm Bushmen of the Ghanzi District. *Botswana Notes and Records*, 7, 161–6.

Gutman, David 1973: The Subjective Politics of Power: The Dilemma of Post-Superego Man. *Social Research*, 40, 570–616.

Habermas, Jürgen 1979: *Communication and the Evolution of Society*. Boston: Beacon.

Hall, John 1982: The Apocalypse at Jonestown. In Ken Levi (ed.), *Violence and Religious Commitment: Implications of Jim Jones' People's Temple Movement*. University Park: Pennsylvania State.

Hall, John A. 1987: *Liberalism, Politics, Ideology and the Market*. Chapel Hill, NC: University of North Carolina Press.

Halperin, David 1983: Group Processes in Cult Affiliation and Recruitment. In David Halperin (ed.), *Psychodynamic Perspectives on Religion, Sect and Cult*, Boston: John Wright.

Handelman, Don 1968: Shamanizing on an Empty Stomach. *American Anthropologist*, 70, 353–5.

Hanfstaengl, Ernst 1957: *Unheard Witnesses*. Philadelphia: J.B. Lippincott.

Heiden, Konrad 1935: *A History of National Socialism*. New York: Knopf.

Heinlein, Robert 1968: *Stranger in a Strange Land*. New York: Berkley.

Herf, Jeffrey 1984: *Reactionary Modernism: Technology, Culture and Politics in Weimar and the Third Reich*. Cambridge: Cambridge University Press.

Hine, Virginia 1974: The Deprivation and Disorganization Theories of Social Movements. In Irving Zaretsky and Mark Leone (eds), *Religious Movements in Contemporary America*. Princeton, NJ: Princeton University Press.

Hirschman, Albert O. 1977: *The Passions and the Interests: Political Arguments for Capitalism before its Triumph*. Princeton, NJ: Princeton University Press.

Holborn, Hajo 1970: *A History of Modern Germany, 1840–1945*. New York: Knopf.

Hoffer, Eric 1951: *The True Believer*. New York: Harper and Row.

Hughes, Richard 1961: *The Fox in the Attic*. New York: Harper and Row.

Hultkrantz, A. 1962: Spirit Lodge, a North American Shamanistic Seance.

In Carl Erdsman (ed.), *Studies in Shamanism*, Abo, Norway: Scripta Instituti Donneriani Aboensis.

——1978: Ecological and Phenomenonological Aspects of Shamanism. In V. Dioszegi and M. Hoppal (eds), *Shamanism in Siberia*, Budapest: Academiai Kiado.

Hume, David 1964: *Essays Moral, Political and Literary*, eds T.H. Green and T.H. Grose (2 vols). Aalen, Germany: Scientia Verlag.

——1978: *A Treatise of Human Nature*, ed. L.A. Selby-Bigge. London: Oxford University Press.

Hunt, Lynn 1984: *Politics, Culture and Class in the French Revolution.* Berkeley: University of California Press.

Huston, T. and Burgess, R. 1979: Social Exchange in Developing Relationships. In R. Burgess and T. Huston (eds), *Social Exchange in Developing Relationships*. New York: Academic Press.

Jacobs, J. 1984: *The Mall*. Prospect Heights, IL: Waveland.

James, William 1929: *Varieties of Religious Experience*. New York: Modern Library.

Jochelson, Vladimir 1926: *The Yukaghir and the Yukaghirized Tungus. Memoirs of the Jesup North Pacific Expedition*, vol. 14. New York: American Museum of Natural History.

Jouvenel, Bertrand de 1958: Authority: The Efficient Imperative. In C. Friedrich (ed.), *Authority*. Cambridge, MA: Harvard University Press.

Kanter, Rosabeth Moss 1972: *Commitment and Community: Communes and Utopias in Sociological Perspective*. Cambridge, MA: Harvard University Press.

Katz, Richard 1982: *Boiling Energy: Community Healing among the Kalahari Kung.* Cambridge, MA: Harvard University Press.

Kennedy, Keven 1985: Manson at 50. *Harper's Magazine*, Sept. 28–9.

Kephart, William 1987: *Extraordinary Groups*. New York: St Martins.

Kernberg, Otto 1967: Borderline Personality Organization. *Journal of the American Psychoanalytic Association*, 15, 641–85.

——1977: Boundaries and Structure in Love Relationships. *Journal of the American Psychoanalytic Association*, 25, 81–144.

——1980: Love, the Couple and the Group: A Psychoanalytic Frame. *Psychoanalytic Quarterly*, 49, 78–108.

Kerns, Phil with Weed, Doug 1979: *People's Temple: People's Tomb.* Plainfield, NJ: Logos.

Kershaw, Ian 1987: *The Hitler Myth: Image and Reality in the Third Reich.* Oxford: Clarendon Press.

Kersten, Felix 1962: *The Kersten Memoirs 1940–1945*. New York: Macmillan.

Khaldun, Ibn 1981: *The Muqaddimah*. Princeton, NJ: Princeton University Press.

Kilduff, Marshall and Javers, Ron 1979: *The Suicide Cult*. New York: Bantam.

Klein, Melanie 1975: *Envy and Gratitude and Other Works*. New York: Dell.

Knox, R.A. 1950: *Enthusiasm: A Chapter in the History of Religion, with Special Reference to the XVII and romance XVIII Centuries.* New York: Oxford University Press.

Kohut, Heinz 1977: *The Restoration of the Self.* New York: International Universities Press.

——1985: *Self-Psychology and the Humanities.* New York: Norton.

Kornhauser, W. 1959: *The Politics of Mass Society.* New York: Free Press of Glencoe.

Kracauer, Siegfried 1974: *From Caligari to Hitler: A Psychological History of the German Film.* Princeton, NJ: Princeton University Press.

Krader, L. 1978: Shamanism: Theory and History in Buryat Society. In V. Dioszegi and M. Hoppal (eds), *Shamanism in Siberia,* Budapest: Academiai Kiado.

Kriegman, D. and Solomon, L. 1985a: Cult Groups and the Narcissistic Personality: The Offer to Heal Defects in the Self. *International Journal of Group Psychotherapy,* 35, 236–61.

——1985b: Psychotherapy and the "New Religions": Are they the Same? *Cultic Studies Journal,* 2, 2–16.

Kroeber, A. 1962: Psychosis or Social Sanction. In A. Kroeber (ed.), *The Nature of Culture,* Chicago: University of Chicago Press.

La Barre, Weston 1970: *The Ghost Dance.* New York: Doubleday.

Lame Deer, John and Erdoes, Richard 1972: *Lame Deer, Seeker of Visions.* New York: Simon and Schuster.

Lan, D.M. 1985: *Guns and Rain: Guerillas and Spirit Mediums in Zimbabwe.* London: James Currey.

Landes, Ruth 1969: *The Ojibwa Woman.* New York: AMS Press.

Langer, Walter 1972: *The Mind of Adolf Hitler: The Secret Wartime Report.* New York: Basic Books.

Lanteneri, V. 1963: *Religion in Context: The Religions of the Oppressed.* London: MacGibbon and Kee.

Lasch, Christopher 1977: *Haven in a Heartless World.* New York: Basic Books.

——1979: *The Culture of Narcissism: American Life in an Age of Diminishing Expectations.* New York: Norton.

——1984: *The Minimal Self.* New York: Norton.

Lasswell, Harold 1960: *Psychopathology and Politics.* New York: Viking.

Le Bon, Gustave 1952: *The Crowd: A Study of the Popular Mind.* London: Ernest Benn.

Lee, Richard 1968: The Sociology of the !Kung Bushman Trance Performances. In Raymond Prince (ed.), *Trance and Possesssion States,* Montreal: R.M. Burket Memorial Society.

Lesse, S. 1969: Revolution Vintage 1968: A Psychosocial View. *American Journal of Psychotherapy,* 23, 584–98.

Letwin, Shirley 1965: *The Pursuit of Certainty.* Cambridge: Cambridge University Press.

Levine, Saul 1984: Radical Departures. *Psychology Today,* August, 20–7.

Levinger, G. 1977: The Embrace of Lives: Changing and Unchanging. In

G. Levinger and H. Raush (eds), *Close Relationships: Perspectives on the Meaning of Intimacy.* Amherst, MA: University of Massachusetts Press.

Lévi-Strauss, Claude 1963: The Sorcerer and his Magic. In Claude Lévi-Strauss (ed.), *Structural Anthropology,* New York: Basic Books.

Lewis, I.M. 1971: *Ecstatic Religion: An Anthropological Study of Spirit Possession and Shamanism.* Harmondsworth: Penguin.

——1986: *Religion in Context: Cults and Charisma.* Cambridge: Cambridge University Press.

Lienhardt, Godfrey 1961: *Divinity and Experience: The Religion of the Dinka.* Oxford: Clarendon Press.

Lifton, Robert Jay 1961: *Thought Reform and the Psychology of Totalism.* New York: Norton.

——1969: *Boundaries: Psychological Man in Revolution.* New York: Simon and Schuster.

Lindholm, C. 1988a: Lovers and Leaders. *Social Science Information,* 16, 3–45.

——1988b: The Social Structure of Emotional Constraint. *Ethos,* 16, 227–46.

——unpublished MS, The Social Anthropology of Romantic Love.

Lipset, Seymour Martin 1979: *The First New Nation: The United States in Historical and Comparative Perspective.* New York: Norton.

Little, G. 1984: *Political Ensembles.* New York: Oxford University Press.

Lofland, John and Stark, Rodney 1965: Becoming a World Saver: A Theory of Conversion to a Deviation Perspective. *American Sociological Review,* 30, 862–74.

Lommel, Andreas 1967: *Shamanism: The Beginnings of Art.* New York: McGraw-Hill.

Ludecke, Kurt 1937: *I Knew Hitler.* New York: Scribner's.

Ludwig, Arnold 1972: Altered States of Consciousness. In Charles Tart (ed.), *Altered States of Consciousness,* New York: Doubleday.

Machiavelli, Niccolò 1988: *The Prince.* New York: Cambridge University Press.

MacIntyre, Alasdair 1981: *After Virtue: A Study in Moral Theory.* London: Duckworth.

McLellan, V. and Avery, P. 1977: *The Voices of Guns.* New York: Putnam.

Martin, David 1978: *A General Theory of Secularization.* New York: Harper and Row.

Mazlich, Bruce 1981: Leader and Led, Individual and Group. In *Psychiatry,* 9, 214–37.

Michelet, Jules 1967: *History of the French Revolution,* ed. Gordon Wright, tr. Charles Cocks. Chicago: University of Chicago Press.

Michels, Robert 1949: *First Lectures in Political Sociology,* tr. Alfred de Grizia. Minneapolis: University of Minnesota Press.

Mill, John Stuart 1975: *On Liberty.* New York: Norton.

Miller, J. 1980: Romantic Couples and the Group Process. In K. Pope (ed.), *On Love and Loving,* San Francisco: Jossey-Bass.

Mills, Jeannie 1979: *Six Years with God: Life Inside Rev. Jim Jones's Peoples Temple.* New York: A & W Publishers.

Mitscherlich, Alexander 1969: *Society Without the Father.* London: Tavistock.

Moore, Rebecca 1986: *The Jonestown Letters: Correspondence of the Moore Family 1970–1985.* Lewiston, MN: Edwin Mellen Press.

Moscovici, Serge 1985: *The Age of the Crowd: A Historical Treatise on Mass Psychology.* New York: Cambridge University Press.

Mosse, George 1964: *The Crisis of German Ideology.* New York: Grosset & Dunlap.

——1968: *Nazi Culture.* New York: Grosset & Dunlap.

Mukhopadhyay, C. 1979: The Functions of Romantic Love. *Behavior Science Research*, 14, 57–63.

Munn, Henry 1973: The Mushrooms of Language. In M. Harner (ed.), *Hallucinogens and Shamanism*, New York: Oxford University Press.

Murphy, Jane 1964: Psychotherapeutic Aspects of Shamanism on St Lawrence Island, Alaska. In A. Kiev, *Magic, Faith and Healing*, London: Free Press.

Nelson, Godfrey 1960: The Spiritualist Movement and the Need for a Redefinition of Cult. *Journal for the Scientific Study of Religion*, 8, 153–60.

Neumann, Franz 1942: *Behemoth.* London: Oxford University Press.

Nietzsche, Friedrich 1964: *The Will to Power*, tr. Anthony Ludovici. New York: Russell and Russell.

——1966: *Beyond Good and Evil.* New York: Vintage.

——1977: *The Twilight of the Idols and The Anti-Christ*, tr. R.J. Hollingdale. Harmondsworth: Penguin.

Noll, Richard 1983: Shamanism and Schizophrenia: A State Specific Approach to the "Schizophrenia Metaphor" of Shamanic States. *American Ethnologist*, 10, 443–59.

Nordland, Odd 1962: Shamanism as an Experiencing of "the Unreal." In Carl Erdsman (ed.), *Studies in Shamanism*, Abo, Norway: Scripta Instituti Donneriani Aboensis.

Nyomarkay, Joseph 1967: *Charisma and Factionalism in the Nazi Party.* Minneapolis: University of Minnesota Press.

Ohnuki-Tierney, Emiko 1980: Shamans and *Imu* Among Two Ainu Groups. *Ethos*, 8, 204–28.

Olsson, Peter 1983: Adolescent Involvement with the Supernatural and Cults. In David Halperin (ed.), *Psychodynamic Perspectives on Religion, Sect and Cult*, Boston: John Wright.

O'Toole, Roger 1975: Sectarianism in Politics: Case Studies of Maoists and De Leonists. In Roy Wallis (ed.), *Sectarianism*, London: Peter Owen.

Ozouf, Mona 1988: *Festivals and the French Revolution.* Cambridge, MA: Harvard University Press.

Peters, Larry 1982: Trance, Initiation and Psychotherapy in Tamang Shamanism. *American Ethnologist*, 9, 21–46.

Pope, Kenneth 1980: Defining and Studying Romantic Love. In K. Pope (ed.), *On Love and Loving*, San Francisco: Jossey-Bass.

Rauschning, Hermann 1940: *The Voice of Destruction*. New York: Putnam.

Rebhan, James 1983: The Drug Rehabilitation Program: Cults in Formation? In David Halperin (ed.), *Psychodynamic Perspectives on Religion, Sect and Cult*, Boston: John Wright.

Reich, Wilhelm 1970: *The Mass Psychology of Fascism*. New York: Farrar, Straus and Giroux.

Reik, T. 1972: *A Psychologist Looks at Love*. New York: Holt, Rinehart and Winston.

Reiterman, Tim with Jacobs, John 1982: *Raven: The Untold Story of the Rev. Jim Jones and his People*. New York: Dutton.

Reston, James Jr 1981: *Our Father Who Art in Hell*. New York: Times Books.

Richardson, James T. 1982: A Comparison Between Jonestown and Other Cults. In Ken Levi (ed.), *Violence and Religious Commitment: Implications of Jim Jones's People's Temple Movement*, University Park, PA: Pennsylvania State.

Riesman, David with Glazer, Nathan and Denny, Ruel 1961: *The Lonely Crowd*. New Haven: Yale University Press. (Abridged, with a new foreword).

Rivera, Geraldo 1988: *Murder: Live from Death Row*. In *Geraldo Transcripts*, 55. New York: Investigative News Group Inc.

Robbins, Thomas and Anthony, Dick 1978: New Religions, Families and Brainwashing. *Society*, May/June, 77–83.

Roheim, Geza 1970: The Origin and Function of Culture. In W. Muensterberger (ed.), *Man and His Culture*, New York: Taplinger.

Rosenblatt, P. 1967: Marital Residence and the Function of Romantic Love. *Ethnology*, 6, 471–80.

——1978: Cross-Cultural Perspectives on Attraction. In T. Huston, *Foundations of Interpersonal Attraction*, New York: Academic Press.

Rubin, Z. 1973: *Liking and Loving*. New York: Holt, Rinehart and Winston.

Sacks, Oliver 1985: *The Man who Mistook his Wife for a Hat*. New York: Harper and Row.

Sandel, M. 1982: *Liberalism and the Limits of Justice*. New York: Cambridge University Press.

Sanders, Ed 1971: *The Family*. New York: Dutton.

Schaffner, Bertram 1948: *Father Land: A Study of Authoritarianism in the German Family*. New York: Columbia University Press.

Schiffer, Irvine 1973: *Charisma: A Psychoanalytic Look at Mass Society*. Toronto: University of Toronto.

Schramm, Percy 1971: *Hitler: The Man and the Military Leader*. Chicago: Quadrangle.

Schreck, Nikolas (ed.) 1988: *The Manson File*. New York: Amok Press.

Schweitzer, Albert 1984: *The Age of Charisma*. Chicago: Nelson Hall.

Segalen, Martine 1986: *Historical Anthropology of the Family*. New York: Cambridge University Press.

Sennett, Richard 1981: *Authority*. New York: Vintage.

Shils, Edward 1965: Charisma, Order, Status. *American Sociological Review*, 30, 199–213.

Shirokogoroff, S. 1935: *Psychomental Complex of the Tungus*. London: Kegan Paul, Trench, Trubner.

Shorter, E. 1975: *The Making of the Modern Family*. New York: Basic Books.

Shupe, Anson 1981: *Six Perspectives on New Religions: A Case Study Approach*. New York: Edwin Mellen Press.

Shweder, Richard 1972: Aspects of Cognition in Zinacanteco Shamans, Experimental Results. In William Lessa and Evon Vogt, *Reader in Comparative Religion*, New York: Harper and Row.

Simcox-Reiner, Beatrice 1979: A Feeling of Irrelevance: The Effects of a Non-supportive Society. *Social Casework*, 60, 3–10.

Simenon, Georges 1984: interview. *New York Times Magazine*, 22 April, 20–3, 60–6.

Sipe, Onjya, with McGrath, Robert 1976: *Devil's Dropout*. Milford, CT: Mott.

Sklar, Dusty 1977: *Gods and Beasts: The Nazis and the Occult*. New York: Thomas Crowell.

Slater, Philip 1976: *The Pursuit of Loneliness: American Culture at the Breaking Point*. Boston: Beacon Press.

——1977: *Footholds*. Boston: Beacon Press.

Smith, Bradley F. 1967: *Adolf Hitler: His Family, Childhood and Youth*. Stanford: Hoover Institution.

Solomon, Robert 1981: *Love: Emotion, Myth and Metaphor*. Garden City, NY: Anchor.

Spero, Moshe 1983: Individual Psychodynamic Intervention with the Cult Devotee. In David Halperin (ed.), *Psychodynamic Perspectives on Religion, Sect and Cult*, Boston: John Wright.

Stern, Fritz 1961: *The Politics of Cultural Despair*. Berkeley, CA: University of California Press.

——1972: *The Failure of Illiberalism*. New York: Knopf.

Stone, L. 1978: *The Family, Sex and Marriage in England: 1500–1800*. New York: Harper and Row.

Swanson, Guy 1978: Trance and Possession: Studies of Charismatic Influence. *Review of Religious Research*, 19, 253–78.

Swidler, A. 1980: Love and Adulthood in American Culture. In N. Smelser and E. Erikson (eds), *Themes of Work and Love in Adulthood*, Cambridge, MA: Harvard University Press.

Tarde, Gabriel de 1903: *The Laws of Imitation*. New York: Henry Holt and Co.

Taylor, A.J.P 1988: *The Course of German History*. London: Routledge.

Tipton, Steven 1982: *Getting Saved from the Sixties*. Berkeley, CA: University of California Press.

Tocqueville, Alexis de 1969: *Democracy in America.* Garden City, NY: Doubleday.

Tumarkin, Nina 1983: *Lenin Lives! The Lenin Cult in Soviet Russia.* Cambridge, MA: Harvard University Press.

Turner, Henry (ed.) 1985: *Hitler – Memoirs of a Confidant.* New Haven: Yale University Press.

Turner, Victor 1982: *The Ritual Process.* New York: Aldine.

Waite, Robert 1952: *Vanguard of Nazism: The Free Corps Movement in Postwar Germany 1918–1923.* Cambridge, MA: Harvard University Press.

——1971: Adolf Hitler's Anti-semitism: A Study in History and Psychoanalysis. In Benjamin Wolman (ed.), *Psychoanalytic Interpretations of History,* New York: Basic Books.

——1977: *The Psychopathic God: Adolf Hitler.* New York: Basic Books.

Wallace, Anthony 1956: Revitalization Movements. *American Anthropologist,* 58, 264–81.

Wallis, Roy 1984: *The Elementary Forms of the New Religious Life.* London: Routledge and Kegan Paul.

Watson, Tex 1978: *"Will You Die For Me?"* Old Tappan, NJ: Fleming H. Revell.

Weber, Eugen 1965: The New Right: An Introduction. In Hans Rogger and Eugen Weber (eds), *The European Right: A Historical Profile,* Berkeley, CA: University of California Press.

Weber, Max 1946: *From Max Weber: Essays in Sociology,* eds Hans Gerth and C. Wright Mills. New York: Oxford University Press.

——1949: *The Methodology of the Social Sciences,* eds Edward Shils and Henry Finch. New York: Free Press.

——1958: *The Protestant Ethic and the Spirit of Capitalism.* New York: Scribner's.

——1978: *Economy and Society,* eds I. Roth and C. Wittich. Berkeley, CA: University of California Press.

Weightman, Judith Mary 1983: *Making Sense of the Jonestown Suicides: A Sociological History of the People's Temple.* New York: Edwin Mellen Press.

Weinstein, Fred 1980: *The Dynamics of Nazism: Leadership, Ideology and the Holocaust.* New York: Academic Press.

Westley, Francis 1982: Merger and Separation: Autistic Symbolism in New Religious Movements. *Journal of Psychoanalytic Anthropology,* 5, 137–54.

Willner, Ann Ruth 1984: *The Spellbinders: Charismatic Political Leadership.* New Haven: Yale University Press.

Wilson, Bryan R. 1975: *The Noble Savages: The Primitive Origins of Charisma and its Contemporary Survival.* Berkeley, CA: University of California Press.

——1976: *Contemporary Transformations of Religion.* Oxford: Oxford University Press.

Winkelman, Michael 1986: Trance States: A Theoretical Model and Cross-Cultural Analysis. *Ethos*, 14, 174–203.

Winnicott, D. 1965: *The Maturation Process and the Facilitating Environment*. New York: International Universities Press.

Wolfenstein, E. Victor 1967: *The Revolutionary Personality: Lenin, Trotsky, Gandhi*. Princeton, NJ: Princeton University Press.

——1969: *Personality in Politics*. Belmont, CA: Dickenson.

Wood, Alan Tate with Vitek, Jack 1979: *Moonstruck: A Memoir of My Life in a Cult*. New York: William Murrow.

Worsley, Peter 1968: *The Trumpet Shall Sound*. New York: Schocken.

Yee, Min S. and Layton, Thomas 1981: *In My Father's House*. New York: Holt, Rinehart and Winston.

Yinger, Milton 1946: *Religion in the Struggle for Power*. Durham, NC: Duke University Press.

——1957: *Religion, Society and the Individual*. New York: Macmillan.

Zablocki, Benjamin 1980: *Alienation and Charisma*. New York: Free Press.

Zaehner, R.C. 1974: *Our Savage God*. London: Collins.

Index

abreaction: and Hitler 106; in new age movement 180; in psychoanalysis 53, 183 among shamans 160, 166;
action: desire for 95, 96; opposing charismatic involvement 152
altered states of consciousness (ASCs): attributes of 77–9, 120; and charismatic immersion 78–9, 120–1; euphoria of 77–8, 199; and hypnotic trance 78; among !Kung 164; in the Manson Family 124; similarity to epilepsy 199; techniques for achieving 79 see also epilepsy; front experience; hallucinogens; hypnotism; !kia; regression; trance ambivalence: of authority figures 45–6; of charismatic relation 7, 88–9; within family 182; of followers 55; Hitler's 107; as human condition 58; toward healers 164; see also
Freud anti-structure 167, 181
artist: charisma of 178–9; charismatic leader as failed 108, 133, 178–9, 202, 205; shaman as prototypical 202
atomization: in Medieval Europe 168; in the modern world 80, 119; in Nazi Germany 111–12; of passions 19; as precursor to charisma 47, 48–9, 82, 119; see also crowd psychology; modernity; rationalization
attachment: to community 71; Durkheim on 28–9; follower's

desire for 66; Freud on 51, 58, 60, 88; need for 82
avarice, as the primal emotion 15, 190

Bettelheim, Bruno, on concentration camps 76
Bion, Wilfred: on the character of leaders 67; on groups as psychotic 63; on rationalization 69; research method of 198
borderline syndrome: and charismatic leaders 65; defined 65–6, 196; evaluation of 166; Hitler as 107; among !Kung healers 164; Manson as 131; modern pressure and 170; shaman as 162; see also charismatic relations; detachment; emotions; narcissism; paraphrenia; regression
brainwashing see thought reform
bureaucratization see rationalization

capitalism, as alternative to charisma 176–7
Catholicism, and charismatic renewal 181
charismatic followers: ambivalence of 55; and ASCs 77–9; as bored 120; and coercion 74–6; and collective effervescence 30–1, 34; demands on leaders 170; ecstatic feelings of 26, 30–1, 34, 57, 58–9, 75, 77–8, 120, 121, 122, 197; as impulsive 45; and love for the leader 44, 46, 56–60, 67, 122–3; as masochistic 46–7, 52, 54–5, 56, 57, 122–3; as

shamanism
contagion *see* crowd psychology
collective effervescence 30–1, 34,
157; among !Kung 163; *see also*
charismatic followers; Durkheim
conformity, in modern world 81, 82,
199; *see also* other directedness
consumption: as alternative to
charisma 176–7; and
entertainment 178
counterculture: 119–23; and desire
for nurturant community 120, 182;
ethic of 121; and the family 182;
hallucinogens and 120–1; and
ideal of self-actualization 121,
122, 187; political radicalism
among 121–2; social conditions
for 119 see also cults; new age
movements
crisis: and charisma 25, 35, 76, 80,
188; economic 177; in Germany
94–5; among the !Kung 165; in
the nation 178; among the
oppressed 167–9
crowd psychology 39–47, 88;
Durkheim on 30–1, 32; Freud on
52; Hitler on 103–4; Le Bon on
40–9; love in 46–7, 56; and media
47–8; Mesmer on 38–9; in the
modern world 27, 33, 47–9, 60–1;
and regression 44–5, 52; Tarde on
40–9; Weber on 26; *see also* Le
Bon; Mesmer; Tarde
cults 119–23; and communes 122;
cultic milieu in Germany 93–5,
98–9; cultic milieu in Medieval
Europe 168, 213; cultic milieu in
US 118–20, 122; definitions of
203–4; ideology of 121, 122,
213; and marketing 212;
membership of 119–204; middle-
class attraction to 119–21; and
new age movements 180, 189,
213; recruitment into 120–1, 212;
and shamanism 158; tendency
toward charismatic leadership in
122–3, 180, 189
culture of narcissism 83–5; *see also*
narcissism

deautomatization: in ASCs 79; and
Hitler 108
detachment and the expression of
strong emotions 201; for Hitler
106, 107; for Jones 141, 152–3;
for Manson 125, 126, in
shamanism 161, 210; *see also*
borderline syndrome; emotions;
narcissism
deviance: as socialization 70; and
labelling 170
Durkheim, Emile 27–35, 88, 183; on
collective effervescence 30–1, 34,
157, 194; on community 29, 34;
and crowd psychologists 40, 47;
on the duality of human nature
28, 34; and emotivism 29; and the
French Revolution 30; general
theory of 28–9, 33, 193; on
leadership 29, 31–2, 35, 183; on
modernity and rationalization 33;
prefiguring psychoanalysis 29, 31;
on the sacred 28, 31, 157, 193;
on sexuality 31, 193; on the
unconscious 29; and Weber 32,
34–5, 157

ecstasy: in battle 96–7, in
charismatic relations 59, 66–7,
157; from crowd density 30–1,
103; in fusion with the mother 58,
66; hallucinogens and 120; in
romantic love 57, 58, 185;
shamanistic 26, 161, 192;
techniques for 26; *see also* altered
states of consciousness; eroticism;
pleasure elite as true believers: in
contemporary cults 211; in Hitler
cult 100–1, 110–11; in Jones cult
146–8; *see also* charismatic
followers
emotions: in abreaction 160; in
ASCs 77–8; attraction of 26; and
borderline syndrome 65–6; in
collective 30–1, 33; and culture of
narcissism 83–4; detachment and
intensity of 201; in family 83,
181–2; Hitler's range of 105–6;
and Hume 13–14; Jones's range of
148, 150; in !Kung healers 164;

reflection 3, 131–2; rejection and 123, 124; revelation of 129–30; role playing of 130–1; as schizophrenic 131; self-pity of 128–9; sexuality of 126, 205; techniques used by 123, 126–8; vegetarianism of 205; as witch 128, 129; on women, 204–5; *see also* charismatic leaders; charismatic relationships; Manson Family

Manson Family 123–36; child training in 131; destruction of 132–5; drug use in 127; emptiness in 131–2; expansion of 133; identification with Manson 132; ideology of 125; indoctrination procedures 126–8; isolation of 128, 134, 205; and love for Manson 127, 134; love within 128, 133, 134; and Manson as redeemer 124; membership in 123; and murder 3, 134–5; play ethic in 127; rationalization of 133; sexuality in 126; time orientation in 126–7; unit of 125, 127, 132, 133; and violence 134–5; *see also* charismatic followers; charismatic relations; Manson

Marxism 85–6

media: and Manson 128, 129; Tarde on 47–8; as undermining beliefs 81

Medieval Europe, charisma in 168–9

Mesmer, Franz Anton 36–9; as a charismatic 36, 42; and crowd psychology 41; and crowds 38–9; egalitarianism of 194; history of 37, 194; influence of 39; precursors of 194; practices of 38; theory of 37; *see also* crowd psychology; hypnotism

Mill, John Stuart, 17–18; on the genius 17–18, 191; as a Utilitarian 17

modernity: and character 81–2; and charismatic immersion 81–5, 83, 87, 175–6, 188–9; and the family 182; and friendship 182–3; and narcissism 83–5; and negative

image of charisma 166–7; and romantic love 185, 187, 188; and the self 82, 187; similarity to 'primitive' society 214–15; sociological view of 71, 80–1, 175; and 'thought reform' 85; the United States as representative of 118–19, 204; *see also* atomization; rationalization

morality: Durkheim on 28–31; Nietzsche's rejection of 18; and the sacred 11; situational 81

narcissism: and charisma 84–5; culture of, 83–5; and ecstatic fusion 58–60; of leader 52, 57, 64–6; and modern character 83–4, 199; and romantic love 57, 59–60, 184, 185, 186; *see also* borderline syndrome; charismatic leaders; Freud; paraphrenia; romantic love

nationalism, as alternative to charisma 177–8, 188

Nazism: as charismatic community 98, 111–12; conversion to 102; distancing from 117; extraordinariness of 80, 117, 175; family and 98, 113, 214; ideology of 101, 113; influence on Manson 125; as religion 102; sexuality in 113, 214; social organization of 111–12; SS in 112–13; symbolism of 101, 201; understandability of 116; *see also* charismatic followers; charismatic relations; Hitler; SS

new age movements: as adaptive 188, 198; charisma in 180, 189, 213; history of 213; ideology of 179, 180, 188; marketing of 179–80, 188, 212; pragmatism of 179; recruitment into 180; *see also* charismatic relations; cults

neo-conservativism 86

Nietzsche, Friedrich 18–20, 87, 88; on civilization 22; and Freud 52, 56; and individualism 20, 89; philosophy of 18–19, 20; on sensation 19; *see also Ubermensch*